P9-AOZ-514

# THE REMASCULINIZATION OF AMERICA

*The Remasculinization of America:*
*Gender and the Vietnam War*
is Volume 10 in the series
THEORIES OF CONTEMPORARY CULTURE
Center for Twentieth Century Studies
University of Wisconsin-Milwaukee

General Editor, KATHLEEN WOODWARD

# THE REMASCULINIZATION OF AMERICA

*Gender and the Vietnam War*

Susan Jeffords

INDIANA UNIVERSITY PRESS
Bloomington and Indianapolis

Manufactured in the United States of America

**Library of Congress Cataloging-in-Publication Data**

Jeffords, Susan
The Remasculinization of America / gender and the Vietnam War
Susan Jeffords.
p. cm.—(Theories of contemporary culture ; v. 10)
Bibliography: p.
Includes index.
ISBN 0-253-33188-9.—ISBN 0-253-20530-1 (pbk.)
1. Masculinity (Psychology)—United States—History—20th century. 2. Patriarchy—United States—History—20th century. 3. Sex role—United States—History—20th century. 4. Vietnamese Conflict, 1961–1975—Social aspects. 5. Vietnamese Conflict, 1961–1975—Motion pictures and the conflict. 6. Vietnamese Conflict, 1961–1975—Literature and the conflict. I. Title. II. Series.
BF692.5.J44 1989
305.3'0973—dc19 88-46019
CIP

1 2 3 4 5 93 92 91 90 89

*To Andrew and Matthew,*
*for whom my dearest hope is*
*that in their lifetimes the*
*issues of this book will*
*become irrelevant.*

# CONTENTS

# Acknowledgments

This book has been a long and deeply felt study for me. There are, as always in these kinds of projects, too many gratitudes to list here, but I would like to name the most important of them, never suggesting that those who are not named are forgotten: Rick Berg, Michael Clark, John Carlos Rowe, and Evan Watkins did perhaps more than they realize to encourage work on this project. I want also to thank Kathleen Woodward for graciously inviting this book to be a part of the series on Theories of Contemporary Culture. The audiences at the Center for Twentieth Century Studies at the University of Wisconsin–Milwaukee, Harvard University, the University of California–Irvine, and the Feminist Colloquium at the University of Washington offered questions and comments that forced me to rethink and refine many of my ideas on this subject. I want especially to thank Robyn Wiegman for her careful and astute reading of drafts of this book and discussions of its ideas; though it may not be a perfect book, without her it would be a lesser one. And finally, I owe a debt to the many feminist critics whose work has enabled me to think about this book at all.

The University of Washington graciously provided me a grant in 1986 to develop these ideas. Earlier versions of parts of this work appeared in other journals. I would like to thank the editors of *Cultural Critique*, *Feminist Studies*, and *The Journal of Popular Film and Television* for kindly allowing me to reprint those portions of chapters 2, 4, and 5 that appeared in their volumes.

At the end, as at the beginning, I want to thank Greg Powell, whose encouragement of both me and my work was unflagging. And above all, for reasons only she will fully know, I thank Betsy Jeffords.

# PREFACE

A segment of the television news program "60 Minutes" on October 4, 1987, was devoted to a college class at the University of Southern California. One of the most popular on campus, it had an enrollment of nine hundred students, and reportedly another six hundred had been turned away. The course that drew such a large number of students was not required, did not relate to business or any career-oriented major, was not even an "easy A." The subject was America's war in Vietnam.

Students in this class heard veterans talk about their experiences during the war and learned about the emotional and personal prices paid by individual soldiers, families, and others who worked or served in Vietnam. The class culminated in a field trip to the Vietnam Veterans' Memorial in Washington, D.C., where the students could see engraved before them the consequences of a war they could only read about.

Why this interest in Vietnam? Why would students who were not even in grade school when the war was over want so much to take this class? Would over a thousand students want to sign up for a class on World War II? the Korean War? the Civil War? Certainly such interest did not exist immediately following the war, or any time soon after. What has taken place in the U.S. in the years since the war that has led to such a response?

This book is an attempt to answer these questions, though not through the political, military, economic, religious, or even ethical paradigms that have often been put forth as interpretive frames for the war in Vietnam. Instead, this study suggests that an important way to read the war, perhaps the most significant way when we think about war itself, is as a construction of gendered interests. Although war might at first seem to be a "man's world" and therefore of little relevance to a discussion of relations between women and men, the arena of warfare and the Vietnam War in particular are not just fields of battle but fields of gender, in which enemies are depicted as feminine, wives and mothers and girl friends are justifications for fighting, and vocabularies are sexually motivated. But more than this, the representational features of the Vietnam War are structurally written through relations of gender, relations designed primarily to reinforce the interests of masculinity and patriarchy.

In the most general terms, I am suggesting here that a study of the representations of the Vietnam War can be used as an emblem for what I call the "remasculinization" of American culture, the large-scale renegotiation and regeneration of the interests, values, and projects of patriarchy now taking place in U.S. social relations. While such a thesis is meant in no way to suggest that patriarchy has ever been absent from American cultures, it does assume that the stability of patriarchal domination shifts, so that its systematic determination of social relations can be more or less embedded. With the advent of women's rights, civil rights, the "generation gap," and other alterations in social relations that occurred during the fifties, sixties, and seventies, the stability of the ground on which patriarchal power rests was challenged. But rather than be negated, that ground shifted, altering its base for relations to a site from which somewhat different but no less forceful relations of dominance could be worked out. A study of representations of the war in Vietnam begins to detail some of the ways in which those shifts occurred. The primary mechanism for this renegotiation of patriarchal relations is through "remasculinization," a revival of the images, abilities, and evaluations of men and masculinity in dominant U.S. culture.

I would like to define several terms as I use them here, specifically "patriarchy," "masculinity," and what I call "the masculine point of view." Gerda Lerner defines patriarchy as "the manifestation and institutionalization of male dominance over women and children in the family and the extension of male dominance over women in society in general. It implies that men hold power in all the important institutions of society and that women are deprived of access to such power."[1] But, as Lerner herself argues about the institution of slavery, "By subordinating women of their own group and later captive women, men learned the symbolic power of sexual control over men and elaborated the symbolic language in which to express dominance and create a class of psychologically enslaved persons" (p. 80), and of class, "Class differences were, at their very beginnings, expressed and constituted in terms of patriarchal relations. . . . class is expressed in genderic terms" (p. 213). In light of Lerner's comments, we can see that any definition of patriarchy in contemporary cultures must include not only "male dominance over women" but the socialized domination of masculine over feminine, in which the patterns of power relations established in the domination of men over women are employed to set systems of dominance over other groups as well. By emphasizing masculinity as a mechanism for the installation of patriarchal structure, it is possible to see the ways in which, through the structural relations of gender, men of color or of the working class or of other groups oppressed via defined categories of difference can be treated as women—"feminized"—and made subject to domination. It is also possible to see how women suffer not only from oppression by gender and structures of difference but also through their positioning as emblem of the "feminine." As *the* category of privilege in patriarchy, masculinity offers to men substantial structural dominance over women even when other forms of dominance are in operation. Yet to limit an analysis of the patriarchal system to relations between men and women is, as Eve Kosofsky Sedgwick has noted, to overlook much of its force.[2]

Within this frame, "masculinity" is used to refer to the set of images, values, interests, and activities held important to a successful achievement of male adulthood in American cultures. While the composition of the masculine can vary from time to time, it remains consistently opposed to the "feminine," those characteristics that must be discarded in order to actualize masculinity. By separating "masculinity" from "men" (and, of course, from male), it is possible to recognize the many ways in which no individual man embodies all of the traits of the masculine (nor any woman of the feminine). One of the goals of this study is to identify some of the ways in which the tensions between "masculinity" and "men" are addressed, tensions worked out and compensated for specifically in relation to women and the feminine.

In attempting to identify some of these separations, I found it useful to suggest a third term, "the masculine point of view," which represents the disembodied voice of masculinity, that which no individual man or woman can realize yet which influences each individually. In this way, it is possible to identify the voice through which dominance is enacted in a narrative representation, though it may not consistently be spoken by any one character. Such a construct is especially important when dealing with relations among men in groups, as is the case in representations of warfare.

The remasculinization I am identifying here takes place primarily through this masculine point of view, the overarching characteristics of which enable individual men to reassert their participation in masculinity. By reaffirming masculinity and thereby the relations of dominance it embodies, other relations of dominance are reinforced as well and the system of patriarchy as a whole is supported.

The six chapters of this book trace some of the strategies by which remasculinization has occurred through the representations of America's war in Vietnam. Chapter 1 sets out some of the narrative mechanisms that are employed in the project of remasculinization: the shift in focus from ends to means, a blurring of the status of fact and fiction, the technologization of the male body, and the elision of viewer and participant. In addition, chapter 1 identifies several topics through which these techniques are formulated: masculine bonding, regeneration of the soldier/veteran, feminization of the government, and reproduction. Each of these topics is the subject of subsequent chapters which attempt to detail the logic of remasculinization.

In order to establish a context for a renegotiation of masculinity, an arena for masculine relations must be set forth. For this purpose, Vietnam representation poses the masculine bond—commitments between men that are seen to cross barriers of racial, ethnic, class, age, geographic, religious, or social differences. As chapter 2 suggests, it is then on this ground that a general cultural proposition of homosocial relations is founded, and relations between veterans and soldiers of Vietnam are used as a basis for reestablishing relations between men in society at large, as, for example, in television programs like "Miami Vice," "Rip Tide," "The A Team," and "Magnum, P. I.," where bonds between veterans are shown to create a sense of community that surpasses legal, bureaucratic, familial, or other social connections.

In order to insure that the value of the masculine bonds is maintained, women must be effectively and finally eliminated from the masculine realm. To this end, chapter 3 discusses how Vietnam representation narrates the masculine appropriation of reproduction, projecting men as necessary and sufficient parents and birth figures. Whether as medical personnel who intervene in the birth process or as paternal figures who act as guides for society, (male) Vietnam soldiers/veterans are portrayed as taking over what is presented as the single remaining feature to distinguish women from men—reproduction. In this way, the self-sufficient community of the masculine bond can be carried over from war to society, from the battlefield to the home, and the men who constitute it can survive and thrive without women. (This is one of the ways in which Vietnam representation can be distinguished from narratives of earlier wars, in which the reinstallation of the heterosexual family unit was prioritized.)[3] Television again provides the best examples of this tendency, as programs like "Full House," "Paradise," "Who's Dad?," and "You Again?" portray single fathers maintaining children and households. The import of these narratives is that men are able not simply to exclude women from their arena, but to take over their functions as well, effectively eliminating them altogether from considerations of value.[4]

With women expelled from the masculine realm, the task fell to Vietnam representation to recuperate the soldier/veteran. Rejected by an American society that came to see these men as emblems of loss, moral failure, or national decline, Vietnam representation could effectively portray them as "victims" of society, government, and the war itself. As chapter 4 argues, it is here that the Vietnam War makes its most effective contribution to the project of remasculinization, as it provided "evidence" of a group of men who were themselves victims, on a par with women, blacks, and other disenfranchised groups. Consequently, it could then be argued that (white) men were not oppressors but instead, along with women and men of color, themselves victims of a third oppressor, in this case the government. For this reason, the chief opponent of the Vietnam soldier/veteran in films like *First Blood, Rambo: First Blood, Part II, Missing in Action, Missing in Action 2—The Beginning,* and *Uncommon Valor* was not the Vietnamese but their own government.

As chapter 5 shows, these arguments of victimization are particularly gendered because the soldier/veteran achieves his renewed status only in opposition to characters or institutions defined as feminine. Specifically, the U.S. government and its representatives are argued as feminine not only in their loss of the war but in relation to their inability to retrieve POWs from Vietnam. Through a posture of negotiation, government figures are shown to be weak, indecisive, and vulnerable, in clear opposition to the now strong, determined, and decisive soldier/veteran. Because so many gains made by women and minorities have been made through legislative or federal action, it is not accidental that a revived masculinity should pose as its feminized opponent those very institutions. Such observations are extremely important in trying to analyze current relationships between masculinity and state power.

This then is the path of remasculinization, the logic of which chapter 6 goes on to explore in relation to other forms of domination than gender, in this case, race. Finally a brief discussion is offered of what I call the "discourse of warfare" now in operation in American cultures. As the vocabulary and structure of warfare gains greater prominence in American society, even as its specific images are being discarded, the relations of dominance that underlie those signifiers play a greater role in shaping general social relations. Consequently, the remasculinization of American manhood is not limited to its most ostentatious forms but is at work in the culture at large through representations of the Vietnam War.

The specific aim of this study is to elucidate the gendered structure of representations of the Vietnam War in America through readings of films, personal narratives, criticism, novels, essays, and short stories, the bulk of them written by men who are themselves veterans of the war, in the hope that, as Kristen Thompson says in her discussion of excess, "An awareness . . . may help change the status of narrative in general for the viewer."[5] In addition, I hope to broaden avenues of feminist criticism, in particular examinations of the specific manifestations and installations of masculinity in culture, as a step toward altering the structures that support and enforce the paradigms of gender. To quote Antony Easthope, "Social change is necessary and a precondition of such change is an attempt to *understand* masculinity, to make it visible."[6] But more than this, I hope to suggest some arguments about warfare in general and its relation to installations of gender in society. Although I refuse to cite any causal connections between war and gender, since an effort to determine causality is itself symptomatic of the system that produces both, I propose that a study of the structural relations between warfare and gender reveals them to be intimately connected, so much so that one does not survive without the other.

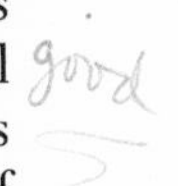

Michael Herr says of the soldiers whose stories he was covering as a journalist that "we were intimate, I'll tell you how intimate: they were my guns, and I let them do it,"[7] suggesting that Herr's ability to survive and write about the war depended primarily on his willingness to let soldiers kill those who might otherwise have killed him. Similar is the relationship between war and gender: it is the crystallized formations of masculinity in warfare that enable gender relations in society to survive, offering territory in which to adjust, test, and reformulate general social relations. As I hope to show in this book, gender and warfare are "intimate, I'll tell you how intimate."

# THE REMASCULINIZATION OF AMERICA

# ONE

# FACT, FICTION, AND THE SPECTACLE OF WAR

The representation in American culture of the Vietnam War, along with that war's aftermath in the shape of returning veterans, POWs and the still embattled question of MIAs, forms a complex of images that seems initially to have become a part of America's past or, at the very least, only one of a multitude of often competing and contradictory factors at work in contemporary culture. Yet I would suggest that such imagery is instead emblematic of the operation of contemporary dominant U.S. cultural formations. More specifically, Vietnam representation is emblematic of the general restructuring and circulation of ideological production in America today. The purpose of this chapter is to indicate some of the strategies by which those operations take place: the shift from ends to means, the proliferation of techniques and technologies, the valorization of performance, the production and technologization of the male body as an aesthetic of spectacle, and the blurring of fact and fiction. The framework through which each of these operations is enacted, I argue, is that of gender.

## I

The popularity of Vietnam representation in contemporary American culture—films, novels, personal accounts, collections of observations and experiences, political and social analyses, and so on—cannot be questioned. In 1983, Edwin McDowell concluded, "Today . . . books about Vietnam are rolling off the presses in record numbers, titles published years ago are being reissued, and bookstores, book reviewers and book clubs are all calling attention to one of the newest trends in publishing."[1] Ballantine, Dell, and Avon each publishes a series of Vietnam titles in paperback, including Robert Stone's *Dog Soldiers*, Philip Caputo's *A Rumor of War* (Ballantine); William E. Holland's *Let a Soldier Die*, Jack Fuller's *Fragments*, Tim O'Brien's *Going after Cacciato* (Dell); and William Pelfry's *The Big V*, James Park Sloan's *War Games*, Charles Nelson's *The Boy Who Picked the Bullets Up* (Avon). *Time*, *Newsweek*, *The New Republic*, and *The New York Times Magazine* all published special issues on the tenth anniversary of the fall of Saigon in 1985. Films like *First Blood*, *Rambo:*

*First Blood, Part II, Rambo III,*[2] *Missing in Action, Missing in Action 2—The Beginning,* and *Platoon* held places at the tops of movie charts, and *Rambo* set records for box office success in its first weeks of release.[3] A popular motif of television heroes is to have nondescript Vietnam backgrounds: in "The A Team," "Miami Vice," "T. J. Hooker," "Magnum, P. I.," "Rip Tide," "Matt Helm," "Gideon Oliver," as well as numerous soap operas. "Tour of Duty" and "China Beach" became in 1987 and 1988 the first television programs to be set entirely during the Vietnam War and in Vietnam: "Tour of Duty" followed a combat unit and "China Beach" focused on the women working in and around an evacuation hospital near Da Nang.[4] In June 1985, a ticker-tape parade was staged in New York for Vietnam veterans, and in May 1987, 100,000 people lined the streets of Los Angeles for a Thank You Vietnam Veterans Parade. Corporations have run advertising spreads celebrating their stockholders who are Vietnam veterans. For example, Southern Company's 1983 two-page ad read as follows: "He flew 191 combat missions. Was shot down over North Vietnam. And came home a hero after 7 years in a P.O.W. camp. But this happy ending was really another beginning. For as George Robert Hall put his energy into civilian life, he also put it into energy itself. As a Southern Company stockholder." Victory Games of New York has produced "Vietnam: 1965–75," a game for two players in which each takes the side of either the U.S. and South Vietnam or North Vietnam and the Viet Cong. Available from Carolco are a duplicate of the Rambo knife priced at $2,250, Rambo action dolls, camouflage makeup, posters, calendars, comic books, and a Rambuddha necklace like that worn by Co and then Rambo in *Rambo: First Blood, Part II.* And in 1986 election campaigns, politicians fabricated Vietnam war records in order to bolster their public image.[5]

Positions on the war vary from publication to publication, image to image, game to game. Many believe that the war was just and could have been won; as John Rambo says in *First Blood,* "We did what we had to do to win, but somebody wouldn't let us win." Some, like Richard Nixon, believe we *did* win the war. As he declares forcefully in *No More Vietnams,* "On January 27, 1973, almost twenty years after the French had lost the first Vietnam War, we had won the second Vietnam War. We signed the peace agreement that ended the war in a way that won the peace. We had redeemed our pledge to keep South Vietnam free."[6] It is only because of the failure of Congress to support U.S. promises to the South Vietnamese government, Nixon argues, that we then "lost the peace" (p. 165). Others, like Norman Mailer, conclude simply that "by every conservative measure . . . the war in Vietnam was an extraordinarily bad war."[7]

Although many current social, historical, and political analysts criticize the war, most have shifted their focus from the political and global issues that were so prominently debated before and during the war—communism versus democracy, American influence in Asia in the face of China's growing power, the viability of colonialism as a feature of France's post–World War II recovery, the strength of the U.S. military, and so on—to an analysis of the way the war was fought. For example, Loren Baritz discusses the bureaucratic and institutional investments of American policy in relation to Vietnam and locates much of the explanation for the loss of the war in the frequently cumbersome, self-serving, and hierarchically overweight structures of the military, the White House, and the U.S. mission in Southeast Asia. As Baritz describes it:

> It was a war with two fronts, one in Vietnam and the other in Washington. The Washington war was bureaucratic, between the White House and the State Department, between State and Defense, between the air force and the navy, between the CIA and everyone else, and between junior employees and their bosses. The failures of the government of the United States during the period of the Vietnam War were the failures that are built into the very nature of the enormous federal bureaucracy. The war in Vietnam revealed how this bureaucracy functions, and fails to function.[8]

In her examination of the "march of folly" that was Vietnam, Barbara Tuchman draws similar conclusions, emphasizing the early dominance of Vietnam policy and strategy by a technocratic mentality that slowly escalated until no amount of contrary evidence about the progress of the war could convince the American government, in what Tuchman calls its "wooden-headedness," of anything different. Behind a litany of "follies," which included overreacting, the "conjuring of specters," an illusion of omnipotence, the simultaneous underestimation of the North Vietnamese and overestimation of the government of South Vietnam, Tuchman finds finally "an absence of reflective thought about the nature of what we were doing" that indicts the bureaucratic structure that integrated and produced these follies. She asks then if "in modern states there is something about political and bureaucratic life that subdues the functioning of intellect in favor of 'working the levers' without regard to rational expectations."[9] Like Baritz, Tuchman locates many of the problems encountered in the Vietnam War in bureaucratic and institutional structures and in attitudes toward that war rather than in the events of the war themselves. Jeffrey Record's critique states this position most succinctly: "America's military malaise stems largely from the substitution of managerial and technocratic values for traditional warrior values that has taken place since World War II."[10]

Arguing many of the same points as Baritz and Tuchman, Richard Halloran and Edward N. Luttwak even more specifically identify where blame for the failure of the American military in recent decades should *not* lie—with the U.S. soldier. Following Tuchman's emphasis on placing blame at the level of an overweight hierarchy, Luttwak concludes:

> American soldiers set out on patrol day after day, through jungle and high grass made for ambushes and man-traps, across swamps infested with blood-sucking leeches, with water up to their chests and soft mud under their feet. Meanwhile the airmen flew their sorties, sometimes twice a day, risking death or foul imprisonment each time, and the sailors aboard ship carried out a routine of

> backbreaking labor, interrupted only by sleep and numbing boredom. *It was not the fault of those young men but of the command structure above them* that the patrols and the sweeps, the air strikes and the warships served ritualistic tactics, vacuous operational methods, and strategies of defeat. [italics added].[11]

Richard Halloran is even more severe in both his praise and blame:

> In adversity, the American GI has no equal. . . . He is unsurpassed in taking initiative and at getting things done with ingenuity. . . . But there is a discouraging contrast between the forces in the field and the high command around the flagpole in Washington. The soldiers and sergeants and combatant commanders who lead battalions and ships and air squadrons guard the nation well. The same cannot be said for those who plan and finance the forces, who are responsible for arming and equipping them, and who dispatch the forces to far corners of the globe where they put their lives on the line every day.[12]

Halloran's shift from an emphasis on the outcome of the war to how it was fought splits, as do the preceding analyses, the government from the soldier, placing blame for the loss of the war on the former while characterizing as innocent the latter.

Philip Beidler's study of Vietnam literature captures this dichotomy in its evaluative slumber:

> Throughout, Vietnam would be a creation of experts, of planners, of programmers, designers and interpreters of packaged death on printouts, flow charts, overlays, graphs, grand collections of statistics, with the crucial screwup factor hidden somewhere neatly below the bottom line. . . . Meanwhile, draftees, mainly, would do the dying, find *their* bottom line on the battlefield.[13]

Vietnam representation faithfully follows this pattern of separating soldier from government. Broad-ranging interpretive critiques of the war in Vietnam take aim at the operation of bureaucratic mechanisms and pay little attention to individuals other than as functionaries. In contrast, the more popular personal narratives and films of Vietnam soldiers focus almost exclusively on the more intimate, individual or collection of separate voices, whether they be of soldiers, journalists, family members, medical personnel, or POWs;[14] they present the government and the military as monolithic and indifferent.

In both perspectives governmental operations are depicted as being either directly or indirectly responsible for the loss of the war. That is, one sees a bureaucracy in which immediate interests in personal promotion or public image impede attention to long-range international situations; there is a failure to move outside of the bureaucracy to gain knowledge and experience of the lives and interests of the Vietnamese; fear of American public response interferes with performance of necessary actions; there is a willingness to sacrifice Vietnam for other American political interests in Europe or Asia; and so on. In contrast, the individual (soldier) is portrayed as having performed well throughout the war and having nothing to do with its loss. (POWs withstood tremendous pressure, torture, and depletion of their minds and bodies to survive and return home; soldiers gave their lives during the war; missionaries, Agency for International Development (AID) employees, and individual soldiers worked with, helped, or came to care for the Vietnamese people; nurses and doctors saved the lives of both American soldiers and Vietnamese citizens; journalists risked their lives to tell the story of the war; and so on.)

This association of the loss of the war with the government and the honor of the war with the soldier reconstitutes one of the principal thematics of U.S. culture, in which individual interests exist in tension with those of the society as a whole.[15] But what distinguishes Vietnam representation from earlier periods in U.S. cultural expression is this shift from focusing on the war's outcome to the way it was fought, in other words, a shift in focus from ends to means. That the first war America lost should be seen in terms of means rather than ends—how we performed rather than that we lost—does not seem coincidental. Yet this shift is more than an opportunistic apologetic for the war. Such a shift is instead characteristic of the general operation of contemporary dominant U.S. culture. Vietnam representation is thus more than a comment on a particular war: it is an emblem for the presentation of dominant cultural ideology in contemporary American society.

One of the chief mechanisms for an elucidation of the shift from ends to means is the focus in Vietnam representation and in contemporary American culture as a whole on the operations and performance of technologies. As Jean-François Lyotard explains, since the Second World War, the "blossoming of techniques and technology" has "shifted emphasis from the ends of action to its means."[16] The characteristics of technology reformulate the methods for "truth" evaluation:

> [Technical devices] follow a principle, and it is the principle of optimal performance: maximizing output . . . and minimizing input. . . . Technology is therefore not a game pertaining to the true, the just, or the beautiful, etc., but to efficiency: a technical "move" is "good" when it does better and/or expends less energy than another. (p. 44)

The goal of such a system is "no longer truth, but performativity—that is, the best possible input/output equation" (p. 46). In such a system, methods of evaluation center on the efficacy of performance rather than on the quality or character of results. The proliferation of technology and the foregrounding of performance as ground for evaluation are thereby intimately linked.

The emphasis on means rather than ends and on performance rather than goals that is a typical feature of Vietnam narrative contrasts to what Roland Barthes describes as the operation of the classic narrative, in which the achievement of the end of the story is one of the key forces that impels the procedure of narrative.[17] The function of the hermeneutic code, Barthes says, is "to articulate in various ways a question, its response, and the variety of chance events which can either formulate the question or delay its answer; or even, constitute an enigma and lead to its solution" (p. 17). In such a context, "truth, these narratives tell us, is what is *at the end* of expectation" (p. 76).

But most Vietnam representation is not interested in the solution to the enigma as much as in the display of the process whereby an ending is unfolded—the "performance" of the narrative. Indeed, in some of its most popular forms—the collected narratives of those who were in Vietnam such as Al Santoli's *Everything We Had*, Mark Baker's *Nam*, Keith Walker's *A Piece of My Heart*, Myra MacPherson's *Long Time Passing*—a "solution" to the narrative does not even exist, as the collected voices echo each other's accounts in a manner that erases even the individual narrative ending. In these cases, the rereading of individual accounts as they coalesce into a collective voice comes to constitute the progress of the narrative. And in films like *First Blood, Rambo: First Blood, Part II, Missing in Action, Missing in Action 2,* and *Uncommon Valor,* the thematics, music, and characterizations of the narratives indicate from the outset the successful rescue of POWs and the thwarting of an indifferent government. The enigma is more directly how the mission will be achieved, not that it will be. Unlike the detective narrative (of which *Sarrasine* would be a type), in which explanation of the mystery is achieved by a "detective" who knows or can deduce the "secret" of the narrative, Vietnam representation is more like the romance, in which the plot variation alters little and readers' pleasure is grounded on the working out of a predictable ending less significant than the events leading to it.[18] Following the pattern of a shift from ends to means, emphasis in Vietnam narrative is placed less on *what* will take place than on *how* it will take place.

> Killing the enemy was not the problem; it was identifying him. Killing him was easy once you found him and identified him. In fact, sometimes it was much easier to do the killing first and the identifying afterwards. Where no answers were possible, no questions were necessary. For many G.I.s the equation became simple. . . . Kill them all and you know for damn sure you're killing the enemy. If they're not VC now, they could fuckin' well become VC. Solve the problem before it starts.[19]

"Truth" has altered from what is "at the end of expectation" to a confirmation of the already known, the already displayed, the already dead.

As in its representations, the "end" of the Vietnam War itself is difficult to identify. Is it with the fall of the Saigon government in 1975? the withdrawal of American troops from battle in 1973? the Tet Offensive of 1968, when, according to many historians, the war was perceived by the American public to be lost? And is its beginning with the large-scale introduction of American troops in 1965? with the commitment of American financing and advisors in 1962? the assumption by the United States government of the debts and institutions of the French in Vietnam in 1945? or the declaration by Ho Chi Minh of an independent Vietnam in 1945? "For most Americans in Vietnam . . . nothing in the war, it seemed, ever really began for any particular reason, and nothing in the war ever really ended."[20] From the soldier's viewpoint, because of the rotation schedule of one-year military service, the war often "began" on the day s/he arrived in Vietnam and "ended" on the day s/he left. The 365-day calendars handed out by the Red Cross emphasized the extent to which the individual soldier's perception of the war was focused on the immediate survival of a given number of days rather than on "winning" the war. "The only kind of distance a GI could think about really, and stay close to sane, was something that could be related to the next step—one more yard sweated out, no mine, no booby trap, no sniper, no ambush."[21]

And while the war seemed to have neither beginning nor end (it still seems in some ways to be going on, with aftereffects of Agent Orange and translation of Vietnam policy into relations with Nicaragua), the goals of such an end became less and less articulable as time went on. John F. Kennedy could declare robustly during his years in Congress that the United States must prevent "the onrushing tide of Communism from engulfing all Asia" and, perhaps less polemically, in his first year in the White House that "we have a problem in making our power credible, and Vietnam is the place."[22] But when Colonel Harry Summers, during the negotiations between North and South Vietnam after the Paris agreement, asked the American embassy in Saigon for a statement on the "American position," an official at the embassy could only reply, "Damned if I know."[23]

The inability to identify clearly marked goals—to tell Vietnam as a classic narrative—translated the strategies of the war into questions, not of whether it was being won but of whether it was being well fought—questions, therefore, of performance. Such an epistemology would explain, for example, the eccentric emphasis placed on the infamous "body count," the military's way of gauging whether it was "winning" the war. The performance of its soldiers in the field was tested by these kinds of numbers, and rewards of three-day passes were often given to those who "produced" the most.

> They were keenly aware that some of the counts were approximations—a patch of blood on the ground, for example, counted as a body on some scorecards if it was six inches or more in diameter—and some were pure fabrications. . . . A rifle counted as a kill in Vietnam; one dead man carrying three rifles counted as three bodies.[24]

That false numbers were reported, that anything counted as a body—arm, leg, torso—and that nonenemy bodies were included in the count confirm the extent to which the technology of performance became ascendant.

Fighting in Vietnam in 1965 and 1966, Michael Clodfelter recalls the pressure of the body count and exemplifies most clearly the relation between performer and audience:

> We had been out several days and all we had to show for our sweat and exertion were robes of mud and waves of frustration. It had been a month now since any

> "Hard Core" glory had come the way of the Second Squad and the body count itch was making life miserable for all the corpse counters all the way up to battalion C.O. Finally, the First Squad scored, wasting an unarmed straggler, and the body count competition intensified. Tate . . . taunted us so unmercifully on our lack of scalps that several members of the Second Squad . . . resolved to count coup and even the score even if it required wasting a slopehead who became VC only after he was dead.[25]

This competition led the Second Squad to a small hamlet where, after some soldiers questioned an old man, three Viet Cong soldiers escaped the squad's bullets. Having promised to return with VC ears, the squad despaired of its reputation.

> But all was not lost; our honor could still be salvaged. The old man with gray cat's whiskers still remained, and his ears . . . were as good as those attached to the skulls of the three nimble Victor Charlies who had escaped. Tate could have his ears, Welch could chalk up a body count, and the squad could maintain its reputation for ferocity. All it required was murder. (p. 654)

In such a system, bodies became only numbers that could be fed back to the military's computerized analyses and killing became a question, not of the enemy or even of survival, but of the demands of the audience for performance.

Because the (enemy) body had meaning only as death, its signification was fragmented—pieces of bodies "counted"; some American soldiers collected and strung Vietnamese ears into ornamental necklaces, severed limbs were bagged and burned at military hospitals. The body became the site for multiple display, as each part became meaningful in itself, not as synecdoche for larger and more coherent forms, but as unintegrated bits of information that did not reassemble themselves into classic narrative. The individual soldiers' view of the war was like these/their body parts—disconnected, fragmentary pieces of a puzzle that did not make a picture. In such a context, meaning rests in the display of the signifier/body part itself, not in its ability to constitute a part of an "explanation" of the war.

The most impressive display of the war in Vietnam—its fragmented body—was the technology of the war, what Jayne Ann Phillips aptly calls its "machine dreams," the "body" that the American military believed would inevitably win the war.

> The memory of World War II concluding in a mushroom cloud was relatively fresh throughout the 1950s. It was unthinkable that America's military could ever fail to establish its supremacy on the battlefield, that the industrial, scientific, and technological strength of the nation would ever be insufficient for the purposes of war. *It was almost as if Americans were technology.* [italics added][26]

The war in Vietnam, "history's most technologically sophisticated war" (p. 31), showed more than any before the overdetermined power of American weaponry, as entire villages were destroyed in response to a single sniper or sprung booby trap.

> Nothing like it ever when we caught a bunch of them out in the open and close together, we really ripped it then, volatile piss-off, crazed expenditure, Godzilla never drew that kind of fire. . . . Charles really wrote the book on fire control, putting one round into the heart of things where fifty of ours might go and still not hit anything. Sometimes we put out so much fire you couldn't tell whether any of it was coming back or not.[27]

Soldiers, journalists, politicians—all comment on the display of technology in Vietnam that pervaded all aspects of the war:

> Distant machine-gun fire sounded in the night. Walden paid attention, first hearing M-60's, followed by the faint crumps of M-79's as the 40-millimeter shells exploded somewhere. . . . North of the city Cobra helicopters fired Mini-Guns; long, arcing, solid-red lines of tracer bullets stood out sharply against the black sky. The electrically fired guns sounded like turbines revving up. The buzzing of the air conditioners took over as they approached, and with its long sandbagged walls and domed sandbagged roof, the dispensary looked like a huge insect squatting in the sand.[28]

What is significant here is not only the intense fascination with technology that pervades Vietnam representation, but also the way that technology is described. In Maurer's account, Vietnam technology is separated from its ostensible function. These machine guns, shells, and mini-guns are not described as killing—whether the enemy, Vietnamese citizens, or American soldiers—or destroying buildings, huts, or military equipment; they are described only as their own display, their own theater. Planes flying overhead were often seen by their American viewers as separate from the bombs that fell from them: "On sunny days their wings flashed as they rolled into inverted dives and then upright again before releasing their bombs. Tiny golden flashes would twinkle against the mountainsides."[29] Divorced from the consequences of their use by the metaphoric rhetoric of "insects" and "golden flashes," these weapons ceased to be seen as instruments of war and became instead objects for display.

Distanced from its context, like the parts of the body that "count," technology, as a deferral of the fragmented body, comes to carry its own aesthetic. Michael Herr, one of this technology's earliest connoisseurs, speaks of helicopter gunships:

> It was incredible, those little ships were the most beautiful things flying in Vietnam *(you had to stop once in a while and admire the machinery)*, they just

> hung there above those bunkers like wasps outside a nest. "That's sex," the captain said. "That's pure sex." [italics added][30]

In an aesthetic that reproduces machinery as objects of display, technology and the body can be rejoined as "pure sex" in an erotic act that fuses the multiplicity of the fragmented body with the unified power of technological display. No longer pieces of body counts and machine guns, the body is reunified through technology as aesthetic: "you had to stop once in a while and admire the machinery."

One of the stages in the production of the aesthetic of technology is the identification of technology as an object of beauty. Linking the production of this aesthetic to sexuality, William Broyles, Jr., touches again on the erotic as the key interpretive feature of the aesthetic of technology: "The seduction of war is in its offering such intense beauty—divorced from all civilized values, but beauty still."[31] In speaking of the link between eroticism and the body, Georges Bataille explains that the sexual act epitomizes the moment of transgression that denies boundaries, specifically, the boundary of death. One of the forms for maintaining and seeming to control this transgression beyond the sexual moment is its projection as objects of beauty:

> We invest the breaking of our barriers with some tangible form if necessary. We try to think of it as a thing. . . . We are incessantly trying to hoodwink ourselves, trying to get at continuity, which implies that the boundaries have been crossed, without actually crossing the boundaries of this discontinuous life. . . . We know that possession of the object we are afire for is out of the question. It is one thing or another: either desire will consume us entirely, or its object will cease to fire us with longing. . . . We can make do with an illusion. If we possess its object we shall seem to achieve our desire without dying.[32]

That in war the mechanisms for death should be seen as objects of and for display, and therefore objects subject to the control of the viewer/audience, should, in Bataille's terms, not seem illogical. To link the body and technology through the erotic locates that object for control in an external frame—the display and beauty of technology—that enables the disavowal of the body's own vulnerability. Technology as display produces not simply continuity but apparent stability out of the transience of death and its enactments, suggesting that the spectacle of warfare and its displaced spectacle of death are "pure" moments in themselves that do not need to be contextualized or interpreted, simply witnessed, in order to be controlled.

Broyles is one of this aesthetic's most eloquent witnesses:

> War *is* beautiful. There is something about a firefight at night, something about the mechanical elegance of an M-60 machine gun. They are everything they should be, perfect examples of their form. When you are firing out at night, the red tracers go out into the blackness as if you were drawing with a light pen.

> Then little dots of light start winking back, and green tracers from AK-47s [the Russian rifles supplied to the North Vietnamese] begin to weave in with the red to form brilliant patterns that seem, given their great speeds, oddly timeless, as if they had been etched on the night. . . . And then the flares pop, casting eerie shadows as they float down on their little parachutes, swinging in the breeze, and anyone who moves in their light seems a ghost escaped from hell.[33]

Although the night is spoken of as supplying the best spectacle, daytime, as Broyles notes, "also has its charms":

> Many men loved napalm, loved its silent power, the way it could make tree lines or houses explode as if by spontaneous combustion. . . . I preferred white phosphorous, which exploded with a fulsome elegance, wreathing its target in intense and billowing white smoke, throwing out glowing red comets trailing brilliant white plumes. (p. 62)

Completely divorced from that for which it is a deferral—death—Broyles's theater is "pure" spectacle, capturing war's technology as an object of beauty, an "illusion" that exists for the value of its own presentation. Francis Ford Coppola obviously recognized the "silent power" of napalm, choosing to close *Apocalypse Now* by filling the screen with the explosion of Kurtz's jungle compound by napalm bombs, what William Eastlake says of mortars, "a phantasmagoria of such bright noise that it was soundless."[34] Coppola's choice to replace the sounds of explosion with an atonal music foregrounds the explosion as spectacle. The blackened screen that follows severs the bombs from their consequences and secures their status as image.

As an aesthetic, the technology of war became a conscious spectacle to the men fighting the war, who stood and watched distant firefights in the night, illuminated by flares, with tracer bullets marking their paths against the sky like a show of fireworks. *The Boys in Company C* includes a scene where munitions become pure theater. When they discover they are being used as a decoy to attract North Vietnamese troops, soldiers call in a fake battle, giving coordinates near their location. As the artillery explodes, they sit on a nearby hillside and cheer the show. And Maureen Walsh, a Navy nurse, recalls, "We would often pull up a chair, grab a beer, and watch the war as we could see it going on in the mountains north and south of us."[35]

One of the most popular Vietnam films, *Rambo: First Blood, Part II*, offers both the spectacle of technology and its "pure" link to the body, revealing not only the extent to which technology is the deferred body, but also how the body, mediated by technologization, can become its own deferral, its own spectacle. While the Russian machinery is deliberately overdetermined—a napalm bomb to kill one man, a computerized helicopter that outflies anything Rambo can get, and what looks like a battalion of soldiers to chase a single man—Rambo's weaponry, though more individualized, is no less sophisticated. His famous fifteen-inch knife (a replica of which is now available in hunting stores) was specially designed for *First Blood* and performs an apparently infinite number of tasks. His most "spectacular" weapon is what stores now call the "Ram-Bow," a collapsible high-tech bow that fires explosive arrows.

But most important is Rambo himself, a man whom Sylvester Stallone calls "a fighting machine."[36] As one veteran summarized of his own experience, "You're trained to perform. I was equipped for anything then."[37] The epitome of this preparation, Rambo is the military's best product, highly trained, adaptable, efficient (in *Rambo: First Blood, Part II*, he kills over forty enemy soldiers and is never even scratched; in *First Blood*, the real display of his skill is that he kills no one, though it is very clear that he could and a less careful man would). He succeeds in his mission, losing no one and decimating the enemy. Rambo fulfills the demands of the logic of technology for performativity as evaluation.

And there is no doubt, as Rambo is the perfect "fighting machine," that his character is presented as spectacle in the same way as the napalm in *Apocalypse Now* or the computerized explosives in *Missing in Action 2*. On the simplest level, Stallone's biceps are foregrounded for display, along with his bulging pectorals and protruding Adam's apple, all fragmented body "counts." David H. Van Biema's joking Rambo quiz—"In the movie, how long is it before Rambo takes off his shirt?" and "When you saw the first extreme closeup of Stallone's arm, what object did you think it was?" (p. 36)—marks only the most superficial way in which Rambo is displayed for the movie's audience. More pointedly, his body is used, not as a vehicle for weapons, but as a weapon itself.

Because it is not limited in its design to one function (like a grenade or machine gun), Rambo's body proves to be the film's greatest spectacle. It can never exhaust its appeal as display because it can always present a new performance, a different look. One of the chief appeals of *Rambo* as a film, enacting its version of the shift from ends to means, is to see how—not who—Rambo will kill next: by strangulation, knifing, burning, with machine gun, bow and arrow. During the scenes in which the Russian soldiers are pursuing Rambo, the spectator is absorbed by the search for Rambo's body. Is it behind a tree? a rock? a waterfall? The film struggles to find new locations for Rambo's body that will enhance both the search and the resulting spectacle of the revealed body. Rambo bursts from beneath the water's surface, leaps from behind boulders, and snakes through dry reeds. But the most startling, and one of the most memorable scenes of the film, is when Rambo's eyes suddenly appear from behind a wall of mud, and his body, completely hidden, springs as if from nowhere, as if from the earth itself.

It is extremely important for the maintenance of the spectacle and the technology it supports that the viewer is just as fooled about Rambo's location as are the Russian soldiers. We do not know until they do where the body will appear. When, for example, Rambo is escaping through a Vietnamese village, we see him enter and then the camera cuts to the Russian soldiers. With the soldiers, the camera moves through huts, over walkways, and into brush, but we do not see Rambo until the killing begins. This strategy of disclosure reinforces Rambo's godlike qualities: he can appear from nowhere, disappear into nothing, and kill with impunity. According to this plan, he cannot be controlled by the Russians, the Vietnamese, the audience, or the camera. He is pervasive, powerful, and inexhaustible.

These are, of course, the characteristics that ideology wishes to present itself as possessing. The spectacle of the body/technology figures the thematics of the film's ideological position in relation to the patriotic, militaristic, individualistic, racial, and economic. The body is the point of intersection of these devices and is constructed to speak its messages, depict its images, and to present them as the holistic gestalt of a functioning efficiency. The body's fluid performance reassures us that these positions work together, are all truly one. By presenting itself as a self-contained object of display, Rambo's body/technology seems to belie the fragmentation of body parts, so foregrounded an aspect of this war. His surprise appearances as he bursts from trees and ground hint that he is "naturally" whole, even that the fragmented images of his body presented by the camera's eye—arm, eye, throat, hand—are (merely) synecdochic, not, as the camera shows, disconnected items of an interchangeable body machinery. Rambo's body, as it carries these emblems, diverts attention from their overt expression through the display of his body as technology: "you had to stop once in a while and admire the machinery." Through him, *as* him, this technology is unchallengeable and its structure of operations seemingly undefeatable. As the camera's intimate examination of Rambo's body declares, this ideology is seamless.

Deferring the body as technology in war reinforces Steve Neale's assertion that "in a heterosexual and patriarchal society, the male body cannot be marked explicitly as the erotic object of another male look," explaining that "that look must be motivated in some other way, its erotic component repressed."[38] By representing Rambo's body as performance, the otherwise erotically suggestive display of his bare chest throughout the film is diverted as an object of military training, "a fighting machine." As Neale recognizes, the chief mechanism in mainstream cinema for deferring eroticism in the heterosexual male body is through establishing that body as an object of violence, so that erotic desire can be displaced as sadomasochism. Rambo's torture by the Russians, his brutal treatment by the Vietnamese, and his flashbacks on having his chest slashed by a Vietnamese prison guard all act to divert attention away from his body to those who mutilate it. (Think here as well of Chuck Norris's torture in *Missing in Action 2*, the Russian roulette scenes of *The Deer Hunter*, and the severed head that stands as castration threat in *Apocalypse Now*.)

But most important for this argument is Neale's final point that the erotic content of the male look can best be diverted

> by drawing upon the structures and processes of fetishistic looking, by stopping the narrative in order to recognize the pleasure of display, but displacing it from the male body as such and locating it more generally in the overall components of a highly ritualized scene. (p. 12)

The aesthetic of technology in Vietnam representation provides just such a displacement. The weapons that Rambo carries distract viewers from seeing the body that carries them as anything more than a part of those weapons itself, the "machine" that is needed in order for them to operate effectively. (This is why Rambo's weapons—his knife, bow, and rifle—require his individual skill to be operated as opposed to the depersonalized weapons of the Russians, which are operated by pushing buttons, turning dials, and employing massive machinery that usually requires more than one man to operate them.) At moments when this war technology is being used, it captures the full attention of the camera "by stopping the narrative in order to recognize the pleasure of display" ("you had to stop once in a while and admire the machinery").

In Vietnam representation, technology does not "stand in for" the (male) body but *is* that body, because the body has ceased to have meaning as a whole and has instead become a fragmented collection of disconnected parts that achieve the illusion of coherence only through their display as spectacle, a point at which the narrative of war stops and signification proclaims itself as self-sufficient and powerful. Power here is not, to return to Lyotard, achieved by the accomplishment of specified goals (death of the enemy or acquisition of territory), but through the display of performance, means rather than ends. Force is not determined by how many are killed, but by the ability to enact display, by the capacity for staging spectacle (think here of American helicopters invading Grenada playing Wagner, "imitating" *Apocalypse Now*).

And finally, because technology is the (male) body,[39] that body achieves not only the illusion of coherence, but its power as well.

> As anyone who has fired a bazooka or an M-60 machine gun knows, there is something to that power in your finger, the soft, seductive touch of the trigger. It's like the magic sword, a grunt's Excalibur—all you do is move that finger so imperceptibly, just a wish flashing across your mind like a shadow, not even a full brain synapse, and poof! in a blast of sound and energy and light a truck or a house or even people disappear, everything flying and settling back into dust.

The (male) body here seems to cease to be an object of erotic desire because it becomes larger than itself, becomes instead a mechanism to control desire that is not channeled into its own forms of erotic display. In two texts that otherwise rarely mention women, the channeling of desire is written so that the eroticism of war is read as strictly heterosexual. Michael Herr recalls how "An English correspondent I knew made a cassette of one of the heavy ones [firefights], he said he used it to seduce American girls";[41] William Broyles, Jr., declares that "Most men who have been to war, and most women who have been around it, remember that never in their lives did they have so heightened a sexuality. War is, in short, a turn-on."[42] By appearing to remove the body from the realm of the erotic and reinscribing it only within the frame of the heterosexual, the aesthetic of technology can divert attention away from the male body as an object of homoerotic desire. In such terms, the power and display of the (male) body/technology outside of the heterosexual is castrating.

## II

The aesthetic of the male body as spectacle, enacted through the technologies of performance, produces the subject of Vietnam representation. Soldiers in Vietnam were not unaware of their own participation in spectacle, from battle to battle, from film to film. In discussing film John Ellis explains that "identification with the cinematic apparatus is a precondition for any cinematic event: it represents the spectator's desire to concentrate him- or herself into the activities of visual and aural perception."[43] For soldiers in Vietnam, this translates into an identification with the frame of the spectacle—the visual display—as precondition for their experiencing the theater that is Vietnam. One of the most consistent motifs of Vietnam narratives is the comparison of the soldier's experience to movies. William Pelfry's *The Big V* is the most insistently referential: "Looking back it was so much like a movie. It always was; as I reminisce, that's the most striking and revolting thing about it."[44] "The MPs were frisking the gooks, feeling their bodies just like a policeman in a movie" (p. 16); "Just like in a damned movie" (p. 23); "Just like the six o'clock news" (p. 23); "The whole thing was so Hollywoodesque" (p. 38); "Kell . . . came skipping back through the bush like John Wayne" (p. 55); "just like in the USO commercials" (p. 61); "like movie stars" (p. 61).

To be conscious of movies as the frame for the Vietnam experience is to be keyed to the dimension of war as spectacle. But what Vietnam representation reveals most insistently is the extent to which the subject not only views the spectacle but is implicated in it, becomes an actor in the spectacle that is Vietnam. Such subjects recapitulate the shift from ends to means; subjects do not identify the actor and remain outside of the action but instead become immersed in the actions themselves, *as* actors. Although many narratives relate episodes of Vietnam in which the subject is watching the theater, as in *The Boys in Company C*, many also acknowledge the extent to which the subject *is* part of that theater, is *in* the movie rather than in the audience.

> I had flash images of John Wayne films with myself as the hero.[45]

> I was John Wayne in *Sands of Iwo Jima*. I was Aldo Ray in *Battle Cry*.[46]

> Oh, my God, this was like a movie! I couldn't conceive that I was really there. I was a participant, but I still didn't feel like I was going to get hit, because I really wasn't there; it was total denial.[47]

These narrative moments reveal the extent to which the subject of Vietnam representation cannot be seen as separate from the construction of that representation.

The subject and representation of Vietnam, like the body and technology, are codefined and mutually validated. One soldier recognizes the structure of that representation as technology: "Somehow, you've carried the wild notion around that all this firepower, all these arms and ammunition, have been assembled not so much to take enemy lives as to protect yours, that the military machine's topmost priority is to lead you safely from harm's way."[48] But this soldier's position as subject for whom the spectacle of Vietnam technology is shown quickly shifts, and he comes to an understanding of the extent to which he exists for the survival of that spectacle as well. He shifts from seeing the technology as being designed for him to recognizing that it is he who is designed for the technology.

> Like any other machine, the green machine [the Army] is impersonal to your life and death. You are only another piece of equipment, like a tank or the M-16 you carry, and your loss would be counted and calculated only in those terms. The machine would not care that a man had died, only that another part of its inventory had been lost and would require replacement, like the destroyed tank. And like the totaled tank, the Army would simply put in another order at another factory—a boot camp, where your replacement was being tooled and trained on a different kind of assembly line. (p. 652)

Both viewer and participant, cause and effect of the machine, the subject of Vietnam representation is split between these two shifting points of view in relation to the spectacle of Vietnam: the subject as viewer and the subject whose body can "count" as spectacle itself.

In Vietnam representation the subject can come to recognize itself only through/as spectacle: subject as spectacle/spectacle as subject. Mikkel Borsch-Jacobsen refines interpretations of Lacanian analysis when he asserts that the self is not determined *in relation to* the Other, to the constructions of discourse with which s/he interacts, but instead is *the same as* the Other, is the shared constructions of the signification of the Other. In such a context, Borsch-Jacobsen goes on, the "subject as representation" is coterminous with "representation as subject."[49] The subject can know itself only through representation.

By both viewing and participating in the movie that is Vietnam, by recognizing itself *as* representation, the subject of Vietnam comes into existence. On entrance into the military and Vietnam, subjects of Vietnam are made to feel severed from other forms of representation, other selves. They are "cherries":

> From that day on they called him Cherry and from the night of that day and on he thought of himself as Cherry. It confused him yet it felt right. He was in a new world, a strange world. . . . It made little difference to him that they

> called every new man Cherry and that with the continual rotation of personnel there would soon be a soldier newer than he and he would call the new man Cherry.[50]

On entrance into the Vietnam theater each subject is immediately redefined, renamed, rerepresented as the Other—"they called him Cherry"—to become an immediate participant of Vietnam spectacle. And Cherry is here both participant—"he thought of himself as Cherry"—and observer—"there would soon be a soldier newer than he and he would call the new man Cherry." He *is* the spectacle to the older soldiers and will validate it *as* spectator for any newer than he. The rotation of soldier's tours in Vietnam for 365 days insured that this representation would be ongoing, that the position of self and other would remain consistently fluid and in process.

John Ellis describes two tendencies in cinematic identification: first, what he calls "dreaming and fantasy identification," in which the subject identifies with various positions in a fictional narrative "across filmic narratives with the various phantasy positions that these narratives invoke"[51] and, second, "narcissistic identification," in which the subject recognizes its self in the images on the screen (p. 43). What Ellis calls "dreaming and fantasy identification" is, as he defines it, a positional relation of the subject to the filmic narrative, one in which the subject takes the part of a functional role in the narrative—hero, villain, victim, and so on. Such positional relations must take place in reference to the structure of the narrative. For as Vladimir Propp made clear in his structural analysis of the Russian folktale,[52] only through narrative can a function be defined, that is, one is a hero only in relation to circumstances that can require a rescue, a noble act, a feat of strength or skill. I thus refer to this form of identification as "structural." Ellis's second category, narcissistic identification, relates to how the subject sees aspects of its self in various images on the screen. These forms of identification are thus separated from the functional positions images have in a narrative, for example "because I have blond hair, I am (like) Robert Redford, whether he is hero or villain." Such identifications divorce the display of an image from its narrative context and lodge it instead in a visual context, in which it functions as an element of and reinforcement for its syntagmatic relations to other images. This type of identification I call "spectacular."

These two categories, the structural and the spectacular, frame Vietnam representation. In the spectacular, Vietnam is seen as display—whether as flares, firefights, or Rambo's body. The structural is the frame for the individual's participation in Vietnam and defines the role, position, or function the individual will take—whether as hero or enemy; as lieutenant, captain, or "grunt"; or as part of a machine. It is important to emphasize that no aspect of Vietnam representation is limited to one or the other form of identification. Technology, for example, can act as both structure—"the green machine," systems management, or computerized logistics—and display—weaponry, bombing, or the body as "fighting machine."

In Philip Caputo's description of his activities in Vietnam as a movie, the structural and the spectacular intersect:

> I had enjoyed the killing of the Viet Cong who had run out of the tree line. Strangest of all had been that sensation of watching myself in a movie. One part of me was doing something while the other part watched from a distance, shocked by the things it saw, yet powerless to stop them from happening.[53]

Caputo describes here both the structural and the spectacular: seeing himself as an actor in the war, a soldier, and watching himself performing those actions as a viewer, separated from his own activities. He is neither representation nor subject but "representation as subject/subject as representation." In this context, Caputo is not simply "the same as the Other," but is both self and other coextensively. Caputo's experience seems to have been framed then not by the structural or the spectacular, but by both simultaneously. He is both *in* a movie and *watching* himself in a movie.

But as Jacques Derrida reminds us, such simultaneity is not possible: "every transgressive gesture reencloses us. . . . One is never installed within transgression, one never lives elsewhere."[54] To claim to be both inside and outside—to be both participant and viewer—is in actuality to posit a third position which can encompass the other two, a position which is itself made available only through the introduction of yet another frame from which these dual positions can be narrated. Caputo accomplishes this, for instance, by positioning himself outside of his experience in Vietnam in the act of becoming a narrator for his past. Inside this narrative frame, Caputo can speak as if he were inside and outside—viewer and actor—only because each position is inside the larger frame of the narrative that he is reciting, a narrative in which his position as narrator is not dispersed but stable.

Judith Hicks Stiehm offers an interesting occasion for the investigation of such participant/viewer relations in her account of the integration of women into the Air Force Academy, *Bring Me Men and Women*. Because of their status both publicly and professionally, she notes, "cadets and academy personnel were used to having an audience." Importantly, "much of that audience was female." Consequently, "when women were integrated into the academy, the audience for men's performance declined. Some of the ex-audience joined the performers. When this occurs previously private behavior becomes known and action becomes self-conscious."[55] Stiehm elaborates in a footnote:

> An audience gives permission and sometimes applause. When there is no audience, actors must question themselves; they require a self-justification they had not needed before. Or their performance must be so good that other actors relinquish their own presentation to watch. (p. 284n)

Unlike previous American wars, the "audience" for the Vietnam War was never as clearly defined or as stable. And Vietnam, unlike Europe, did not supply its own audience for American displays, lacking the receptive and grateful citizenry that often lined the streets of European towns to greet American "heroes." Instead, American soldiers more often tell of being met with sales pitches (for anything from watches to women), suspicion, or outright hostility. In such a context, they would "require a self-justification they had not needed before." The significance of Stiehm's comments is that this self-justification did not come in terms of increased social or political rhetoric, but in increased display, "superb enough to gain an audience of fellow-workers" (p. 284n). Likewise, for Vietnam soldiers, this lack of an audience was not replaced by augmented patriotism or even explanations for American presence in Vietnam, but by an enhancement of the war's display, with its warriors as audience, soldiers watching themselves fighting a war. And, as Stiehm reports of the Air Force cadets, "their performance must be so good that other actors relinquish their own presentation to watch." More than almost any individual performance, the war's technology/body achieved this end.

Heroes like Rambo and Chuck Norris's Colonel Braddock (*Missing In Action* and *Missing in Action 2*) had their own audiences provided by their narratives—the captured POWs who were waiting and watching, hoping to be rescued by these "fighting machines." In *Missing in Action* and *Missing in Action 2* Braddock is numerous times the object of POWs' attentions, as they watch from behind the bars of their cages Braddock accomplishing superhuman feats of endurance, strength, and will. Rambo as well has his own audience, not just in the men he rescues, but in the soldiers of the base camp who are monitoring his radio communications.

But both Rambo and Braddock are occupying, like Caputo, the shifting positions of observer and participant: they who are now actors were once themselves POWs, once members of their own audience. Similarly, in the opening scenes of Oliver Stone's *Platoon* (1986), the new soldiers, the "cherries," watch as seasoned soldiers pass by them. Both are occupying positions of exchange, as these new soldiers are on display for the old, who are now members of an audience they once performed for. Like the Air Force cadets, they cannot remain in one position but must relinquish it at times for other performers. In order to maintain the existence of an audience—and therefore of the validity of their own performances—they must be willing to accept the role of viewer as well as actor, must, in Stiehm's words, "relinquish their own presentation to watch."

The pretense of occupying two positions simultaneously is one of the primary features of Vietnam representation. It functions primarily to promote a strategy of blurring: (con)fusing categories *at the same time* the categories are being maintained. For Caputo, this means speaking of the self as both actor and spectator, without seeming to abandon either position. Yet the consequence of such action for Caputo is clear: "shocked by the things it saw, yet powerless to stop them from happening." The strategy of blurring categories leads, not to a challenging of categories, but to a sense of powerlessness, or an inability to alter the frame (movies/representation) within which the categories are presented. Films like Oliver Stone's *Platoon* effect this blurring as an audience position as well, rarely allowing the distancing camera shot that gives perspective, offering only the close-up that isolates viewers in the positions of soldiers—confused, lost, helpless. This blurring operates to distract attention from the third position within which the two categories (inside/outside) are fixed, to prevent the reader/viewer/soldier from recognizing the position from which the categories are being presented and defined. It leaves the reader in a state of paralysis, unable to challenge the text on its (unspoken) grounds, able only to shift back and forth from one prescribed position to another. You are either in the movie or in the audience, but you are not producing the theater.

This feature of shifting from movie to audience is interestingly valorized in much contemporary literature as a feature of "literariness" rather than ideology. Cecelia Tichi suggests, for example, that contemporary writers of "new fiction" like Ann Beattie, Bret Easton Ellis, Bobbie Ann Mason, Tama Janowitz, and others frequently featured in magazines like *The New Yorker* employ this technique as part of "a full revolt against the traditional structure of beginning-middle-end because it is false to their perceptual experience."[56] But this "revolt" produces, ironically, the same situation as Caputo describes, what Tichi identifies as "a location where characters can be forever poised for action rather than engaged in it" (p. 13). Tichi labels this an effect of a television culture in which

> TV viewers become sojourners in several video realms and in the material world too. In transit, they may feel self-possessed only at the point of juncture between worlds. In the new fiction, that threshold is more often than not *the* place to be, the only firm place, both a point of poise for the author and the locus of attention for the reader. (p. 13)

What Tichi's comments reveal is that this feature of placing subjects at a "point of juncture" belongs neither to "high" nor "low" culture, neither to literary nor popular writing, neither to the avant-garde nor to the colloquial but to the general operation of dominant cultural representation in American society.[57]

It might also seem at first that the multiple relations Vietnam subjects have to their representations could provide a position from which to critique those representations. Teresa de Lauretis argues, for example, that the contradictory positions women are asked to hold within ideology enable them to gain, through the disruption produced by these contradictions, a distance from that ideology, one that men, whose positions in relation to ideological constructions are formed with more coherence and stability, are less able to experience.[58] But these contradictions are not the same as the positions of viewer/participant held by subjects in Vietnam representation. While de Lauretis suggests that women can become aware of these contradictions and use this awareness to reexamine ideology, the viewer/participant in Vietnam representation is instead diverted from such analysis through the representation of spectacle. The subject is recaptured in the coherent and stable narrative position from which the viewer/participant roles are recounted, is diverted by the display of the hero who wills their "escape" from such positions. When Rambo and Braddock release the POWs, it is not to challenge the structures that placed the prisoners in such positions, but to enable them to regain their ability to become performers once again.[59] The display of the technology/body of Vietnam representation diverts attention away from these multiple positions themselves to the spectacle that surrounds them and leads, not to any radical questioning of ideology, but to a paralysis in the face of that ideology. The contradictory subject of Vietnam representation is reinscribed in narrative by the display of the new hero, the enhanced spectacle of war.

Thus, rather than the Vietnam experience challenging the current structures of American society, it seems only to enhance them. John Wheeler's account of how the training soldiers received is transferred to stateside jobs reveals this replacement. Federal Express founder Frederick W. Smith, for instance, constructed his company in the plan of the delivery system for Vietnam. Tellingly, Wheeler insists, "*If you have overnight mail and courier in a war zone you can have it in the States*."[60] Wheeler's own experience mimics this transference: "My perceptions had been honed by war service. The article [written in law school on computer technology he learned in Vietnam] led to a surprise offer to join the staff of the SEC as an assistant general counsel to work on computer applications to securities regulation" (p. 51). Vietnam became in many ways a testing ground for systems and organizations that would later be adapted to civilian use. As such, its participants became reinscribed within the larger "systems analysis" of American society. Such reincorporation prescribes a narrative position that disenables the expression of accounts of contradictions or repositionings in relation to ideology and allows only a repositioning in relation to spectacle.

In *Touched with Fire* Wheeler exemplifies this strategy in his analysis of the effect Vietnam has had on American society:

> For ten years, I have found myself wrestling with the question of how the events of the Vietnam era shape America. It seems clear to me that the war itself was both catalyst and fuel for the social, economic, and political change in America since 1960. It also seems clear that the events of the war years are interconnected, and they feed each other in their effects. (p. 3)

A catalyst is something added to a mixture that causes other reactions to occur. It cannot be both that mixture and its additive; it cannot be both the fuel and that which ignites it. Wheeler suggests that events are both interconnected and causal, that they relate both spatially and linearly. His study of Vietnam is thus premised on a strategy that confuses not only categories but also the relations between them. Rather than "explain" the war, this type of argument (re)presents it in such a way that the process of explanation itself becomes blurred.

This is an indication of the shift from ends to means with which this chapter began; it is more pointedly shown here as a shift from working toward a specific explanation to restructuring the way in which explanations (don't) take place. Consequently, the proliferation of Vietnam representation in contemporary American culture must be read, not as increasingly refined attempts to arrive at an explanation of the war, but as increasingly deferred logics that produce a (con)fusion from which explanation cannot occur. The strategy of these representations, as we have just seen, is not to provide contradictory or inexplicable information—on the contrary, Vietnam representation suggests, if anything, that its information is incontrovertibly clear, that, like the MIAs, it is there if one wishes to find it. Instead, the strategy of these representations is to produce, not an incoherent object, but a confused subject, one that is positioned by its representations in such a way that it is incapable of acting on the information it seems so clearly to hold. In this way, the display of spectacle negates dissent so that the Vietnam subject, though in possession of "information," will be unable to offer a contrary explanation for its appearance, will be unable to do anything other than evaluate its performance.

## III

## Chevvys and Fords

> "It's been proven!" someone said. "You take and put a Chevvy in a Ford and a Ford in a Chevvy and they *both* go faster. It's been proven!"[61]

Norman Mailer's *The Armies of the Night: History as a Novel, The Novel as History* (1968), Michael Herr's *Dispatches* (1978), and Richard Nixon's *No More Vietnams* (1985) are some of the best-known works written on the Vietnam war. They are presented from what appear to be excluding positions. Herr's text is written during the early years of the war about his experiences at the height of the war's escalation, Mailer's about one of the largest demonstrations against the war, and Nixon's about the end of the war and the collapse of the Saigon government. Herr is a journalist, Mailer a novelist, and Nixon a politician and (in this context) an historian. Herr talks of the futility of the war, Mailer writes of ending it, and Nixon of how we could have "won" it. Mailer speaks from a "liberal" point of view, Nixon from a "conservative," and Herr from a nonpolitical perspective defined by the political uncertainty of the war itself. These texts, then, are opposed in point of view, literary style, interpretation, and political interest.

But to focus on foregrounded political positioning in reading the representation of Vietnam is to ignore the way in which those positions are themselves constructed and represented. Although each purports to take a specific stance on the Vietnam war, these texts share a strategy of representation that becomes a spectacle itself, one that paralyzes rather than enables effective political action. Mailer's, Nixon's, and Herr's texts employ the same tactic for argument: (con)fusing fact and fiction, which leads the reader to a point of paralysis. Political orientation thus becomes only another aspect of the spectacular that diverts attention away from the structural aspects of representation. Such an analysis reveals that it is not political declaration that structures representation as much as a strategy of spectacle that cuts across political posturing to position the subject in similar rather than contradictory relations to reality.

*The Armies of the Night* is an autobiographical account of Mailer's participation in the 1967 Pentagon protest against the Vietnam War. In it he recounts the performances of speakers like Paul Goodman, Robert Lowell, and Dwight MacDonald, as well as his own speech at the Ambassador Theater, the demonstration itself, his own arrest and release, and the ensuing news accounts of the demonstration. Mailer's subtitle for the book, *History as a Novel, The Novel as History,* establishes his sense of the structure of the text. The first half describes the October march from Mailer's point of view, emphasizing his own anxieties, frustrations, and reactions to the protest. The second half uses an omniscient narrator who treats Mailer as only one of several actors in the event, using for its sources accounts from magazines, newspapers, and other eyewitnesses. In Mailer's words:

> Yet in writing his personal history of these four days, he was delivered a discovery of what the March on the Pentagon had finally meant, and what had been won, and what had been lost, and so found himself ready at last to write a most concise Short History, a veritable précis of a collective novel, which here now, in the remaining pages, will seek as History, no, rather as some Novel of History, to elucidate the mysterious character of that quintessentially American event.[62]

It was Mailer's autobiographical account then that presumably enabled him to write a history that could explain "what the March on the Pentagon had finally meant." His own impressionistic and subjective account is being somehow replaced by a factual and objective one in the second half of the book.

But toward the end of *The Armies of the Night* Mailer challenges his own oppositional treatment, admitting that "the conceit [that] one is writing a history must be relinquished" (p. 283). "It is obvious," he continues, "the first book is a history in the guise or dress or manifest of a novel, and the second is a real or true novel—no less!—presented in the style of a history" (p. 284). As a result, the original presentation of "novel" and "history" is reversed, so that Mailer's personal account itself becomes a "document," being "to the best of the author's memory scrupulous to facts," whereas the history becomes a "collective novel"—which is to admit that an explanation of the mystery of the events at the Pentagon cannot be developed by the methods of history, only by the "instincts of the novelist" (p. 284). The categories of fact/fiction and objective/subjective have been reversed.

Mailer opens his book with the following proposal: "From the outset, let us bring you news of your protagonist. The following is from *Time* magazine, October 27, 1967" (p. 13). Mailer then quotes an article entitled "A Shaky Start" that characterizes him as a drunken, publicity-seeking "antistar" of the protest, "spewing obscenities as he staggered about the stage." Returning to his own narrative after this lengthy quotation, Mailer concludes his opening chapter: "Now we may leave *Time* in order to find out what happened" (p. 14).

It is clear at this point that Mailer is prepared to (con)fuse fact and fiction on several levels, challenging the *Time* version of his behavior with his own version of "what happened." Contrary to his later statements that only after he had written his autobiographical account had he "found himself ready at last" to write history, Mailer already claims to be writing the more "factual" account of the demonstration and the events surrounding it. He has already begun to (con)fuse categories in his narrative voice: "let *us* bring *you* news of *your* protagonist" (italics added). The omniscient narrator of part two—"the novel as history"—fuses here with the subjective narrator of part one—"history as a novel"—as Mailer presents himself as carrying the voice of both the individual and the collective, both the historical and the novelistic. Importantly, neither voice includes the position of the reader—"*your* protagonist" (italics added). While other categories are being fused, the reader is being distanced.

Two of Mailer's assumptions typify Vietnam narratives: first, that personal experience is the "documentary" of the war and, second, that histories written about the war should be "collective novels." In the first category fall works like Philip Caputo's *Rumors of War* (1977), Michael Herr's *Dispatches* (1978), and Tim O'Brien's *If I Die in a Combat Zone* (1973). In the second category are works such as Mark Baker's *Nam* (1981), Al Santoli's *Everything We Had* (1981), Zalin Grant's *Survivors* (1975), Wallace Terry's *Bloods* (1984), and Kathryn Marshall's *In the Combat Zone* (1987). In these collections, a war that seems to have no single interpretation is re-presented in its dissonance by a plethora of voices.

These assumptions, operating to various degrees in Vietnam representation, vivify the spectacular and the structural. Collective personal accounts generally recall the most significant part of each individual's memory of the war—its atrocities, racial incidents, firefights, fear, gags, mistakes, sexual encounters, torture, and so on. Presented as they are out of context and in fragmented form, these micro-narratives are like Rambo's body, held up for display as objects separated from the person who experienced them. With so many names, actual names become nameless. Experiences seem self-embodied; like Rambo, they spring from nowhere, and the reader is preoccupied with what will come next rather than with how or why they happened.

And this is precisely the point. Blurring fragments of narratives into a collective novel creates the appearance of a whole as if these disparate pieces all fit together as a unit. This is the structural tactic of Vietnam narrative: to create the illusion of a collective experience (in a war in which soldiers fought only for a year [the Marines for thirteen months] and rotated in and out of units), as if there were a common bond behind the varied incidents recounted in these narratives. As I discuss in chapter two, this collective novel as structure subsumes disparate elements into the framework of the masculine bond. When everything else is different—background, race, ethnicity, class, military rank, and expertise—these soldiers share the common experience of the masculine bond. Mailer's insistence on the collective novel and the reproduction of Vietnam narrative as collected fragments of individual experience is the structural equivalent of the masculine bond; these collected narratives create the illusion of a shared bond, if only by appearing as the "same" text.

Like Mailer's use of "we" and "you" to distance the reader from his various narrative positions, these characteristics of Vietnam narrative—the documentary validity of personal experience and the historical validity of the collective narrative—function as well to distance the reader from representation. Lyotard identifies as one of the primary rules for the production of scientific knowledge "the rule that there is no reality unless testified by a consensus between partners over a certain knowledge and certain commitments."[63] The same can be said of cultural "knowledge" in Vietnam representation. Through the "we" of the collective narrative, a reality is created and simultaneously validated, but this reality, as Mailer makes clear, is not available to readers except as they participate in the consensus of the narrators.

William Broyles, Jr., in his account of his return to Vietnam in 1986, *Brothers in Arms: A Journey from War to Peace*, makes these exclusionary lines clearest. Eliding all political differences between veterans of Vietnam, Broyles insists that the lines of separation are not drawn by politics or judgments about the war but by "being there": "Many veterans of the Vietnam War helped in different ways in the course of my writing this book. . . . Several of them have written their own books, and most would probably disagree with at least some of what appears in this one. No matter. All of us were there."[64] Kathryn Marshall, in the introduction to her collection of narratives of women in Vietnam, *In the Combat Zone: An Oral History of American Women in Vietnam*, makes the same point: "Just as there is no 'woman's position' on war, there is no single position on the Vietnam War in this collection. . . . [A]ll they had had in common was that they had gone to the Vietnam War."[65] Broyles insists that such lines obtain in all wars. After recounting the story of the battle of Gettysburg by a captain in the Confederate Army, Broyles concludes,

> The language is different, but it is the same story. And it is a story that I would imagine has been told for as long as men went to war. *Its purpose is not to enlighten but to exclude. Its message is not its content but to put the listener in his place.* I suffered, I was there. You were not. Only those facts matter. Everything else is beyond words to tell. [italics added][66]

For Broyles finally this exclusion goes beyond any political or national boundaries, for "War stories . . . are all, at bottom, the same" (p. 195). This exclusion aligns him with all men who fought in battle, for whatever side, against all of those who took the "part of staying behind" (p. xi): "I discovered that I had more in common with my old enemies than with anyone except the men who had fought at my side. My enemies and I had shared something almost beyond words" (p. 275).

As with Mailer's, Herr's, and Nixon's narratives, political questions take second place to identification and maintenance of the collective. The exclusion of those who did not participate marks a stronger and more permanent boundary than any formed by nations, parties, communities, or families. Even President Reagan is excluded from Broyles's "brotherhood," because he too, for all of his sympathy with veterans, "hadn't been there" (p. 202). In such a context, the documentary collective narratives of Vietnam establish in their telling an exclusion at all levels of the very person who is reading the accounts. For even those who were "there" were not in these particular circumstances, did not share these identical experiences; and even those whose stories are being told are distanced from their narratives through the telling, through shaping them as narrative in retrospect. There is thus an ongoing process of collective-formation as the narrative is being told *and* a process of exclusion as the reader is distanced from the events through narrative. For this reason, Vietnam narrative can never be completely "told" and the lines of exclusion never firmly established. This is why the market for Vietnam literature can bear appearance after appearance of a "new" collective narrative of Vietnam. The process of exclusion, which is the very premise of the narratives, requires their retelling in even slightly varied forms, even to those who were "there."

Michael Herr's narrative of his Vietnam experience, *Dispatches*, is a tale of becoming a part of this consensus. He opens his narrative as Mailer does, by explaining how "facts" are not absolute, but interpretable:

> It was late '67 now, even the most detailed maps didn't reveal much anymore; reading them was like trying to read the faces of the Vietnamese, and that was like trying to read the wind. We knew that the uses of most information were flexible, different pieces of ground told different stories to different people. We also knew that for years now there had been no country here but the war.[67]

The "we" here, "now," is an excluded one, someone who is unable to interpret the war, to "read" Vietnam. His distance is compounded when he hears a soldier tell his own "war story":

> "Patrol went up the mountain. One man came back. He died before he could tell us what happened."
>
> I waited for the rest, but it seemed not to be that kind of story; when I asked him what had happened he just looked like he felt sorry for me, fucked if he'd waste time telling stories to anyone dumb as I was. (pp. 4–5)

Obviously not a part of the consensus that could comprehend this "reality," Herr makes it clear that he did come to understand the story later: "it took me a year to understand it" (p. 4).

Isolated from the Vietnam narrative in the beginning, Herr soon identifies himself with the soldiers he follows in the war. He becomes a part of their story:

> I was in many ways brother to these poor, tired grunts, I knew what they knew now, I'd done it and it was really something. (p. 220)

He even becomes a part of their war:

> But of course we were intimate, I'll tell you how intimate: they were my guns, and I let them do it. . . . We covered each other, an exchange of services that worked all right until one night I slid over to the wrong end of the story, propped up behind some sandbags at an airstrip in Can Tho with a .30-caliber automatic in my hands, firing cover for a four-man reaction team trying to get back in. (pp. 70–71)

During Tet, he confesses, "I wasn't a reporter, I was a shooter" (p. 71). The day after, he wonders whether he killed any of the bodies he saw lying in the field after the firefight. The structural and the spectacular merge:

> And for the next six years I saw them all, the ones I'd really seen and the ones I'd imagined, theirs and ours, friends I'd loved and strangers, motionless figures in a dance, the old dance. Years of thinking this or that about what happens to you when you pursue a fantasy until it becomes experience, and then afterward you can't handle the experience. Until I felt that I was just a dancer too. (pp. 71–72)

At first an outsider who can't even understand a war story, Herr becomes "just a dancer too," one of the fragmented pieces of Vietnam representation. He has merged with the "reality" of the war by accepting its consensus, assuming its voices. Like Mailer, his personal experience enables him to write history, as he leaves the individual and identifies with the collective: "Where else could you go for a real sense of the war's past? There were all kinds of people who knew the background, the facts, the most minute details, but only a correspondent could give you the exact mood that attended each of the major epochs" (p. 241). The mark of the transition from outsider to member, from individual experience to history is being able to speak with the voice of the collective. For Mailer, it is using the "instincts of the novelist"; for Herr, the "mood" that only a journalist could capture; for the "collective novel," it is speaking for all of the soldiers whose stories weren't told. As the editors of *Charlie Company: What Vietnam Did to Us* explain:

> We had chosen Charlie Company almost out of a hat. It was only as our reporting progressed that we found the close family resemblances between our

> small, unscientific sample and a 1,380-interview profile of Vietnam veterans by the Center for Policy Research in the most authoritative study now extant.[68]

The collectivity of Vietnam voices is so unified that even a random, "unscientific" account can speak for its "family."

In each of these cases, the structural *becomes* the spectacular, as the individual stories function both as display—representing individual events, images, and so on—and as structure, as the fragmented pieces of the spectacle are gathered into a collective narrative that gives them the appearance of one voice, a "we" that can reliably tell the history of the war. The spectacular is collapsed onto the structural in order to present an aesthetic of war.[69] Broyles asserts that "War *is* beautiful" and goes on to explain: "The seduction of war is in its offering such intense beauty—divorced from all civilized values, but beauty still."[70] The masking of the contradiction of his argument—that beauty, a socially defined construct, cannot exist outside of "civilized values"—is elemental to his production of an aesthetic that depends for its (re)presentation on an appearance of self-definition and enclosure—"we" and "you." In positing its own aesthetic, positioning its readers, and establishing its own method of history, Vietnam representation succeeds in (re)presenting itself and the war with which it is associated as autonomous, able to set forth its own standards of evaluation, criteria for validation, and framework for judgment.

Richard Nixon's *No More Vietnams* epitomizes these portrayals and habits, employing the same strategies and techniques as Mailer's *Armies of the Night* and Herr's *Dispatches*, though for a different political purpose. Like Mailer and the collective novels of Vietnam soldiers, Nixon presents a version of an autobiographical narrative, writing both "objective" history—"How the Vietnam War Began"—and a personal account of his own acts as vice-president, president, and advisor during the years of the war: "I had been intimately associated with the history of Vietnam for twenty years."[71] Because of his "intimate" connection with the war ("I'll tell you how intimate: they were my guns, and I let them do it"), Nixon's personal narrative and his account of the war's history merge. The objective and the subjective intermingle and the documentary becomes the personal.

Nixon begins his narrative by claiming that "No event in American history is more misunderstood than the Vietnam War" (p. 9). Citing the numerous articles, books, films, and documentaries of Vietnam, Nixon introduces a litany of popular statements about the war by stating, "The great majority of these efforts have portrayed one or more of the following conclusions as facts" (p. 9). Included on that list are: "The Vietnam War was a civil war"; "The Buddhist protests in 1962 against Diem resulted from religious repression"; "The Johnson administration was the first to send American troops into combat in Vietnam"; "Most American soldiers were addicted to drugs, guilt-ridden about their role in the war, and deliberately used cruel and inhumane tactics"; "American blacks constituted a disproportionate number of the combat casualties"; "The antiwar demonstrations in the United States shortened the war"; "The domino theory has been proved false"; and "Life is better in Indochina now that the United States is gone" (pp. 9–10). Nixon concludes this opening section by declaring: "All of these statements are false" (p. 10).

Nixon thus opens his narrative in a pattern identical to Mailer's quotation of the *Time* article and subsequent effort to "find out what happened": the inversion of "facts" and "myths" as preface to an exposition of "history." Nixon's strategy becomes even more confusing when he elides exaggerations with misstatements of well-documented situations as if they were equivalent. Thus he states, "American soldiers . . . deliberately used cruel and inhumane tactics" and "American blacks constituted a disproportionate number of the combat casualties." Wallace Terry's figures are reliable. According to Terry, the black soldier "was dying at a greater rate, proportionately, than American soldiers of other races. In the early years of the fighting, blacks made up 23 percent of the fatalities. . . . [In 1969] Black combat fatalities had dropped to 14 percent, still proportionately higher than the 11 percent which blacks represented in the American population."[72] For Nixon to suggest that all of his characterized statements about the war are equally "myths" is to deny a basis for challenging his argument as a misrepresentation of situations. Like Mailer's narrative, Nixon's (con)fuses the status of fact and fiction as a route to bypass and paralyze the reader/audience.

Nixon's first three chapters, "The Myths of Vietnam," "How the War Began," and "Why and How We Went into Vietnam," are largely explanatory and constitute his "novel as history." The last chapters, "How We Won the War," "How We Lost the Peace," and "Third World War," are Nixon's own analyses of the war and projections for how future incidents should be handled differently. They are based primarily on Nixon's personal diplomatic and political experience and constitute his "history as novel." He first presents the "facts" about the war and then reinterprets them in a fiction of how the outcome could have been different: "On January 27, 1973, almost twenty years after the French had lost the first Vietnam War, we had won the second Vietnam War" (p. 164). In so doing Nixon succeeds in rewriting, seventeen years later, the plan of *Armies of the Night*, thereby inverting the status of fact and fiction. As a result, he is able to redefine the meaning of "winning" a war:

> But *win* must be properly defined. We are a defensive power. We are not trying to conquer other countries. That is why we must have a policy in which we will fight limited wars if they are necessary to achieve limited goals. We *win* if we prevent the enemy from winning. (p. 225)

Consequently, Nixon is able to assert that the statement that America lost the war in Vietnam is no longer a fact, but a myth, a conclusion "portrayed . . . as facts." Thus we have "history as a novel, the novel as history."

And, Nixon concludes, "*we* win." While he acknowledges his own "intimate" involvement with the war, Nixon moves, like Mailer and Herr, from an "objective" account to an inclusive "we." While his first two chapters purport to be factual summaries of the events leading up to America's involvement in Vietnam, the next three chapters move quickly and subtly away from a distanced objectivity to an "intimate" correspondence. Nixon slides from "they" to "we" on both the historical and the rhetorical planes, historically as the "we" coincides with America's escalated participation in the war and rhetorically as "we" becomes the constructed narrative position of Nixon's account.

## "Facts No Longer Exist"

The position of the reader/viewer/soldier in Vietnam narrative is constructed by the (con)fusion of the status of fact and fiction. The resulting paralysis of response can then be overlaid by the "new" "facts" of the narrative: "they" become "we," the viewers and participants slide together. There are three stages to this process: denying previous concepts of fact, offering the narrator/author as authority/guide for the new definitions of fact, and having the narrator/author predetermine and occupy the reader's position. All work toward positioning the reader in a kind of paralysis in relation to textual interpretation.

(1) "All of these statements are false." When Mailer shifts to tell "what happened" and Nixon moves to demystify conclusions "portrayed . . . as facts," they are declaring to their readers that previous notions of fact are henceforth invalidated. Readers, if they choose to continue reading, are thus from the outset asked to abandon previous standards of judgment and analysis, not only about the specific information presented as fact and fiction, but about the very concept of a fact and its related "truth." A poem by Bill Tremblay, "Evening with Novelists at Crown Point Estates," captures this aspect of Vietnam representation. At a party, a veteran plays a tape of bomber pilots during a mission in Cambodia while Nixon's announcement of an end to hostilities is being piped into their cockpits.

> Besides, he says, everything he could ever say about a theory of
> fiction is embodied on that tape. Facts no longer exist. The record is
> simply a fabric of conflicting fictions which are believed in absolutely
> because not to believe them would mean that everything we've
> done we've
> done wrongly. That is our morality, the necessity to stick to our fictions
> because the consequences would be more than we could bear without
> them.[73]

Michael Herr's declaration that "trying to read the faces of the Vietnamese . . . was like trying to read the wind" reinforces the (con)fusion of the status of fact and fiction by suggesting that Vietnam was an unfamiliar world in which expected definitions and conclusions would appear alien. A common feature of Vietnam representation is to oppose "the World" to "the Nam," a place where values, actions, and lives have different meaning. *The 13th Valley*'s Daniel Egan explains: "Takin it personal is for people back in the World. We got a separate culture out here. And in some respects it's better."[74] This "separate culture," as the glossaries appended to many Vietnam narratives attest, has its own language, its own way of using words, its own way of determining meaning. The reigning feature of this discourse is that what was taken for a fact in the World has an entirely different meaning in the Nam. Definition of the "enemy" was particularly ambiguous. As one soldier explains, "In this type of fighting it was almost impossible to know who the enemy was at any one time. Children were suspect, women were suspect. Frequently the ARVNs themselves were on two payrolls."[75] The same villagers would, at different times, be friend or enemy, fact or fiction.

Philip Caputo makes the clearest statement on the status of "facts." He and several members of his platoon are on trial for the premeditated murder of a Vietnamese informant whom they questionably mistook, in their own frenzy to retaliate for the recent deaths of their friends, for a Viet Cong. After discussing the case with his lawyer, Caputo learns of "the wide gulf that divides the facts from the truth."[76]

> I was fascinated by the testimony that was produced by our Socratic dialogues. . . . There were qualifying phrases here and there . . . but there wasn't a single lie in it. And yet it wasn't the truth. Conversely, the attorneys for the enlisted men had them convinced that they were all good, God-fearing soldiers who had been obeying orders . . . issued by a vicious killer-officer. And that was neither a lie nor the truth. The prosecution had meanwhile marshaled facts to support its argument that five criminal marines, following the unlawful orders of their criminal platoon leader, had cold-bloodedly murdered two civilians. . . . And that was neither a lie nor the truth. None of this testimony, none of these "facts" amounted to the truth. (pp. 312–13)

For Caputo, who had the "sensation of watching myself in a movie," his position in relation to the "facts" is equally as confused as his sense of his own self in relation to them. Fact and fiction have become fused. Without a place from which to view them, Caputo cannot tell whether they are in or out of the movie.

(2) "The instincts of the novelist": In a place where "the uses of most information were flexible," the reader is in need of a guide. With the facts from "the World" no longer applicable, the reader is left with no firm basis for definition and evaluation. The reader must then depend on the narrator to establish new "facts" and new standards for their determination. Consequently, the narrator's ability to define fact and fiction becomes more significant than the distinction itself.

Faced with this dilemma, Mailer falls back on "the instincts of the novelist," as Herr does on the perception of the journalist, and Nixon on the intimacy of the politician. In each case, it is the quality and character of the narrator's position that is privileged, not the status of the information/narration they supply. In such a context, the reader's relation to the narrative is constructed in Lyotard's frame of modern technology—it is performance rather than "truth" that counts. The narrator is to be judged on the basis of how well s/he performs the process of narrating—of constructing the "collective novel"—not on the basis of the assessment, production, or validity of information.

Mimicking Mailer's retreat to "instinct," one soldier, when faced with a similar dilemma of (con)fusion, resorts to another kind of power: "In the Nam you realized that you had the power to take a life. . . . That godlike feeling you had was in the field. It was like I was a god. I could take a life, I could screw a woman. I could beat somebody up and get away with it."[77] Such control extends, as another soldier realizes, to the war itself. "I began to realize many months later that *we* were the war. If we wanted to go out and chase people around and shoot at them and get them to shoot back at us, we had a war going on. If we didn't do that, they left us alone."[78] Events, meaning, the war itself—all happen at the will of the narrator/soldier/journalist/president. (One thinks here of Johnson's insistence that he personally approve every bombing target during his presidency.) Once in "the Nam," Mailer, Herr, and Nixon are like gods, with the ability to determine what is myth, what is history, what is truth.

This narrative position lends itself to the interests of the structural, the power to make the war happen, to stage its events, to tell its story. But at the same time, it reproduces the spectacular as well. The narrator embodies the narration in his/her power to determine the status of fact and fiction and thus becomes a focus for display as well as for the production of structure. Like Caputo, Mailer, Herr, and Nixon find themselves both on the stage and in the audience. They are both participants in the events they recall and witnesses to their outcome.[79]

Mailer is narrating events in which he took part, detailing his own experiences and chronicling his participation in the march, building from "the author's memory" (p. 284) "a history of himself over four days" (p. 241). The book, written by Norman Mailer, presents a protagonist, Norman Mailer, whose story is told by an objective narrator, presumably also Norman Mailer. Mailer is clearly taking part in the narrative.

But at the same time, he is watching himself play that part. Mailer's opening excerpt from *Time* presents himself as a subject viewed by a reporter in the audience for Mailer's part in the pre-march rally. The first chapters of the "history as a novel" section recount Mailer's performance at the rally as well as his activities during the march. He is seen as an actor taking part in the staging of a Vietnam protest. Oriented toward publicity, toward being seen, the organizers of the protest invite Mailer because of his ability to attract attention, to fulfill his role as display. When the march begins, "Lowell, Macdonald, and Mailer were requested to get up in the front row, where the notables were to lead the March, a row obviously to be consecrated for the mass media. Newsreel, still, and television cameras were clicking and rounding and snapping and zooming before the first rank was even formed" (p. 123). When Mailer finally arrives at the Pentagon, the stated goal of the march, he steps deliberately over a rope that marks his trespass onto Pentagon property. As he does so, he and Caputo exchange seats: "It was as if the air had changed, or light had altered; he felt immediately much more alive . . . and yet disembodied from himself, as if indeed he were watching himself in a film where this action was taking place" (p. 149). Even in his "autobiographical" section, "history as a novel," Mailer does not speak in the first person but instead refers to himself as "Mailer," "he," and "your protagonist." While he is telling his story, he is distanced from himself as if he were watching his own actions.

For Nixon, the plan is similar in that he narrates both as audience and actor. Nixon employs the shift from objective to subjective narration and back again to skillfully construct his own "history" of what took place in Vietnam. His final (con)fusion of the subjective and objective narration parallels and is erected on his early reversal of the status of fact and fiction.

The opening chapters of his book present the "history" of the war (in contrast to the "myths" of his early pages) as it would appear to an "objective" observer. These are "facts" that anyone would know—Diem's assassination, Ho Chi Minh's communist education, French and Japanese occupation of Vietnam, and so on. Nixon here takes the position of any member of the audience for Vietnam, viewing its unfolding actions from a distance.

When Nixon moves to the central chapters—"How We Won the War" and "How We Lost the Peace"—he begins the account of his own involvement as president during the Vietnam war. He shifts to a first person narration: "I became the fifth American President in twenty-three years to deal with the problem of Vietnam" (p. 98). In this section, presentations of historical information are always framed by Nixon's subjectivity. An analysis of his predecessors' reasons for involvement in Vietnam is seen through Nixon's point of view: "As I reviewed the record of the previous twenty-three years, I found that each of my predecessors had been motivated by different considerations in formulating his Vietnam policy" (p. 98).

But in the final chapters, Nixon drops the first person narration of his account of the fall of Saigon, the subsequent takeover of the South by the North, and the mass executions, starvation, and exodus from Cambodia. At this point, and in his final chapter, he becomes "we," speaking for "our" interests, goals, and involvements. Dissociating himself from the tragedies of Vietnam, Nixon speaks of those who, in his reading, brought on these events. "The possibility of retaliating against North Vietnam evaporated by the end of April 1973. It was not a failure of presidential will—I was willing to act—but an erosion of congressional support" (p. 178). "Congress turned its back on a noble cause and a brave people" (p. 202). "A generous view of the antiwar movement's position would be that there was no way they could have known what would happen in the wake of our defeat. But it *was* known—and they *should have* known" (p. 208).

Nixon thus moves from his early references to "the United States" to "I" to "we," from observer to participant to that "godlike feeling" recalled by one soldier. Nixon can accomplish this final step only by identifying a "they" from which "we" can now be distinguished. These are the members of Congress who failed to support his policies, the antiwar demonstrators, journalists and others who highlighted Watergate. Significantly, at the very point when he is making this transition from "I" to "we," Nixon reminds us of the "facts":

> Worse still, antiwar critics were naively ignorant of the fact that diplomacy cannot succeed without power to back it up. Diplomacy involves our getting another country to take certain actions against the wishes of its leaders. Foreign leaders who oppose our course of action are seldom brought along by reason and persuasion alone. If it is a minor dispute with a pliable adversary, diplomatic prodding may suffice. If it is a military conflict with an implacable foe—as it was in Indochina—diplomacy is helpless unless combined with direct military pressure. Nothing would convince Congress of this simple fact of international life in 1973. Simple facts had somehow lost their persuasive impact. (p. 179)

Nixon, who opened his narrative by challenging the very idea of a fact, now blames the loss of the war on the apparent dissolution of the status of facts. The (con)fusion of the status of fact and fiction intersects here with the manipulation of the reader through the construction of the narrative position. Those who are opposed to "our" interests are also those who, Nixon claims, have lost the ability to distinguish fact from fiction. "We" "know" (as the antiwar demonstrators "should have" known) what "facts" are. "They" do not. But what Nixon fails to remind his reader of here is his own complicity in the reorganization of fact and fiction and his own manipulation of that (con)fusion to reassert his position as "godlike" narrator. Through the inversion of fact and fiction, and the shifting of point of view from actor to audience, Nixon has achieved a reconstruction of the position of the reader.

(3) "Powerless to stop them from happening": Nixon's comments on diplomacy translate the position of the reader. "Diplomacy [read: narration] involves our [the narrator's] getting another country [the reader] to take certain actions [accept certain interpretations] against the wishes of its leaders [against the reader's previous system for interpretation, in this case, a fact/fiction synchrony]." In a bald statement of the case, "Foreign leaders who oppose our course of action are seldom brought along by reason and persuasion alone." Consequently, "diplomatic prodding" or "military pressure" are needed in order to get these "foreign leaders" to accept "our" notion of the "facts." The "prodding" Nixon and Mailer apply is their initial gambit of reorienting the attention to "facts." As Mailer wrote, "Now we may leave *Time* in order to find out what happened." The "pressure" is the exclusion of the reader who does not accept the redefinition of fact and fiction supplied in the narrative: "it *was* known. And they *should have* known."

The position of the reader as delineated in these narratives is open to such "prodding" and "pressure" because, from the opening lines of each text, the reader has been asked to abandon any previous basis on which a variant position could be established. It is important that Nixon, Herr, and Mailer attack the *idea* of a fact and not simply individual bits of information. Single disputes of events, dates, characters are still handled within the frame of a shared system of what is accepted *as* event, date, character. But a dispute about the idea of a fact disenables debate about individual items and instead requires a full-scale reinterpretation of what can be discussed. In such a context, the reader is led to assume the position defined by the text in order to engage the text at all.

This is why Mailer, Nixon, and Herr assume the position of both actor and audience in their narrations. Such shifting not only reinforces the (con)fusion of the status of fact and fiction but also insures the definition of the position of the reader in relation to their texts. The reader cannot forge his/her own position in relation to the texts because the position is already occupied. It is not the reader but Herr who hears the cryptic story about the patrol; not the reader but Mailer who reads *Time* magazine; not the reader but Nixon who understands presidents' motivations. As a result, the reader is left with nowhere to move, with only paralysis in relation to textual interpretation.

The thematic that underlies the (con)fusion of fact and fiction and its resulting paralysis in Vietnam representation is thus not political orientation, "experience," or any aspect of what are viewed as the historical and political circumstances of the war in Vietnam. Instead, as an examination of the paradigmatic form of the war novel in Vietnam (and cultural) representation will show, that key is gender.

## IV

William Eastlake's novel, *The Bamboo Bed* (1969), opens as well with the overt (con)fusion of the status of fact and fiction, this time focusing not on Vietnam or *Time* magazine or the voices of protesters but on a single woman:

> Madame Dieudonné arose, stark and stripped, in her underground villa at 0600 as was her wont, turned on the shortwave radio and heard the report from Laos that Captain Clancy was dead, then she walked, still naked, to her jewel box, removed a small, black, heavy object, raised it to her head and blew her pretty French brains out. Pas vrai. Not true.

And then, like Mailer's opening gambit with *Time* magazine,

> That's the way the papers had it, but they did not get it right. They never do. The newspapers seldom get anything right because they are not creative. Life is an art. . . . The newspapers made a good story. But there is a better one. The truth.[80]

Eastlake's novel then takes off on a surreal adventure through Vietnam, combining a "literary creation and the process of cultural myth-making at large" that Philip Beidler finds capable of telling "about an experience more 'real', finally, than any one that ever existed in fact."[81] Beidler celebrates Eastlake's novel and those like it for their straightforward challenging of the boundaries between fact and fiction, finds this indeed to be the literary style most appropriate to the experiences of Vietnam:

> Whatever their ostensible qualities of perspective and mode, the narrative works, predictably, that got closest to Vietnam from the beginning were those that somehow came upon a recognition, given the peculiarities of their special task of sense-making, of the essential interchangeability of art and life—an explicit, centralizing vision of the literary process as self-conscious heuristic, a medium not of predication but rather of complex creative discovery. (p. 49)

In this way, Beidler goes on, *The Bamboo Bed,* one of the "three early important novels of Vietnam" (p. 51), claims rights to suggesting "that there may be other and even better ways for fictions to accrue factual authority than by claiming it outright" (p. 52).

Although Eastlake may well establish, as Beidler claims, in these opening lines "the relationship between truth and literary falsehood as a central thematic issue" (p. 52), if we read on a few more lines, we can discover the thematic that underlies the (con)fusion of the status of fact and fiction in Vietnam representation: the construction, confirmation, and presentation of the status of gender. Most straightforwardly, where fact and fiction are inverted as an opening strategy, the (con)fusion rests in the characterization of the feminine. Herr's Vietnam is unreadable, shifting, and fragmented ("different pieces of ground told different stories to different people"); Mailer's *Time* magazine is personalized, petty, and avoids political issues behind his activities; and for those who "misreported" Vietnam as Nixon sees it, "rarely have so many people been so wrong about so much. Never have the consequences of their misunderstandings been so tragic," revealing for Nixon their inability to think rationally and independently, as well as a propensity to act as a mass rather than an individual.[82] Each of these narratives codes what Eastlake seems to present boldly—that the locus for the (con)fusion of fact and fiction rests in the feminine.

But Eastlake's characterization of the feminine goes further to reveal the intricate and complex constructions, not simply of the feminine, but of gender relations, in Vietnam representation. He links a presentation of the feminine as female body to a thematization of male aggression, depicting (hetero)sexual intercourse as a means to rise above violence caused by male competitiveness. Specifically, *The Bamboo Bed* exemplifies how, in Vietnam representation, the feminine exists only in relation to and as a function of the masculine and how, at the same time, the masculine feels dependent for its definition on the feminine.[83] In such a scheme, as in the narration of the participant/viewer exchange, both positions can be posited only from a third, what I call here the masculine point of view, the point of view from which genders in American culture, both masculine and feminine, are presented and constructed.

Madame Dieudonné, who had arisen "stark and stripped," did not blow her brains out but instead took the pistol and returned to her bamboo bed, where she "stared at the naked picture of herself in the great mirror" over her bed

> at the mirror image of a body *that had not betrayed her.* It was still good. The body of herself that was still firm in all the right places and sloping and undulating and good in all the right places. But a body is for someone else. A body is never for yourself, so that the mirror of herself became a vanity, an indulgence, *that was nothing at all because it was mirrored back to no one.* Nothing. *No man at all*. [italics added] (p. 2)

Madame Dieudonné in effect has no "body" because she has "no one" to verify its existence, "no man" to see and touch it. She cannot, clearly, verify this herself (her not-self), for she has only her "self" as seen in a mirror, a self that is "good" only if it appears so in the mirror. This body had not "betrayed her," we can conclude, because there never was a "her" to betray, anything more than a body to see.

It is easy to see how such a body can become a repository for the exchange of fact and fiction. First, such a body has no constitution of its own and appears therefore flexible, unlike Rambo's body, so that, in Herr's words, "different pieces of ground told different stories to different people." Second, this body denies the existence of "fact" in its existence only as mirror image, as reflection of a man's gaze. And finally, because the body's status is defined by its viewer, it "is" only fact or fiction as the viewer dictates, as the man sees.

Eastlake's novel, an otherwise deliberately dissociated narrative that contains an explicit critique of the senselessness of war, is linked by a plot to search for Captain Clancy's dead body and a thematics of male aggression being tamed by contact with women, preferably through sex. This is a war of pointless battles between soldiers who are lost and disoriented. "We are not lost," a deserter declares, "if an elephant knows where we are" (p. 246). Eastlake provides the following conversation between soldiers flying above the battlefields in a helicopter as a sample of his warriors:

> "How can we lose the war," Batcheck said, "when we can see everything?"
> "We can manage," Knightbridge said.
> "I can't see a damn thing," Lavender said, "except the tops of the trees." (p. 149)

Above this war and confusion flies "the Bamboo Bed," a Search and Rescue helicopter in which Captain Knightbridge and Lieutenant Janine Bliss have joyful sex while the war goes on. "The Bamboo Bed darted, danced above the Friendly and Unfriendly in erratic flight, then paused, a great butterfly surprised at some flash movement below in the continuous jungle" (p. 378). Lieutenant Bliss articulates the "solution" to war that the Bamboo Bed carries within it, an emblem of love in a war of hate:

> Love is the greatest survival device. It is the best. Love is the long-time ecstasy. Death is short but very sweet in the jungle. An escape route.
>
> When you are surrounded on all sides and there is no direction to turn, when there is no love, you accept death. (pp. 121–22)

If only she could explain this to the men, "Everyone could go home and live happily ever after. She would no longer have to have sex at ten thousand feet to prove anything. Everything would be proved. Love approves of everything" (p. 122).

But what stops Janine's "bliss" is her realization of Eastlake's primary explanation for war, that "it was a man's jungle. It was a jungle of pride. . . . A jungle of man. They want to confront each other. Confrontation. Confrontation in the bright and dark jungle. A jungle of men" (pp. 122–23). Men are, the women in this novel realize in a voice that echoes Eastlake's, "competitive, acquisitive, possessive. Wonderful. And necessary to a woman. But they will not share. They want all or nothing" (p. 121). Unlike men, women "would rather fuck than fight" (p. 249), because "women are able to sublimate their aggressions with business," whereas "A man needs the real thing. A man has got to go out and kill someone to prove that he is alive" (p. 362).

The only way men can avoid this painful cycle of killing and war, Eastlake implies, is through women. At the close of the novel, when Clancy, who has been dying in the jungle throughout, comes to new insights about war and death, he does so through Madame Dieudonné, through a woman, as must all men:

> There comes a time in everyone's life, Tiger, when he must begin all over again. Knightbridge did it. But he had Nurse Bliss. Well, I had got Madame Dieudonné. A man must start from scratch. Starting from scratch is an untrue cliché, Tiger. A man has got to start from something. A woman. And if a man's any good he ends with a woman. (pp. 389–90)

It is only after this qualifying epiphany that Clancy, who had been lying in the jungle throughout, is picked up by the Search and Rescue helicopter, the Bamboo Bed.

But before he is picked up, Clancy's insight is enacted, not so that he "ends with a woman," but with a man. A Vietnamese peasant, himself dying of battle wounds, finds Clancy in the jungle.

> They were tied together now against all the rest of life. One Friendly and one Unfriendly had joined together to constitute an army of two. . . . They would recapture Red Boy together and then make secret plans. . . . One plan might be to discover a new language. . . . Another plan would be to save something. Save what? Save something, that's all. Everything is not being saved and they would save something. They would be the great saviors. (pp. 392–93)

When the Bamboo Bed comes down to rescue Clancy, it finds "Clancy and the peasant, and their hands were gripped together" (p. 393). Finally, the Bamboo

Bed rises again above the war, this time bearing in its cargo a "new language," "something" to save from the war. "Everyone was on the Bamboo Bed," "the Friendlies and the Unfriendlies," in a "final trip" that seems to carry its once separate and now unified cargo out of the "jungle of men."

And yet, what became of "ending with a woman"? Mike, a ubiquitous reporter/CIA figure who seems to speak the truth of war, declares, "If a man wants to find out about a man he should go to a woman" (p. 118). Thus, if Eastlake's novel claims to investigate the reasons behind men's aggression, behind war itself, it should "go to a woman." But for all of the importance given to women as mediators, as bearers of love, as entrances to a place out of war, this narrative does not "end" with them, but with men, rejoined as brothers in battle, carried away from war. Women are finally only that mirror image that drew so much of Madame Dieudonné's attention, that image that "mirrored back no one" because there was "no man at all." A novel that presents as its solution to war to start and end with a woman starts in fact with a woman who is only a mirror image of a man's desires and ends with that man joined in death to his brother in battle.

In such a context, Eastlake's location of the (con)fusion of fact and fiction must be reexamined. He has opened his novel, not with a woman, but with an aesthetic inversion of life and art (she is, the narrative tells us, alive, not dead); and closed that novel, not "with a woman," but with a mythic bonding of brothers that supersedes the antagonisms of war. Rather than follow Clancy's final insights into overcoming war ("A man has got to start from something. A woman. And if a man's any good he ends with a woman"), Eastlake enacts Mike's very early suggestion, "If a man wants to find out about a man he should go to a woman." Madame Dieudonné and all the women of the novel are not beginnings and ends, but passages, means through which men reach each other. And they are because "a body is for someone else," because their bodies are for the translations of men.

But this is more than Rene Girard's pattern of triangulated desire, in which men achieve their relations and identification with other men through the objects (principally women) those men desire.[84] And it suggests a slightly different reading of narrative than Eve Sedgwick offers in her theory of male homosociality, in which she states that the narrative of ideology "is necessarily chiasmic in structure: that is, that the subject of the beginning of the narrative is different from the subject at the end, and that the two subjects cross each other in a rhetorical figure that conceals their discontinuity."[85] Typically, she adds, they cross each other in "woman." But, while the immediate subject of *The Bamboo Bed* may be "different" at the end of the narrative than at the beginning—the shift from Clancy's war-making to the "bliss" of the bamboo bed—as an examination of the position of women makes apparent, there is no "difference" from beginning to end in the construction of the masculine bond. It has, if anything, become reinforced by its passage through women, by its appropriation and rejection of women's bodies as the place to "start" or "end."

As Nancy Hartsock convincingly argues, there is no discontinuity in what she calls the "negative eros" of the masculine community: the intellectualization and rationalization of the body, the denial of sensuality, and the channeling of creativity through the rational and external.[86] In such a scheme, the move from aesthetic inversion to masculine bond is neither unmotivated nor unexpected. It is, instead, drawing to full circle the cloak of the masculine around an "experimental" narrative.

This consistent masculine thematic both opens and closes *The Bamboo Bed* and characterizes the masculine point of view. Whereas the masculine gender can be portrayed within the narrative as "confrontational" and needing to "kill someone to prove that he is alive," while women "don't have to go to war to prove something" (p. 85), what the masculine point of view reveals, *separate from the characterization of the masculine as gender*, is that such confrontation and divisiveness are finally subsumed under the collective brotherhood of "Friendlies" and "Unfriendlies" that rises above (the war of) gender. Women, rather than having a radically alternate epistemology (of war), are merely points of transience through which these bonds can be enacted. What Madame Dieudonné is responding to in her mirror is not herself, but this masculine point of view that introduces, into this space between the mirror and the body, the narrative of masculine bonding.

Although focusing on the construction and presentation of the immediate subject, as in Girard and Sedgwick, accurately identifies the force and operation of masculine bonds, it leaves the expression of the masculine bond as aesthetic intact. What Sedgwick calls homosociality, the bonds formed between men for the production and maintenance of power, is an important step in the task of identifying the operation of men's dominance. But by focusing on men rather than the masculine Sedgwick does not specify the shifting relations of the masculine position in relation to the more stable interests of the masculine point of view, does not explore the occupation of that position by females or its rejection by males all as expression of a masculine point of view lying behind the narrating of gender.

In such narratives, the masculine point of view is voyeuristic. Kaja Silverman, in her reading of fashion in the eighteenth century, indicates that "exhibitionism plays as fundamental a part within the constitution of the male subject as it does within that of the female subject" and that "voyeurism, which is much more fully associated with male subjectivity than is exhibitionism, is only a secondary formation, or alternative avenue of libidinal gratification,"[87] specifically as "the male subject see[s] himself . . . as 'the one who looks at women'" (p. 143). In such a context, *both* the masculine and feminine as genders are objects of spectacle, presented for the display/diversion of ideology. It is the masculine point of view that assumes the secondary level of relation, the voyeuristic, and it is this point of view from which gender—both masculine and feminine—is narrated.

Eastlake's strategy of (con)fusing fact and fiction is then not to be read as an aesthetic but as a gendered move, one which is designed, not to alter the relations between "life and art," but to maintain the relations between men and women through the invocation of the voice of the masculine point of view cloaked as aesthetic. Such gambits, foregrounded only in the opening passages, serve to divert attention away from the narration of gender that is being begun by suggesting that all bounds of usual narration are being cast aside and "new" stories are being told, as if the story were being told by "no man at all."

A reading of Eastlake's novel offers a way of interpreting Herr, Nixon, and Mailer in such a way that it becomes apparent that what all are (re)telling, in their politically diverse and seemingly antithetical accounts of the Vietnam War, are the narrations of gender. Such a reading foregrounds the extent to which the operations identified at the opening of this chapter—the shift from means to ends, the valorization of performance, the aesthetic of spectacle through the male body as technology, and the (con)fusion of fact and fiction—are all mechanisms at the service of a structure of gender that underlies the formations of Vietnam representation in contemporary dominant U.S. culture. A return to their texts through the frame of gender will show how each of these writers is establishing, in his display of facts and fictions, an aspect of the masculine point of view from which relations of gender are displayed in Vietnam representation (each of which will be the focus of subsequent chapters): Herr, the masculine as bonding and collectivity; Nixon, the feminine as negotiation, weakness, and inaction; and Mailer, the efforts of the masculine to appropriate gender through reproduction.

## V

## "That Men without Women Trip"

Herr says of his "intimacy" with Vietnam's journalists:

> We shared a great many things: field gear, grass, whiskey, girls (that Men Without Women trip got old all the time), sources, information, hunches, tips, prestige (during my first days there bureau chiefs from *Life* and CBS took me around to introduce everyone they could think of, and somebody did as much for other new arrivals), we even shared each other's luck when our own seemed gone. (p. 242)

Although Herr admits that there were "all kinds of girl reporters" (p. 239) in Vietnam, it is clear that his "brotherhood" (p. 238) was one of men, men who could "share" girls. The borders of the bond are marked by gender, for they are "Men Without Women." Women enter into the bond only through the relations defined by brotherhood. They are permitted, not as journalists, but as "girls" who can be shared within the framework of the bond, much like field gear and whiskey. And to insure the perpetuation of the bond for a rapidly rotating clientele, older members introduced the newer ones to the operatives of the brotherhood, "and somebody did as much for other new arrivals."

Herr's brotherhood captures gender as the structural. "Girls," information, prestige—all were interpreted and distributed within the framework established by the act of sharing, introductions to "everyone they could think of." The defining feature of Herr's group is not the field gear, grass, whiskey, information, tips, and so on that were available to any correspondent, but the prestige and the "Men Without Women trip" that could not be shared by all. As a frame for Vietnam narration, Herr identifies our narrators, bureau chiefs from *Life* and CBS, and the form of narration, the trip. Herr's passage as a narrator from the uninitiated and naive "I" who could not understand the LURP[88] story to the experienced and confident "we" who is "intimate" with the soldiers in the field and firing guns himself is a passage negotiated by gender. In Herr's narrative, the terms of the passage are most often those of (hetero)sexuality.

Just before he tells his cryptic story, the LURP soldier finds out that Herr is a reporter. "'Tits on a bull,' he said. 'Nothing personal'" (p. 4). But toward the end of his narrative, after Herr has become "intimate" with the soldiers, he is given a compliment by those same soldiers that marks his transition:

> Even the ones who preferred not to be in your company, who despised what your work required or felt that you took your living from their deaths . . . even they would cut back at the last and make their one concession to what there was in us that we ourselves loved most: "I got to give it to you, you guys got balls." (p. 221)

From "tits" to "balls," from feminine to masculine,[89] Herr's narrative is demarcated by these signs of sexual identification. Herr's shift from "I" to "we" is an expression of the more narratively "intimate" structuration of gender. The plot of his narration is thus the story of how to enter the masculine, how to get on the "Men Without Women trip." And like the LURP's story, the narrative of gender "seemed not to be that kind of story," not an overt telling of a tale, but instead a hidden and cryptic story that can be told only within the frame of its own initiation.

In between the "tits" and the "balls" Herr tells another story, about a soldier who receives a letter from his wife telling him that the baby she is carrying is not his and was conceived after he left for Vietnam. Orrin's response—"There's gone be a death in my family. Just soon's I git home"—prompts these remarks from Herr:

> After that, he was the crazy fucking grunt who was going to get through the war so he could go home and kill his old lady. It made him someone special in the company. It made a lot of guys think that he was lucky now, that nothing could happen to him, and they stayed as close to him as they could. I even felt some of it, enough to be glad that we would be in the same bunker that night. It made sense. . . . When I remembered Orrin, all I could think of was that there was going to be a shooting in Tennessee. (p. 135)

Initially apart from this story—"Mayhew had a friend named Orrin from somewhere in Tennessee" (p. 135)—Herr becomes "intimate" with Orrin after hearing his tale—"glad that we would be in the same bunker that night." It is this story of reproduction that marks Herr's transition from the feminine to the masculine bond, for it is a story of exclusion and of a bonding that will combat it. Gone to Vietnam, Orrin's place has been taken by another man, another father to his child. And Herr, along with the other men in the company, unites with Orrin against his exclusion from his wife's reproduction. But in keeping with the frame of a gendered narration, it is not the replaced father that Orrin will kill, but the mother. Orrin responds to his exclusion from within the frame of gender by reacting against the woman who is outside of the brotherhood. And the men of his company support him, feel that he is "lucky," that he is charmed to survive the war. It is the repulsion of women from the masculine bond that enables survival in Vietnam. And Herr here subscribes to that strategy—"It made sense"—and passes into the position of the masculine—"you guys got balls."

## "Act before the Fighting Breaks Out"

Nixon characterizes those who oppose or derail his policies as weak, inactive, in favor of negotiating to the exclusion of fighting, and responding out of emotion rather than reason—all features that Vietnam representation affixes to the position of the feminine. More to the point, it is these characteristics that are responsible in Nixon's framework for the loss of the war.

Nixon identifies what he calls the "Vietnam syndrome" prevalent in American society since the war. Its features are isolationism, an unwillingness "to use power to defend national interests" (p. 13), and Americans who are "ashamed of their power" and feel "guilty about being strong" (p. 19). One of the principal consequences of the Vietnam War for Nixon is America's hesitation to stop Communist takeovers around the globe for fear that they will metamorphose into "another Vietnam." On the contrary, Nixon insists, "The surest way to prevent another Vietnam is to act before the fighting breaks out" (p. 227).

One of the reasons, according to Nixon, for the outcome of the war was the extent to which a negotiating stance both harmed U.S. credibility to act and bargained away important safeguards of South Vietnamese integrity. In reference to the Ho Chi Minh Trail, for example, Nixon states, "The Geneva agreement on Laos in 1962 paved the way for the Communist victory in South Vietnam in 1975" (p. 60). Likewise, the War Powers Act hampers presidential ability to act decisively in the face of Communist aggression:

> The outstretched hand of diplomacy will have a very weak grip unless a President holds the scepter of credible military power in his other hand. . . . He cannot wait on the 535 members of Congress to make these quick, tough decisions for him. . . . As Charles de Gaulle observed shortly before his death, members of parliaments can paralyze policy; they cannot initiate it. Congres-

> sional leadership means leadership by consensus, and consensus leadership is no leadership. (p. 226)

The process of negotiation, agreement, consensus, and compromise is antithetical to an effective foreign policy as designed by Nixon. When Nixon was engaged in the Paris negotiations and working toward an effective peace, congressional action, he tells us, tied his hands: "it was impossible for us to hold out for more favorable terms with Congress poised to legislate an end to our involvement on Hanoi's terms" (p. 170). This same congressional stance led to the defeat of the South Vietnamese troops, because "our South Vietnamese friends were asking us to give them the tools so they could finish the job" but "Congress would not" (p. 202). Policies that are negotiated by consensual action are, in Nixon's terms, destructive. According to him, only the individual can act efficiently and effectively. Nixon's thesis is picked up by Vietnam narratives like *Rambo: First Blood* and *Missing in Action*, in which a negotiating government is stalled in its efforts to retrieve POWs but a determined individual who acts can bring them home.[90]

As Nixon shows, there is a difference between the "consensual" and the "collective." Consensus is a situation in which each individual expresses a particular position and then accepts a final compromise that addresses that position as well as those expressed by other members of a group. In contrast, the kind of collective Herr participates in and that is discussed as masculine bonding in chapter 2 is instead one where (previous) difference has ceased to exist and the group shares a single opinion. Nixon claims to be acting for such a collective, what he called the "silent majority." Negotiation and compromise are antithetical to such claims and the kinds of action they enable.

Negotiation and legislation are, according to Nixon, least effective against those who do not fight by the same rules of engagement as the U.S. The Viet Minh, for instance, "adopted the tactics of the weak—constant skirmishes, hit-and-run attacks, ambushes along jungle roads, always avoiding anything approaching an even test of strength" (p. 26). Guerrilla warfare in general "is a tactic of the weak" (p. 83). Terrorists, like guerrilla fighters, dare not risk "an even test of strength" but must instead use their primary tool of creating fear, the ploy of "a tiny minority who have resorted to violence in pursuit of their objectives" (p. 223). (These "acts" are not given the same value as presidential acts of violence.) The U.S. cannot fight them because "our military forces can only fight an enemy they can see. All the military power in the world is useless against shadows" (p. 222). Against those who adopt the "tactics of the weak," diplomacy, as used in Vietnam, is least effective: "Terrorists will not be deterred by UN resolutions or expressions of outrage by leaders and legislatures" (p. 223).

Part of the Vietnam syndrome is the emotional response to the war. Such emotion has led, Nixon concludes, to inaction, the fodder of Communist aggression: "While we wrung our hands and agonized over our mistakes, over

100 million people were lost to the West in the vacuum left by our withdrawal from the world stage" (p. 13). Antiwar activists, the "self-proclaimed humanitarians" (p. 12) of the United States, reacted to bombings, napalm, escalation, and so on with outrage and emotional fervor, but their emotion later brought them only shame and guilt: "They cannot bear to look in the mirror, because if they do, they will see who must share the blame: those who opposed the U.S. war effort and in doing so gave support to the Cambodian communists—who, once they came into power, pulled the triggers and dug the mass graves" (p. 12).

Emotion, weakness, inaction, negotiation, compromise—all are painted with the palette of blame in Nixon's schema. Such attitudes led, inevitably according to Nixon, to the loss of a war that did not need to be lost, to the murder of millions of innocent people, and to the havoc and turmoil of contemporary international relations. Although Nixon does not call them such, most Vietnam representation, as we shall see, does not flinch from labeling these as the characteristics and features of the feminine and does not hesitate to blame the feminine for the loss of the war.

## "False Labor"

Mailer closes *The Armies of the Night* with this plea:

> Brood on that country who expresses our will. She is America, once a beauty of magnificence unparalleled, now a beauty with a leprous skin. She is heavy with child—no one knows if legitimate—and languishes in a dungeon whose walls are never seen. Now the first contractions of her fearsome labor begin—it will go on: no doctor exists to tell the hour. It is only known that false labor is not likely on her now, no, she will probably give birth, and to what?—the most fearsome totalitarianism the world has ever known? or can she, poor giant, tormented lovely girl, deliver a babe of a new world brave and tender, artful and wild? Rush to the locks. God writhes in his bonds. Rush to the locks. Deliver us from our curse. For we must end on the road to that mystery where courage, death, and the dream of love give promise of sleep. (p. 320)

Mailer's characterization of America, not as "she" (a commonplace gendered reference) but as giving birth, marks the play of reproduction in Vietnam representation. The close of his autobiography of the Vietnam protests, the completion of his merging of history and novel, the end to his exploration of his own subjectivity—all are drawn together in Mailer's final chapter, "The Metaphor Delivered," in which Mailer's writing gives birth to his final metaphor for America as laboring mother.

Throughout *The Armies of the Night*, Mailer has been constructing a narrative of America and/as woman. Mailer first explains America's involvement in Vietnam as a result of the technologization of America, one which subsumed America's small towns and opened them up to "the bypasses and the supermarkets and the shopping centers." Small towns were valuable because it was there that the "fever"—"the fever to travel was in the American blood, so said all, but now the fever had left the blood, it was in the cells, the cells traveled, and the cells were as insane as Grandma with orange hair"—of America could expend itself:

> Enough of the old walled town had once remained in the American small town for gnomes and dwarfs and knaves and churls (yes, and owls and elves and crickets) to live in the constellated cities of the spiders below the eaves in the old leaning barn which—for all one knew—had been a secret ear to the fevers of the small town, message center for the inhuman dreams which passed through the town at night in sleep and came to tell their insane tale of the old barbarian lust to slaughter villages and drink their blood. (p. 173)

But with the advent of technology, the message came, not "by the wind" but "by the wire," and

> the American small town grew out of itself, and grew out of itself again and again, harmony between communication and the wind, between lives and ghosts, insanity, the solemn reaches of nature where insanity could learn melancholy (and madness some measure of modesty) had all been lost now, lost to the American small town. (p. 173)

Consequently, "the nightmares which passed on the winds in the old small towns now traveled on the nozzle tip of the flame thrower." Because "technology had driven insanity out of the wind and out of the attic," it could only be found "wherever fever, force, and machines could come together, in Vegas, at the race track, in pro football, race riots for the Negro, suburban orgies—none of it was enough—one had to find it in Vietnam; that was where the small town had gone to get its kicks" (p. 174). With no repository for its madness, America sought out Vietnam as an arena for the display of its technological "fever."

Mailer's metaphor for the American small town is the visceral body. The problem that became Vietnam arose when this body got out of control, lost its "harmony," and gave way to "fever, force, and machines." It is a problem of unrestrained reproduction: "the American small town grew out of itself, and grew out of itself again and again." Self-generating, without beginning or end, without frame or control, this body has lost even its own shape and is now only cells that travel independently of each other, independently of a plan. It is this that Mailer fears, this "technology" that has gone out of control, this reproduction that grows on its own without shape.

Not against all wars, Mailer differentiates between Vietnam—a "bad war"—and a good war:

> Certainly any war was a bad war which required an inability to reason as the price of retaining one's patriotism; finally any war which offered no prospect of improving itself as a war . . . was a bad war. A good war, like anything else which is good, offers the possibility that further effort will produce a determinable effect upon chaos, evil, or waste. By every conservative measure . . . the war in Vietnam was an extraordinarily bad war. (pp. 208–9)

Vietnam is a "bad war" because it springs from the very chaos it is to suppress; it "grows" from the uncontrollable, the unreasonable, and the unstructured. It cannot have an effect on chaos because it *is* chaos.

But Mailer loves America anyway, just as he loves his wife, whose "attractiveness . . . came from her presence so quintessentially American":

> Mailer came finally to decide that his love for his wife while not at all equal or congruent to his love for America was damnably parallel. It was not inconceivable to him that if he finally came to believe his wife was not nearly so magical as he would make her . . . why then he would finally lose some part of his love affair with America. (p. 193)

It is important for Mailer's strategy of gendered representation that he compare America with his love for his wife, because America is, as Mailer has lamented, becoming unavailable to control or reason. To liken this uncontrollable America to a woman in relation to whom Mailer holds a position of possession and a type of control—his wife—is for Mailer to attempt to regain some of the lost control of America, to reshape it in a knowable form, to keep its cells from traveling. It is, then, for Mailer to attempt to control reproduction.

The purpose of Mailer's final chapter is thus to appropriate reproduction to himself through narrative. In line with Marilyn French's statement that "Patriarchal cultures . . . attempt to take over as their own the very physical functioning of women's procreation, by assigning children to men and diminishing the role of women in procreation (p. 72),"[91] Mailer presents an America that is pregnant, on the verge of reproduction, but now in a known shape, the body of woman, no longer the cells themselves. Mailer is attempting to control this birth by predelimiting its outcome—either totalitarianism or "a new world" but nothing of its own choosing. But more than this, he is attempting to control that birth—to possess its reproduction, to possess reproduction itself—through his narrative. His final chapter title, "The Metaphor Delivered," places Mailer in the position of having, after "delivering" his own narrative/autobiography/history, the ability to deliver the metaphor of America as woman that he has been erratically building throughout the text. He has succeeded, through the play of his own metaphors, in "reproducing" America from chaos to form, from cells to body. Like Nixon, he has redefined winning so that it can now seem as if he has "won" the war of Vietnam by reintroducing form onto chaos, by controlling the "evil" and "waste" that are that war/woman.

Mailer's strategy then of (con)fusing the status of fact and fiction is only a prelude to the achievement of his metaphor, to the repossession of reproduction. Through his elision of fact and fiction as a narrative strategy, Mailer has established a structural plan for inversion and confusion. It is on this plan that he builds the metaphor of America as woman/as woman reproducing. More important, it is on this plan that he builds his own position as narrator. Initially disjuncted, Mailer's narrator/protagonist has, by the close of the narrative, completed his "rite of passage" (p. 318) in the march and arrest and come to a point where he can relieve himself of his narrative, moving away from the specificity of history on which the narrative is based to the abstraction of metaphor.

*The Armies of the Night* then is Mailer's attempt to (re)produce his own personality—dispersed through television, media, and his own writing—as a unified voice, to join his own history with his own novels. In order to accomplish this, Mailer projects himself onto "America" (writing in the third person) as it struggles with its own dispersal writ large in Vietnam and poses America against "chaos, evil, and waste" as he perceives himself posed against his own misrepresentation. For Mailer, as for most Vietnam representation, this project is achieved through gender. He creates the metaphor of Mailer/America, and, in order to remove himself from its operation and thereby control it, he transposes the metaphor to America/woman, with the linking term being the process of reproduction. By setting himself outside of the metaphor as the producer of metaphor—outside of gender—he is marking a move that is familiar to Vietnam representation: positioning the masculine outside the (re)production of gender and therefore in control of its definition and operation and, more significantly, not subject to its determinations. When Mailer "delivers" his metaphor, he is in effect delivering himself outside of gender, apart from reproduction, divorced from the process of metaphor: "Deliver us from our curse," he writes. His success in confusing fact and fiction has enabled him to disorient his own metaphors and to (con)fuse the positions of masculine and feminine, to rewrite them as metaphor.

Mailer reintroduces the masculine into his metaphor, not as a direct characterization, as he does woman, but in a manner typical of Vietnam representation, through the rules by which the masculine marks its possessions: "She is heavy with child—no one knows if legitimate." The question of the child's legitimacy, the law by which its father is known, reminds us of the father's existence. Like Mailer in relation to his own metaphor, the father here has been abstracted—"no one knows"—but has not disappeared. His anonymity all the more removes him from the birth itself, especially if Mailer's "no one" includes the mother herself; if she too is unaware of the father's identity, his abstraction is complete and Mailer has succeeded in removing "himself" from the structure and performance of his narrative, succeeded in removing the masculine from the (re)production of gender. "[A]ll I could think of was that there was going to be a shooting in Tennessee."

## VI

The blurring of categories is the strategic premise through which Vietnam is (re)presented in contemporary American culture. What on the simplest level seems a mere difference in point of view or political orientation—"liberal" or "conservative"—is in fact a structural feature that has numerous parallels in

Vietnam representation: America/"the Nam," participants/observers, Americans/the enemy, soldiers/civilians, and so on. Mailer, Herr, and Eastlake translate these oppositions into aesthetic terms by overtly discussing the status of fact and fiction, history and myth, truth and falsehood. The terms change and are given different weight in different interpretations, but the pattern of relations remains the same. With such evidence, it is not unreasonable to conclude that the very subject and method of Vietnam representation is difference, a difference that is presented as hierarchy ("All of us were there").

The most obvious expression of difference in Vietnam representation, and often therefore apparently that of least notice, is gender. The defining feature of American war narratives is that they are a "man's story" from which women are generally excluded. For such narratives, gender is the assumed category of interpretation, the only one that is not subject to interpretation and variation of point of view, experience, age, race, and so on. But as Frederic Jameson cautions about coherent narrative, only by reading back from the narrative to its excluded possibilities can we comprehend the ideological operations of such narratives: "Just as every work is true at the point at which we are able to reckon its conceptual situation, its ideological distortion back into it, so every work is clear, provided we locate the angle from which the blur becomes so natural as to pass unnoticed."[92] For the representation of Vietnam in American culture, that angle is the "blur" of gender.

Although this structuration might at first seem to be a product of men's narratives, women's narratives of Vietnam, a numerically smaller category of Vietnam representation, are equally dependent on an assumed structuration of gender that determines the genre. Although these narratives focus on different locations, relations to the war, and levels of participation, collections of women's narratives, such as Kathryn Marshall's *In the Combat Zone: An Oral History of American Women in Vietnam* and Keith Walker's *A Piece of My Heart,* still present women's narratives as if they were compensatory and marginal, having already been excluded. The point of narration, so firmly lodged in the personal and subjective, continues to be defined by gender.

How is this assumption of gender suppressed? The answer takes the shape of both the structural and the spectacular. The numerous oppositions that mark Vietnam narratives operate as diversionary spectacles from gender as opposition. In the debate over Republican versus Democrat, negotiation versus bombardment, elimination versus pacification, North versus South, killing versus capturing, winning versus losing, gender as opposition is never debated, only assumed as a stable category. Soldiers argue about killing and befriending, politicians contest peace and battle plans, journalists highlight political positions and military reactions, but the extent to which the constructions of gender affected the production of the war is not discussed. And because these diversionary issues are treated as politically and historically localized, gender—a construction that has pervaded Western cultures for centuries—is not perceived as an historical "event."

But while gender is suppressed as background to perceptually more immediate oppositions in Vietnam representation, it is equally suppressed through foregrounding it as a subject of its own display. In Vietnam representation, gender is rephrased as sexuality and presented as its own spectacle. Rambo's body, the Playboy Bunnies of *Apocalypse Now,* the helicopter of *Dispatches,* the bar dancing scene in *The Deer Hunter,* the sensual effeminacy of the Vietnamese negotiators in *Missing in Action*—all divert attention from the constructions of gender by drawing attention to the sexual characteristics of their images. By eliding (hetero)sexuality with gender, these representations suggest that gender is being addressed at the same time that they dismiss the need for its discussion.

Structurally, gender is suppressed through the strategy of blurring that typifies Vietnam representation. (Other) difference is foregrounded as spectacle and then (con)fused. Vietnam representation is punctuated by questions of confusion: the undefinability of the "enemy"; the vague goals of American involvement in Vietnam; the taking, relinquishing, and then retaking of the same village or hill; the indeterminacy of responsibility for actions; the status of fact and fiction; the reliability of subjectivity. In each case, what seemed to be a clearcut opposition before the war—friend/enemy, victory/loss, truth/falsehood, actor/observer—is muddled so that it is impossible to determine which construct is which and only individual will/assertion/declaration/death can "answer" the question of definition. "Where no answers were possible, no questions were necessary. For many G.I.s the equation became simple; they . . . tagged all Vietnamese as the enemy, every damn one of them [. . .]. Kill them all and you know for damn sure you're killing the enemy. If they're not all VC now, they could fuckin' well become VC."[93] In the face of such indeterminacy, definition becomes both impossible and implausible.

In Vietnam representation, blurring becomes its own spectacle, drawing attention to itself *as* confusion, *as* indeterminacy, *as* undecidability. *Platoon* accomplishes this most effectively with its close-in camera, preventing shots that offer the individual soldier/viewer any perspective on situations (until the closing shot from the helicopter, a false closure that merely appears to tie the fragmented narrative together), providing only the immediate perimeter of fear, anxiety, darkness, and jungle.[94] And though one of the film's most tense scenes, the brink of another My Lai, stages the confrontation between Elias and Barnes that marks the poles of good and evil in the film, we leave the village, now sure about what is good but still not knowing whether or not the villagers were helping the Viet Cong.

*Time* magazine writes of *Platoon,*

> Welcome back to the war that, just 20 years ago, turned America schizophrenic. Suddenly we were a nation split between left and right, black and white, hip and square, mothers and fathers, parents and children. For a nation whose war history had read like a John Wayne war movie—where good guys

> finish first by being tough and playing fair—the polarization was soul-souring. Americans were fighting themselves, and both sides lost.[95]

Read as a "schizophrenia" in which "both sides lost," Vietnam is then only the undecidable, the indeterminate. And, as Richard Corliss writes, this war was not like other wars for America, in which decisions were apparently clearcut and "they" would lose.

Thus, although war is a formation of gender, this *particular* strategy of (con)fusion is not typical of war itself but more characteristic of the Vietnam War. Consequently, Vietnam representation's presentation of gender must be historically localized in order to read accurately its permutations of the general structure and representation of gender in Western culture. Because the war in Vietnam is interpreted in U.S. culture differently from other wars, it can provide insight into the ways in which the structure of gender is both maintained as a general frame and altered in relation to specific cultural circumstances. In particular, it has been altered to produce, validate, and secure what I call here a "remasculinization"—a regeneration of the concepts, constructions, and definitions of masculinity in American culture and a restabilization of the gender system within and for which it is formulated.

While Vietnam representation often displays the apparent dissolution of traditional forms of power—race, family, politics—as Jean-Joseph Goux suggests, "the breakdown of a form of power can easily imply its replacement by other newly-emergent forms of power."[96] Consequently, Vietnam can at the same time be the location for the presentation of a "new" form of power. Dana Polan, in elaborating Goux's position, describes how that power operates: "the new mass culture may operate by offering no models [of behavior] whatsoever, preferring instead a situation in which there are no stable values, in which there are no effective roles that one could follow through from beginning to end" (p. 182). This is a power that takes as its mode of operation the position of (con)fusion I have been discussing here and positions its audience in relation to that model for the purpose of diverting attention from the structure that enables that operation—the construction of gender.

Rather than a wholly new form of power, Vietnam is then the historical site for a permutation of power. If forms of power other than gender are attended to, it would seem that Vietnam is a point of genuine transformation, but with gender the focus of analysis, it becomes clear that Vietnam is instead a point of translation, one in which the specific manifestations of gender relations may appear to be altered, but in which the masculine point of view from which gender is presented is maintained. The apparent breakdown of the order of logic in Vietnam opens the way for a reconstitution of the phallic order *apart from* logic. Such a breakdown appears to offer, as Polan suggests, "no models whatsoever," only as it maintains the model of gender. Divorced from logic, presentations of gender and other expressions of power relations appear to be unstable, challengeable, and alterable. But with the separation from logic, the masculine point of view is now free to maintain and impose itself solely through its own representation and display. Disburdened of a responsibility to logic (a strategy that could be used against it), its power is not decreased but increased and now appears more inaccessible and unlocatable.[97]

A theory of the spectacle as masculinity can offer a language in which to read the forms of power present in Vietnam representation and constructions of gender. As Guy Debord writes of capitalism,

> in the spectacle, one part of the world *represents itself* to the world and is superior to it. The spectacle is nothing more than the common language of this separation. What binds the spectators together is no more than an irreversible relation at the very center which maintains their isolation. The spectacle reunites the separate, but reunites it *as separate*.[98]

The masculine point of view represents itself to the world as gendered, as diverse, as multiple. Within this context, the masculine as gender appears to be vulnerable and alterable with historical conditions, but the point of view from which gender is narrated remains relatively stable. Because it presents itself as concrete and diverse in gender, and because it presents gender as spectacle, the masculine point of view remains less available to challenge, to reading its operation. "The spectacle presents itself as something enormously positive, indisputable and inaccessible" (p. 12).

The spectacle of blurring that is the chief diversion of Vietnam representation, because it draws attention to itself *as* confusion that is unresolved, is not then deconstruction.[99] Although both deconstruction and blurring depend for their progress on the presentation of constructed oppositions, there are several key differences between them. Deconstruction reveals the insufficiencies of categories that present themselves as inexhaustible and originary ("man") by (re)membering the suppressed term of opposition that is denied and rejected ("woman"). It moves through this given opposition toward the projection of a position in which that opposition is understood as a structural and not an absolute feature of a system of thought (what Derrida calls in a discussion of gender the "sexual otherwise"), thereby collapsing the logic built on that opposition (law, religion, and so on). In contrast, blurring maintains oppositions by (con)fusing them. Rather than challenging the sufficiency of the categories themselves, blurring rests in point of view, as the reader/viewer/soldier is individually unable to discriminate between concepts/objects/enemies. As Richard Ohmann observes of American novels of the fifties,[100] this strategy of placing blame for dissatisfaction on individuals rather than the social system in which they exist is ideologically oriented to inhibit any questioning of that system and its failures to satisfy its members. Likewise, blurring produces paralysis, an inability to act because the positions for action are clouded. Rather than the "otherwise," blurring produces only the same, but in a disguise (it produces gender, for example, and calls it sexuality).

There are two important consequences of this (con)fusion: first, the reader/

viewer/soldier is unable to question the definition of categories and the determination of oppositions because the ground from which they could be questioned is constantly shifting—"If they're not VC now, they could fuckin' well become VC"; second, the production of difference as opposition is clouded, so that these oppositions seem to have sprung from themselves and have a life of their own, are "natural," and therefore unchallengeable.

These strategies and the oppositions they employ are the mechanisms for the repression of gender as difference. But gender is not simply another of the many oppositions that mark Vietnam representation. It is *the* difference on which these narratives and images depend because it is the single difference that is asserted as *not* participating in the confusion that characterizes other oppositions. While friends may be uncertain, enemies unidentifiable, and goals unclear, the line between the masculine and the feminine is presented in Vietnam representation as firm and unwavering. As John Wheeler declares, in contrast to American culture as a whole, "In Vietnam masculinity did not go out of fashion."[101]

As a result, though Vietnam representation displays multiply diverse topics for its narratives and imagery, gender is its determining subject and structure. It is what Vietnam narrative is "about." Gender is the matrix through which Vietnam is read, interpreted, and reframed in dominant American culture. More to the point, the insistent popularity of Vietnam novels, films, characters, and associations can best be understood, not in relation to its all too apparent military promotions, but in a context of changing roles, definitions, and relations of masculine and feminine and of male and female in contemporary American culture. Wheeler's suggestion that the "commitment" learned by soldiers in Vietnam can be productively carried over to American society as a whole is no more than a textured euphemism for the desire to bring this certainty about gender "home" as well. The unspoken desire of Vietnam representation, and its primary cultural function, is to restage "the Nam" (read: gender) in America.

# TWO

# "THAT MEN WITHOUT WOMEN TRIP"

## Masculine Bonding and the Ideology of Collectivity

### I

In his 1982 novel, *The 13th Valley,* John Del Vecchio describes American soldiers in Vietnam:

> The restless infantrymen in the trenches and their clustered sergeants and lieutenants and captains on the landing strip represented a collective consciousness of America. These men . . . were products of the Great American Experiment, black brown yellow white and red, children of the Melting Pot. . . . What they had in common was the denominator of American society in the '50s and '60s, a television culture, the army experience—basic, AIT, RVN training, SERTS, the Oh-deuce and now the sitting, waiting in the trench at LZ Sally, I Corps, in the Republic of Vietnam.[1]

What Del Vecchio here calls the "collective consciousness of America" is a prominent motif of Vietnam films, personal narratives, novels, and analyses: the military unit in wartime as a location for the eradication of social, class, ethnic, and racial boundaries. Whether as "human beings,"[2] "grunts" (the title of Charles R. Anderson's novel is *The Grunts*), "brothers in soul,"[3] or, in Vietnam's simplest terms, "the herd,"[4] soldiers fighting in Vietnam have, in these representations, successfully eliminated hierarchical difference by subordinating it to the broader value system of "survival." As Daniel Egan, Del Vecchio's obligatory truth-speaking soldier, explains, "Takin it personal is for people in the World. We got a separate culture out here. And in some respects it's better. Fuck Man, an AK round don't care what color your paint job is" (p. 444).

Del Vecchio's invocation of America's "collective consciousness" follows immediately on a litany of Army hierarchies, an exacting description of the battalion down to individual squad members: "A squad consisted of seven riflemen, a thumper man (M-79 grenade launcher), an M-60 machine gunner and an assistant gunner (the AG carried an M-16), an RTO (carried an M-16) and a squad leader" (pp. 137–38). Including a name-by-position graph of the entire company, Del Vecchio's encoded recital establishes a rigidly defined structure of Army relations. Only after this framework has been reaffirmed does he present the imagery and rhetoric of collectivity, suggesting that its story—the assertion that there are no real boundaries separating human relations—depends first and foremost on a (hidden) contract of differentiation as separation and hierarchy which enables the story to be told.

Whereas in Hollywood films about World War II the boundaries dissolved between soldiers were primarily those of ethnicity,[5] Vietnam narratives focus more deliberately on race and class. The chief story of Vietnam representations is to show how these barriers are overcome in the face of battle. Wallace Terry's *Bloods* (1984), a collection of narratives by black soldiers who were in Vietnam, contains numerous references to black soldiers feeling that, in battle at least, there were no color lines: "I use the term 'brother' because in a war circumstance, we all brothers."[6] There was a common feeling that "racial incidents didn't happen in the field. Just when we went to the back."[7] Though there was little off-duty contact between blacks and whites (different bars were patronized by whites and blacks in Saigon, as well as different groups of prostitutes in Hong Kong), attitudes reported during battle were much like those of Sergeant Major Edgar A. Huff: "I knew I might get killed saving a white boy. But he was my man. That's what mattered."[8] As Richard Halloran's study of the American military concludes, "Relations between whites and blacks were often tense, openly antagonistic, and sometimes violent. The exception was blacks and whites under fire—the fight for survival wiped out color lines in the foxholes and rice paddies."[9]

In William Turner Hugget's *Body Count* (1973), Red, "a white boy from Minneapolis" (p. 35), becomes close friends with Big John, a black soldier whose father had been a Southern sharecropper. Both are part of a listening post overrun during a Vietnamese attack. They are found dead the next morning, lying together, holding hands. Because Red's body is still warm, we are to conclude that he found Big John and took his hand. And the 1967 film *The Boys in Company C* (dir. Sidney Furie), concludes with Tyrone Washington, a black soldier from Chicago's streets, forcing the white Billy Ray Pike from Galveston, Texas, into an ambulance so that Pike can return home safely to his new baby. Perhaps the best statement of interracial unity comes from Huggett's Big John, who, in his colloquial English and apparently simple thought, epitomizes the unrefined "truth" of "brotherhood":

> People ha' t'be ohvur heahr in Vee-et Nam before dey could see wha' life is really like. An' they got t'come ta d'bush before they can see how it *should* be. Jus like playin' ball. Yo'all a *team*. T'aint you'hr *color*, it's you'hr *ability*. . . . But afta' two doods been in d'bush a while they tugethur. They jus' like brothers; they *know* one's goin' ta protect the ohthur. An' it doan make no diffronce wh' color they ahr. One gives the ohthur a drink of his water. They drink outta the same canteen. They eat with the same spoon. They sleep unna the same poncho-linna. They doan care. The'ahr tugethur. The'ahr brothers. (pp. 197–98)

Like Egan's, Big John's description implies that Vietnam provides a separate and more real world in which true human nature (a caring and collective, not an aggressive and divisive one) can surface. In such a rationale, war becomes not only a necessary but a beneficial complement to society as well.

It is in war, William Broyles, Jr., tells us, that we discover "a love that needs no reasons, that transcends race and personality and education—all those things that would make a difference in peace."[10] Consequently, the war in Vietnam, in its most intense moments of combat, reinscribes the values and conditions of "peace." Paradoxically, it is only at the core of war that peace can be realized. By foregrounding collectivity, Vietnam representation thus succeeds in insuring its own perpetuation, insisting that peace in its purest forms can only be produced within its *apparent* contradiction—war.

Even a narrative like William Eastlake's *The Bamboo Bed*, in which racial tensions are openly acknowledged, concludes by subsuming them to the brotherhood of the battlefield. The novel introduces onto a winless battlefield "black sergeant Pike" who "had led the Detroit race riots" and who now plans to surrender his squad of white soldiers to the enemy: "There is no greater honor on this earth to a black man than to hand white men to yellow men for killing."[11] Pike here articulates a different set of bonds than those suggested by collectivity, bonds that link him to other races oppressed by whites, for, he asserts, "There is no stronger bond. The bond of suffering. The bond that binds people of color the whole world over. The bond of pain" (pp. 61–62). Pike even realizes that in the collectivity of the military "the game is this—everyone in the army is equal. The interdependency in the common great death is the big equalizer. Each individual is bound to all of humankind in the fraternity of blood that flows out" (p. 62). In saying this, Pike seems to disclose and openly contradict the "game" of collectivity on which bonding in wartime is based.

But then the fighting starts, and one white soldier, Peterbilt, throws himself over Pike to protect him from a mortar round; Pike lives, Peterbilt dies. And suddenly, "There was not a God damn white guy in the outfit who was not a human being. Whitey had become people" (p. 63). In combat, Pike finds, it is not race that is the problem, but survival, "the problem of remaining alive" (p. 64). Under this new criterion for evaluating human relations, Pike discovers, not that whites deserve to die, but that "a man can't help being born the color he is born. That a man has no control over being born white" (p. 69). Finally, as the NVA attack, Pike stays to defend his squad of white men so that they can escape and survive. The satisfaction that before would come from "hand[ing] white men to yellow men for killing" now becomes the satisfaction that "if a man can't . . . make it himself, then he must see someone else . . . make it" (p. 72). As the mortar rounds come in, Pike dies defending "His boys. His Whiteys" (p. 72).

Captain Clancy, the "eternal warrior" (p. 352) of *The Bamboo Bed*, dies, not with a black soldier from his own army, but with a Vietnamese soldier. Both dying, both alone in the jungle, the Vietnamese peasant finds Clancy and lies down next to him. "They were tied together now against all the rest of life. One Friendly and one Unfriendly had joined together to constitute an army of two . . . They would be the great saviors" (pp. 392–93). It is this "army of two," Eastlake implies, that can constitute a new kind of struggle, one that can overcome the "competitive, acquisitive, and possessive" (p. 121) masculinity that leads to war. Combat can thus yield bonds not only between races who fight together but between races who are enemies. The collectivity of war, we are to understand, encompasses all men who engage in battle on any battlefield and overcomes all barriers between races.

In this interracial boundary crossing, many Vietnam narratives insist that the American soldier is more like his Vietnamese enemy than like those Americans who did not participate in combat. Tony 5 in Robert Roth's *Sand in the Wind* comments about Viet Cong soldiers: "They're just a bunch of slant-eyed marines. You know how they tried to make us in boot camp? Well that's how the NVA are—hard-core motherfuckers."[12] And James Webb's *Fields of Fire* claims that grunts are "closer to Gooks" than to the people who give the orders that get them all killed.[13]

But William Broyles, Jr., pursues the cross-race ties more fully than anyone in his account of his return to Vietnam in 1986, *Brothers in Arms*. For Broyles, the meaning of war *is* this bond that transcends barriers: men "loved war for many reasons, not all of them good. The best reason we loved war is also its most enduring memory—comradeship."[14] Comradeship, Broyles explains, "makes war intelligible for the citizen soldier," for comradeship "writ large, is patriotism" in a system where to be a patriot is "to believe that there are values greater than one's own life, values worth dying for" (p. 76). Within this frame, "a comrade in war is a man you can trust with anything, because you trust him with your life" (p. 199). But most importantly, "comradeship isn't a particularly selective process. Race, personality, education—anything that would make a difference in peace—count for nothing. It is, simply, brotherly love" (p. 199).

While Broyles senses this bond with the men he fought with during the war, only with his return to Vietnam did he realize that he shared it with his enemy as well. Broyles develops a grudging respect for his enemy as he realizes their determination to fight, like Americans, for "values greater than one's own life":

> The Communist leaders were ruthless and insulated from suffering. Death did not deter them. And these soldiers they kept sending down the trail were prepared to die. . . . Whatever the reason—ideology, romanticism, patriotism, brainwashing, or the herd instinct—they saw death not primarily as tragedy but as part of a higher purpose. *Like the Texans who fought to the death at the Alamo,* they were ready to sacrifice themselves. [italics added] (p. 91)

The Vietnamese enemy is then not only like the American soldiers Broyles met in battle in Vietnam but like any American soldier as well, even American heroes of the highest sort. There is no racial barrier here, or any political or economic ones, only the barriers between those who believe there are "things worth dying for" and those who do not.

Facing the grave of a Vietnamese soldier who dies during the time Broyles was in Vietnam, Broyles realizes, "if only an AK-47 round or a mortar had taken a slightly different course, or if my footsteps down a slippery paddy dike had fallen an inch or two differently and set off the mine waiting beneath the mud," he could have been in the same grave. "[B]y *the ultimate accident of birth,* he lay here in a muddy paddy . . . And I stood, a tourist from the land of his old enemy, and looked upon his grave and thought how it might have been my own" [italics added] (p. 273). Like Pike's admission that "a man can't help being born the color he is born," Broyles's "accident of birth" absolves him and the society that sent him to fight of any responsibility for the racial animosities that so intimately underlay American motivations for entering Vietnam.[15] At the same time, because none of the barriers separating soldiers seem to spring from anything other than mere "accident," war, in its restructuring of the usual hierarchies of social evaluation, can cut through such accidents and produce collectivity, a collectivity that finally leads Broyles to conclude that "I discovered that I had more in common with my old enemies than with anyone except the men who had fought at my side. My enemies and I shared something almost beyond words. . . . We had tried to kill each other, but we were brothers now" (p. 275).

In Vietnam narratives class difference is erased as well. Joe Galimore, a black veteran in J. C. Pollock's *Mission M.I.A.*, concludes: "It was different over there. . . . It wasn't what you had in the bank that mattered; it was what you had inside."[16] Charles Anderson's *The Grunts* (1976) offers an understanding of class differences that expands to include, like Broyles's interracial brotherhood, the Vietnamese:

> The grunts knew there were things that caused people to lead different lives. From their parents they had heard the nervous excuses, the flashes of resentment when they had first asked why some people lived in bigger houses than others, why some people wore dress-up clothes to work. A few of the grunts now saw their dead enemy as comrades in the struggle against the realities of weakness within themselves too painful to admit, brothers in the struggle against the faceless and nameless forces of circumstances which could send them to the union hall instead of the country club, which would keep them at the gas station, the factory. In killing the grunts of North Vietnam, the grunts of America had killed a part of themselves.[17]

This superficial and convenient explanation for class—that it is determined somewhere else by "faceless and nameless forces"— suggests that all soldiers, in fact, all people are victims of an unalterable class structure. Like the "accidents of birth" that make men different races, soldiers of different economic backgrounds are in this scheme absolved of any responsibility for the attitudes and actions of their class, for it is not they, but these "faceless and nameless forces" that determine class relations. In facing this structure (which clearly cannot be fought), all are joined, effacing class lines through a common victimization that only war, in its revelation of "things worth fighting for," makes apparent.

Like race, class differences are most readily forgotten during battle. Typical of Vietnam narratives, *Body Count* groups in a single platoon the college-educated Chris Hawkins, whose father's company gained its wealth through defense contracts; Robert Wilson, whose father was a mail carrier; "Chief," Screaming Sky Eagle, who was raised on a reservation and educated at Berkeley; Martin Logan, who lives with his divorced father on a Texas ranch; Carlysle, who grew up on the streets in Washington, D.C.; and Big John, whose father was a sharecropper. (It should not be overlooked that these soldiers' class backgrounds are established through their fathers, reinforcing the determination of the masculine bond as basis for meaning.) In this case, as in so many other Vietnam narratives, such as *The 13th Valley, The Boys in Company C, M,* and *Uncommon Valor,* these soldiers, divided at first by disparate class and social backgrounds, as well as perceptions of racial difference, become a cohesive and supportive military unit by the close of the narratives. It is, according to the logic of these stories, the war itself which brings them "tugethur."

Vietnam narratives typically pose against "the World" at home the "strange," "new," and for some, "better" world of Vietnam. It is a place in which values (such as the value of human life) are radically different and the definitions, vocabulary, and discourse of "the World" no longer obtain: "We got a separate culture out here." It is in and through this new world that barriers of race and class can be overcome: "Takin it personal is for people back in the World." But while race, class, and ethnic variety populate Vietnam, one difference is not presented, one boundary is not broken, and that is the difference of gender. "[Comradeship] does not demand for its sustenance the reciprocity, the pledges of affection, the endless reassurances required by the love of men and women. It is, unlike marriage, a bond that cannot be broken by a word, by boredom or divorce, or by anything other than death."[18] Although Vietnam narratives show the bonding of soldiers from diverse and often antagonistic backgrounds, those bonds are always and already masculine. At no point are women to be included as part of this collectivity. And, given American prohibitions against women in combat, prohibitions based largely on sexual difference, such exclusions take on the appearance of the "natural" rather than the social. It is through this elision—"America's collective consciousness" is a masculine consciousness—that the claim of collectivity is most safely made, as the firmly established structure of gender difference maintains a frame within which other change can (apparently) occur, change circumscribed by the masculine bond.[19]

Collectivity fulfills the structural in Vietnam representation through the imagery and frame of the masculine bond, "that Men Without Women trip." As structure, the masculine bond insists on a denial of difference—whether black or white, wealthy or poor, high school or college-educated, from north or south, men are the "same"—at the same time that the bond itself depends for its existence on an affirmation of difference—men are not women. The motif of this structure is thus one of exclusion, and its primary shape is a hierarchy defined by participation in/exclusion from the experience of war. Marilyn French identifies exclusion as one of the means by which patriarchal interests isolated women from men and from each other in early societies, valorizing the bonds between men over those between women and within families: "By excluding women from the public realm, men prevented them from forming alliances there."[20] In American society this hierarchy is not *based on* gender, that is, a development or variation of it, but *is* gender: on the simplest level, men go to war and women don't. The hierarchical structure of Vietnam representation is one of the narratives generated by the desire of gender to tell its story, to make its story the only one that can be told.

As Judith Hicks Stiehm reports in her analysis of the integration of women into the Air Force Academy, *Bring Me Men and Women*, "The prejudice against women in the military and especially in combat is so profound as to amount almost to a taboo."[21] A Navy report on integrating women into the Naval Academy explained: "the waging of war is by its nature different [from sports or professions] and requires professional attributes and characteristics which are the antithesis of what we in this society consider essentially feminine qualities" (p. 31). More revealing is the report on women in combat by the Hoover Commission following World War II: "women might, indeed, be trained to think and act as men but that to so train them might seriously alter society's equilibrium, which depends upon a male-female or rather a military-nonmilitary balance" (p. 294).

But rather than taking such arguments as recording "natural," biological, or essential social differences, Stiehm suggests that the exclusion of women from combat is designed to insure the maintenance of the boundaries of the masculine as a representational and functional category. "The military competes on behalf of a nation just as an athlete competes on behalf of a school, yet women are not often included in either of these forms of ordeal. Is this so because women only represent women? Is representation of a nation or an institution basically a male prerogative?" (p. 148). What Stiehm's questions pinpoint is not simply that the masculine is capable of representing institutions and structures of power relations in a way that the feminine is not (because the feminine, as we see in chapter 5, is certainly a characteristic ascribed to institutions in a negative sense, institutions that have "failed"), but that the masculine, as opposed to the feminine, is meant to be synonymous with them. And in order to maintain the stability of this institutional power, the masculine must by necessity exclude from its arena that against which it defines itself. As Eve Kosofsky Sedgwick writes, "In the presence of a woman who can be seen as pitiable or contemptible, men are able to exchange power and to confirm each other's value even in the context of the remaining inequalities in their power."[22]

Stiehm discloses the fallacies of biological or social arguments against women in combat and pinpoints the institutional investments behind them.

> Everyone agreed that in a national emergency everyone would do whatever was required. Women *would* fight if needed. This meant, of course, that what women were most excluded from, and what men were most closely guarding, was the *peacetime* military. In a sense it was the role; the posture, the career, the profit—not the actual activity—that was being protected.[23]

Nancy Hartsock investigates the grounding of this "posture" of the masculine bond in the traditions of Western politics and philosophy, specifically in the association she defines between masculinity and the *polis*, the rhetorical community of laws and social relations in ancient Greece. Because the warrior-hero's role lies at the heart of the formation of the *polis* as political community, "the establishment of the *polis* takes place through a process of domesticating and subordinating the dangerous and threatening female forces that surround what is to become the political community."[24] In such a context, the female must by necessity be excluded from the enactment and maintenance of this masculine community. Representing the body, the appetitive, necessity, the domestic, and the mundane, the female stands in direct contradistinction to that which the masculine presents itself as being: the abstract, the immortal, the unchanging, the public. Anchoring these dualities in the psychoanalytic development of children consequent on the sexual division of labor in childrearing,[25] Hartsock elaborates on the constitution of the masculine:

> Material reality as experienced by the boy in the family provides no model, and is unimportant in the attainment of masculinity. Nothing of value to the boy occurs within the family, and masculinity becomes an abstract ideal to be achieved over the opposition of daily life. Masculinity must be attained by means of opposition to the concrete world of daily life, by escaping from contact with the female world of the household into the masculine world of politics or public life. (p. 241)

As Stiehm articulates it, "men do not fight to the finish; they fight to establish hierarchy and to create order" (p. 293).

In light of such historical and psychoanalytic suggestions, Stiehm's conclusion that "it was the role; the posture, the career, the profit—not the actual activity—that was being protected" in the military's exclusion of women from combat can be read as indicative of more than an attitude peculiar to the military in its exclusion of women from the activity of combat. This posture of protection/exclusion is indeed typical of the masculine as it perceives itself in relation to the feminine, in effect maintains the feminine as distinct and separate in order to insure its own constitution, its own continued viablity. That posture is most identified in a community of men: "while men are gentlemenly in the presence of women, men are more likely to consider themselves *really* men in all-male groups."[26] But while the masculine feels most "itself" in its own presence, it is able to do so only in the knowledge of what it is not, that it is not the feminine. Thus Stiehm asks, "Is it possible that 'warriorship' somehow requires female exclusion? Are women essential as an audience? as a justification" (p. 276)?

The masculine has thus turned into itself: the *polis* was generated to incorporate and secure the role and position of the warrior-hero in a stable community in ancient Greece, a community within which the complex institutionalization of the exclusion of women took shape; in contemporary American culture, the warrior "is the only role that is now exclusively [men's]" (p. 296), and the institutionalized exclusion of women is seeming less clearcut and enforceable.[27] In such a context, it becomes clear that the representation of the soldier and combat in contemporary American culture is more than simply a resurgence of militarism or nationalistic fever, but is instead a forum for the reaffirmation and reconstitution of the masculine in the modern *polis*. Consequently, Vietnam narratives are to be read, not as a subgenre of popular fiction, but as an emblem of a cultural reformulation of masculinity.

## II

## "Unless You've Been Humping the Boonies, You Don't Know"

Bobbie Ann Mason's *In Country* (1985), a novel written by a woman and told from a woman's point of view, confirms collectivity as a function of the masculine bond. The narrative of a teenager whose father was killed in Vietnam during the war, *In Country* begins with a group of characters who are disoriented, confused, aimless, and separated from each other. Samantha Hughes's mother has remarried and moved away; her uncle, Emmett, cannot hold a job or a relationship and has symptoms of Agent Orange contamination that he will not discuss with other veterans; Samantha has not seen her father's parents in two years, and, having graduated from high school, she cannot decide on a direction for the rest of her life. As the novel progresses, "Sam" becomes more involved in Vietnam, reading books, attending veterans' gatherings, arguing with the VA about Agent Orange, reading her father's Vietnam diary, and dating a Vietnam veteran. She finally leaves home to live in a swamp to enable her to have the feeling of being "in country," in Vietnam.

Sam's attempt to duplicate her father's Vietnam experience finally reunites her with her family. She travels with her uncle and father's mother to Washington, D.C., where they visit the Vietnam Veterans' Memorial and touch her father's name engraved in the granite monument. Sam is confirmed as part of this collective when she finds "her" own name listed in the memorial directory, a soldier whom she doesn't know: "Sam Alan Hughes PFC AR 02 MAR 49 02 FEB 67 Houston TX 14E 104."[28] More important, her name becomes an emblem for an American collectivity: "She touches her own name. How odd it feels, as though all the names in America have been used to decorate this wall" (p. 245).

This quiet collectivity recapitulates Del Vecchio's more strident "collective consciousness" of America, using the Vietnam Memorial as a focus for collective identity. In spite of the novel's apparent focus on women, the mechanism for the generation of collectivity is still, as for Del Vecchio, the masculine bond, a bond that must be confirmed before the closure of collectivity can be presented.

Although Sam Hughes's life is suffused with Vietnam, and she knows more about Agent Orange and many aspects of the war than her uncle who fought in it, she is constantly denied real knowledge of the war because she is a woman. "Stop thinking about Vietnam, Sambo. You don't know how it was, and you never will. There is no way you can ever understand. So just forget it. Unless you've been humping the boonies, you don't know" (p. 136). When she suggests to her uncle that "some vets I could name are afraid of women," he reminds her of women's exclusion: "'Women weren't over there,' Emmett snapped. 'So they can't really understand'" (p. 107). Sam's own arguments against this exclusion simply reaffirm it:

> "Well, Mom took care of you all those years, and you think she didn't understand?" Sam said angrily. "And what about me? I feel like there's a big conspiracy against me. Like something the CIA would be in on." Sam grabbed up one of her Vietnam books from the table and shook it at him. "But I know about stuff that went on." (p. 107)

Although women can "understand" the war, it is only through men or books written about men's experiences, not from the experience itself. Gaining knowledge from "her Vietnam books" and veterans she talks to, she still cannot achieve the qualification of "humping the boonies."

When Sam presses too hard for information, she is treated like a child and separated even further from any Vietnam experience. After she questions Tom Hudson about his war experience, he replies, "It's hard to talk about, and some people want to protect you, you know. They don't want to dump all this stuff on you" (p. 95). Her attempts to continue their conversation are met only with "I think you're cute." Even after her stay in the swamp, where "she was in her father's place" (p. 217), Emmett reminds her, "You think you can go through what we went through in the jungle, but you can't. This place is scary, and things can happen to you, but it's not the same as having snipers and mortar fire and shells and people shooting at you from behind bushes" (p. 220).

Sam's "reunion" with her father is then only a superficial one that exists through the inanimate stone of the Vietnam Memorial. The "wild" independence that she boasts of in earlier sections of the novel is left in Cawood's Pond, where her final exclusion from the masculine bond defined by war is confirmed. She ceases fighting against the "conspiracy" that excludes her and allows Emmett, previously unable to act on anything, to take over. Indeed, the very motivation for the trip to the memorial—the location for the generation of collectivity—comes from Emmett: "Then Emmett announced a plan. They were going to see the Vietnam Memorial in Washington. He was so definite about it, as though he were an executive making a big decision that would mean millions of dollars for his company" (p. 230).

Sam's name lends itself to the confusion of collectivity that is generated by the masculine bond. Her nickname, Sam, suggests a man's name and was chosen by her father, who wanted a boy—"Samantha was an afterthought" (p. 182). More indirect is a nickname that some of the veterans use, Sambo, a name that has clear racial (and racist) connotations. Her character thus embodies challenges to a masculine collectivity from women and blacks and suggests that, in her reunion with her father and her appearance in the stone of Vietnam, she represents all of those who have been excluded and are now brought back. That Sam and America can only join in this masculine bond through a name carved in stone suggests the rigidity of positions defined by that bond. Now dead and reborn as "Sam Alan Hughes," Samantha Hughes is no longer excluded from Vietnam.

As a rule, when women appear in Vietnam narratives, it is never as part of the "brotherhood" that is created in battle. They are instead usually trying to stop their husbands, sons, or lovers from going to Vietnam.[29] In *Uncommon Valor*, Mrs. Wilkes tells the men who have come to ask her husband to join a POW rescue mission that will return them to Vietnam: "Listen, my husband doesn't want to talk to you." When Wilkes agrees to go on the mission, we see how little she understands the masculine bond that draws him to his former unit, we see that her opinions are disregarded by it and her interests excluded from it. And while Rick Donatelli's father responds to his son's need to return to Vietnam to help rescue his former sergeant from a POW camp by saying, "you do what your heart tells you,"[30] Phil Houser's girlfriend can only plead, "Don't you care how I feel about this?" (p. 94).

In these positions of pleading, fear, and loneliness, women in Vietnam narratives fulfill Sedgwick's prescription for the maintenance of masculine power: "in the presence of a woman who can be seen as pitiable or contemptible, men are able to exchange power and to confirm each other's value even in the context of the remaining inequalities in their power."[31] Class and race differences can be "overlooked" in a masculine bond that foregrounds the value of masculinity itself and privileges that value above all others. But Sedgwick's situational enactment limits the display and enforcement/encouragement of the masculine to the presence of women. One of the functions and achievements of Vietnam narrative is to expand those individual circumstances to an exhaustive feature of the Vietnam stage, one where the position of women is only and exclusively "pitiable and contemptible." Women who might have seemed strong at one point, like Sam Hughes, are finally forced into the position of being "pitiable and contemptible" in order for the narrative to progress. Reading her father's letters to her mother and his diary puts Sam, not in her father's place, but in the place of the excluded women who read them, who are not and cannot be "in country," in the place of the women who waited for men, cried for them, and were unable to understand them.

## The Mystery of the Orient

Whereas differences between men (or those who take on the positions of men) can be overcome by the power of the masculine bond, differences between women and between women and men are accentuated by it. In the world of the masculine bond, it is most important that these differences be marked in sexual terms. By perceiving women through a prism of sexuality, women's difference from men is made to appear "natural" whereas the differences between men—class, race, and ethnicity—are made to seem circumstantial. The logic of Vietnam decrees that "natural" differences cannot be overcome, whereas social ones not only can but should. In an argument that admits the social construction of difference—"The grunts knew there were things that caused people to lead different lives"—it is all the more necessary that the social construction of gender be translated into terms that will not allow gender to be considered in the same light as class or ethnicity, as one of the "faceless and nameless forces of circumstance" that govern people's lives, but instead be seen as predetermined and incontrovertible.

After having sex with a Vietnamese prostitute, *Body Count*'s Chris Hawkins watches her squat in a corner and douche herself with a pan of water: he "watched the girl as if she were something in a sideshow. How crude that looked. I wonder if that's the difference in Oriental women or just the difference in class. Somehow it would be impossible to picture a cultured girl back home doing something like that. The incongruity of the two images made him laugh" (p. 179). Once he has asserted that women are separated from each other—American women are not like Vietnamese—and that difference does exist, Hawkins can move quickly and infallibly to the differences between women and men, differences that are framed in strictly sexual terms. During his meeting with the prostitute, Hawkins asks one of the most insistent questions of *Body Count:* "Was it really sideways?" (p. 177). The pursuit of the answer to this question (pre)occupies much of the novel and moves beyond the superficial differences of class originally proposed, concluding in an R&R in Hong Kong, when Wilson and Chief assault a prostitute hired by Wilson in order to "solve the ancient mystery of the Orient" (p. 340). Turning her upside down and forcing her legs apart, Chief announces "in a mighty chant," "The great riddle is solved. Look. Look. Oh, the whole wide world, look. Oriental pussy is *not* sideways" (p. 340)! Chief, a Native American, and Wilson, a black, announce their conclusion from a position that does not recognize the racial and class differences that separate them—"men are able to exchange power and confirm each other's value even in the context of the remaining inequalities in their power." Joined by the masculine bond, Chief and Wilson, rejoicing in their inclusion, notice only their difference from women.

Racial differences disappear here for women as well, since "Oriental pussy is *not* sideways" and thus all women are physically alike. This makes their exclusion then not a matter of race, class, ethnicity, or other forms of difference, but of direct and observable physiology. And while the American soldier can cross racial barriers to share the bond of war with his enemy, he is still alienated from women, who also share cross-racial bonds, but only with other women, not with men. John Clark Pratt's *The Laotian Fragments* recounts a conversation overheard through a listening device between an NVA lieutenant and nurse in which "he was putting the make on her, and she was being coy *like all women anywhere*" [italics added].[32] Affirming difference only in sexual terms so that the constructions of gender can be denied, the barriers between all men and all women are reinforced. "Nevertheless, he finally scored" (p. 149). The denial of class, race, or national differences between women disallows any possible grounding for the formation of bonds between men and women who might share the oppression of race or class. Instead, women, "like all women anywhere," share a profoundly determinate physical difference that irreversibly and consistently divides them from men.

As *Body Count* proceeds, the search for an answer to the "mystery of the Orient" takes on a force equal to that of the war itself; it is, in fact, *the* story of the war. One might speculate that an (unconscious) motivation for American and other national military involvements in various parts of the globe might well be to ascertain that women are, in fact, not like men *anywhere* and that the structure of gender difference is "universal" (for the U.S., from Europe to Asia to the Middle East, Africa, and now Latin America). Groups of (exclusively) men colonize geographic regions in order to "engage the enemy" where s/he lives and both assert and appropriate her difference.

In contrast to their physical consistency, women are shown in Vietnam narratives to be emotionally and psychologically inconsistent, not in relation to other women, but in their relations to men. They change their minds about divorces, pregnancies, marriages, and so on. When Lieutenant Brooks hears that his wife wants a divorce, Doc proclaims, "Women. They all the time doin somethin jus so you can't expect why. . . . If you expects them in the valleys they's gonna be on the hills and if you expects them on the hill they's gonna be in the valley. Women like that. They figure out what you expects then they do jus the opposite" (p. 103). Although the physical difference might seem sufficient to differentiate women from men, the simultaneous awareness that this difference links *all* women makes the bond of their distinction more threatening. Thus, other boundaries need to be distinguished as well, boundaries that can affirm, not only that women are different, but that they are lesser than men. But because these differences are "inconsistent" and "unpredictable," they can never be concluded. Here we see the validation for the continual social oppression of women, controlling not just women's bodies but their behavior as well.

In contrast to the "inconsistencies" of women, men in Vietnam narratives are profoundly consistent:

> All the collective lessons of ten years of American involvement snapping into place in his head, all the collective lessons learned, forgotten, relearned by tens of men, by tens of thousands. The lessons were there in Egan's mind, there from almost eighteen months of combat duty, there from his heritage as an American, as a man, as a human being. All that need be done was to relax, allow the mind to shift, to tap the data banks of 10,000 years of human warfare perhaps 100,000 years perhaps for the entire age of man perhaps earlier. . . . And his enemy . . . they too would bring the collective lessons of tens of millions of men from tens of thousands of years of fighting, of fighting North against South, brother against brother, the same pattern from antiquity to post-Geneva, the enemy had a mind-set developed by tens of billions of man-years of war. (p. 179).

As Del Vecchio's analysis makes clear, the consistency of men is a consistency of war—"tens of billions of man-years of war"— while the consistency of women is not social but biological—"Oriental pussy is *not* sideways!"; "like all women anywhere." In such terms, the consistencies of men depend on and are framed by the bond of masculinity, of which war is a chief expression.

Doc concludes his diatribe by reaffirming the lines between men and women: "Sometime a dude got plenty of brains for dealin on dinks but he *loses his powers* when applyin it to pussy" [italics added] (p. 103). To quote Andrea Dworkin, "the first rule of masculinity is that whatever he is, women are not."[33] The real threat of women's inconsistency is that they confound men's "powers" by disallowing them a stable basis for control—"They figure out what you expects then they do jus the opposite." In going to the new world that is Vietnam, soldiers are entering the apparently timeless, stable, and undifferentiated world of the masculine bond, a world that women, by inscribing difference, both sustain and destroy or, more accurately, sustain by threatening to destroy. The belief that women not only will but want to destroy the bonds between men is necessary to insuring the constant tensions that bound masculine bonds and prevent their dissolution from within through a recognition of other forms of difference. The pressure of difference demands that wars be fought and re-fought, presented and represented so that the control produced in the artificial environment of the masculine bond can be maintained.

## III

## "I Am a Man-God"

> From that day on they called him Cherry and from the night of that day and on he thought of himself as Cherry. It confused him yet it felt right. He was in a new world, a strange world. . . . It made little difference to him that they called every new man Cherry and that with the continual rotation of personnel there would soon be a soldier newer than he and he would call the new man Cherry.[34]

When James Chellini enters Vietnam, he abandons his name from "the world" and takes on the nickname he is assigned by his comrades, his name as a character in the narrative of Vietnam—"cherry," the virginal, the uninitiated, the untouched, the feminine. "Cherry" invokes the difference of gender at the moment when other differences presumably disappear, maintains this difference as a basis for eradicating all others. It is not only a naming, a translation that others use in relation to him; it is the way "he thought of himself." The category is not simply identifying but is a mode of identity necessary for entrance into a world that structures its hierarchies of value around the masculine bond.

Once the structure of difference has been established, the logic of collectivity can be initiated. Chellini, whose name is replaced by the gender structure itself—"Cherry"—comes to symbolize the path of that structure in Vietnam narrative. As he gradually becomes more experienced, he becomes progressively more violent and insensitive to the consequences of that violence. He becomes intoxicated by battle, moving through the jungle, chanting his own rhymes of war:

> Men at war, once again,
> Peace's a bore,
> Let's have fun. (p. 603)

Finally, as his name signifies gender difference, so his story fulfills its logic. He becomes the masculine-bonded collective—its voice, embodiment, and spirit:

> If Jesus Christ was a man and all men are brothers, does not that mean Christ was my brother. He is the Son of God. Then it follows that I too am the Son of God and thus a God myself. I am immortal. I am immune to destruction. I am a man-God. If I get blown away I will resurrect myself. . . . My friends, we have become one being. Your cells are my cells, my cells are yours. I have this love in me for you, in me, through me, with me, in the power and the spirit of this man-god you are resurrected and you shall live. I am the Mangod and ye shall not raise false gods before Me. (p. 604)

From virgin to God, Cherry's immaculate conception depends for its unfailing procedure on the difference that gender proclaims as it simultaneously preaches its religion of "indifference," a world in which all men are brothers, are gods.

This dependence of the logic of collectivity on gender difference explains the tension in war narratives provoked by homoeroticism. Because gender is seen within the vocabulary of the masculine bond as a sexually defined category, the efforts to reaffirm male sexual identity are unavoidable repercussions of its definition. Only through the constant reaffirmation of such sexual difference can the conservative structure that frames the collective be maintained. More important, sexual difference is insisted on as an aspect of the collective, something that men share together *in the same ways*. It is here that the collective becomes the spectacular, as the sexuality that confirms the masculine bond is displayed with insistence and, on occasion, with a vengeance.

Susan Brownmiller's summary of rape and atrocities toward women during the Vietnam War underscores the extent to which rape functioned both as confirmation of masculine bonds and as display. The very frequency of accounts of gang-rape in soldiers' narratives of the war is only one symptom of the violent force of the spectacular, of how the spectacle functions through violence to release tensions of difference. Soldier after soldier remarks that he was aware that others were watching him commit the rape: "They only do it when there are a lot of guys around. . . . You know, it makes them feel good. They show each other what they can do—'I can do it,' you know. They won't do it by themselves."[35] In some cases this knowledge impelled them to commit an act they would otherwise have avoided. As one soldier who participated in a rape confessed, "Okay, let's say you are on a patrol. These guys right here are going to start laughing you out. Pretty soon you're going to be an outcast from the platoon" (p. 102). Far from something to hide, rape became, for some, spectacle on a grand scale. One helicopter pilot recalled his first view of the My Lai massacre from the air:

> Flying over a rice paddy, Ridenhour and his pilot sighted a body on the field below. . . . "It was a woman," Ridenhour later said with emotion. "She was spread-eagled, as if on display. She had an 11th Brigade patch between her legs—as if it were some type of display, some badge of honor" (p. 105).

Gang-rape combines collectivity and display as the masculine bond performs as a group, with itself as audience. (Recall here Judith Hicks Stiehm's conclusion that when the community of Air Force cadets lost women as its external audience, it became, by necessity, its own.) "One gang rape and murder of a peasant woman, set upon while she labored in a field with her baby at her side, had even been photographed step by step by one of the participants with his Instamatic camera" (p. 103). With soldiers both viewers and participants, rape as collective reaffirms Caputo's experience of paralysis. In turn raping and watching others rape leaves no position for any other action within the bond; if you challenge the rape, question the display, you risk being rejected by the collective. Phan Thi Mao was abducted from her village by force by a five-man patrol for five days of "boom-boom," after which, they admitted, she would have to be killed. The one man who did not participate in the rape or murder was ostracized by his peers, "derided by the patrol leader . . . as a chicken and queer" (p. 102), and believed he was almost killed by the men he accused of rape. Gang-rape is testimony to the function of display in establishing and enforcing the status of the collective. Collectivity is finally nothing more, and nothing less, than its power to create and re-create spectacle.

As gang-rape makes clear, sexuality is displayed through the prism of the collective. Rape is the most violent extreme of the enforcement of the collective in Vietnam narrative, the promise of the consequences of denying the demands and definitions of the masculine bond. Larry Heinemann's *Paco's Story*[36] traces the path between collective violence as gang-rape and violence toward individual women. In one of the harshest scenes of all Vietnam narrative, Heinemann details the gang-rape of a Vietnamese sniper who has killed two men. A sergeant of the platoon, Gallagher, ties the woman's arms with wire looped over the beam of a bombed building, presses her body into a table strewn with "chunks of tiles and scraps of air-burst howitzer shrapnel,"[37] and rapes her.

> And when Gallagher finished, Jonesy fucked her, and when Jonesy was done, half the fucking company was standing in line and commenced to fuck her ragged. . . . watching one another while they ground the girl into the rubble. . . . Dudes still ambled over to the doorway to watch, to call out coaching, taking their turns, hanging around the side of the building after—some getting back in line. (pp. 180–81)

Afterwards, Gallagher shoots her in the forehead.

This is the memory that the novel's protagonist, Paco, a man covered with scars from an artillery and air strike of his platoon's position, tries to forget, tries to relieve. "And he's just a man like the rest of us, James, who wants to fuck away all that pain and redeem his body" (p. 173). To do so he plays a game of voyeurism with the niece of a hotel keeper who lives behind the diner Paco works in after his return from Vietnam. He watches her undress in her window, overhears her make love to her boyfriend, and

> has the incredible, shivering urge to sneak into Cathy's room and stalk up behind Marty-boy as bold as brass, grab him by the hips and yank him off, shake him out and set him aside. . . . Cathy would be pulling at her own hair by then; grinding her hips in the air, straining her legs and belly. (p. 173)

Cathy's diary records her own dream of making love to Paco, but it is one that reveals the violence implicit in Paco's desire, a violence that connects Cathy to the Vietnamese sniper:

> He's done, but still between my legs. He . . . then begins to peel the scars off as if they were a mask. . . . I close my eyes and turn my head, and urge him off me with my hips—but I think now that he must have thought I wanted to fuck more. . . . Then he's kneeling on my shoulders . . . and he's laying strings of those scars on my face, and I'm beginning to suffocate. . . . And he lays them across my breasts and belly—tingling and burning—lays them in my hair . . . And when each scar touches me, I feel the suffocating burn, hear the scream. (pp. 208–209)

By having this second rape be Cathy's dream, not Paco's, Heinemann constructs a complex narrative in which Paco and Cathy both stand in for the collective experiences of and about veterans, with Paco a living monument to the war's damage to men's lives and Cathy's dream a record of the nonveteran's inability to understand or feel the pain of those who fought in the war. Paco's is a collective experience, one that the rape of the Vietnamese sniper epitomizes, while Cathy's is typical, not collective, one that her own rape epitomizes.

For Heinemann, rape is the figure of the violence of the war. But in a novel where everyone is guilty, rape loses its gendered force and seems to achieve status as a collective metaphor of American involvement in the Vietnam War. But individual violence in *Paco's Story* happens in only one direction, in the collective rape of women by men. Such notions of a collective function not to reveal the operations of masculine bonds, but to offer the spectacle of masculine violence as ground for all experience.

Sexual relations of any sort are displayed in the same terms in Vietnam narrative, with the hint or threat of violence never far away. In one of the most detailed displays of Vietnam narrative, Lieutenant Brooks, a black soldier whose wife is divorcing him, has a fantasy of seeing his wife with another man:

> In his mind Brooks entered the bedroom of a penthouse bachelor's pad. . . . She did not know he had returned. It was his first day back. They were giggling on the bed. The lights were low. Lila, her sensuous mocha-colored body naked on the Jody's legs, her mouth on his large penis. . . . Brooks snapped his right hand toward the bed. The spoon flew from the grenade with a metallic ting.

But suddenly, this scene of revenge becomes a scene of passion, only the actors have changed:

> He was in bed with the Jody. The Jody was Egan. . . . Lila kissed Rufus passionately. . . . Then Egan began rubbing his giant cock against her face. . . . Then the cock slid into his mouth. Lila held Rufus' face to it.[38]

Brooks has, in the now-familiar pattern of Vietnam's display of gender, changed from observer to participant, occupying again both positions of the bond, reassuring his membership in it as well as his inability to act outside of it. Racial difference—Brooks is black and Egan white—seems to play no part in this scene, in fact it reassures the collectivity of the masculine by drawing the men together against (a) woman. Lila betrays her husband by making love with another man, but Egan remains loyal to the masculine bond by becoming Brooks's "Jody."

Although Egan's and Brooks's fantasy sexual encounter achieves the satisfaction that Brooks's relations with his wife do not, thereby reinforcing the strength of their relation over that of man and woman, their eroticism must reenact heterosexual imperatives, with Egan as the male "Jody" and Brooks as the female, taking Lila's place. "Fucking requires that the male act on one who has less power and this valuation is so deep, so completely implicit in the act, that the one who is fucked is stigmatized as feminine during the act even when not anatomically female."[39] Replying to the anxieties about homosexuality (that is, there are still masculine and feminine roles), this episode underscores the extent to which masculine bonding, at its most intimate, is sanctioned only in a gendered framework. Luce Irigaray explains: "[Male] homosexuality is the law that regulates the sociocultural order. Heterosexuality amounts to the assignment of roles in the economy. . . . sex, and different sexes, would exist only as prescribed by the successful conduct of (business) relations among men."[40] The gendered relations that determine Vietnam narratives take place through the insistent heterosexualities on which masculinity depends for its enactment. The goal of these theatrical pieces is to reestablish the collective bonds of masculinity that exclude any need for women. It is at the same time their limitation that they require the role of the feminine through which they must act. To quote Terry Eagleston: "man is what he is only by virtue of ceaselessly shutting out this other or opposite [woman], defining himself in antithesis to it. . . . Man therefore needs this other even as he spurns it."[41] Although Brooks eliminates Lila to get to Egan, he must become Lila to have sex with Egan; although Chellini forsakes "the World" to become part of the masculine collective of Vietnam, he must become feminine—"cherry"—in order to achieve it.

Frightened by his own fantasy, Brooks broaches the subject with Egan, who quickly explains that "everybody does that," reassuring the collective about the ambivalence of its sexual displays. So common that Army psychiatrists had even labeled it the "Nam Syndrome" (p. 539), it is a necessary fulfillment of the logic of gender difference defined in sexual terms. While sexual images must be foregrounded in order to act as constant reminders of the structuration of gender that reinforces the ideology of collectivity, they pose a constant risk of displaying the dependence of that collectivity on the very relation it denies—the association with women. For this reason Vietnam narratives are replete with sexual encounters, pornographic images, and sexually motivated vocabularies. Because they are grounded on that which they deny, the narratives of masculine collectivity, trapped in the inevitability of their own logic, must constantly rework themselves. They can never completely achieve their separation from the feminine and so must constantly retell their relations to it.

But as Sedgwick explains, the explicit sexualization of homoeroticism in homosexuality is only one pole of a continuum of male homosociality that permeates a patriarchally defined society. Consequently, "for a man to be a man's man is separated only by an invisible, carefully blurred, always-already-crossed line from being 'interested in men'."[42] The "Nam Syndrome" suggests that this is an aspect of all masculine relationships, one that cannot, because of the need to maintain gender difference, be resolved. Richard Klein, in summarizing Freud's explanation of homosexuality, concludes that "heterosexuality in the male . . . presupposes a homosexual phase as the condition of its normal possibility."[43] With Freudian theory thus acting as an apologetics for homoeroticism as a heterosexual matrix, the Nam Syndrome becomes a necessary part of male development, an essential phase to be passed through on the way to the "normal." At a time when other arenas for masculine bonding in American culture are being "invaded" (by the integration of professional sports, the enactment of Title IX, requiring all-male schools to become co-educational, all-male clubs to accept women as members, the racial and gender integration of traditionally male professions, and so on), war can be perceived as the last "pure" theater for the masculine bond. In this context, war, as the most efficient structural space for the figuration of gender difference, can be defended as necessary for the enactment and development of the masculine bond.

More precisely, war *is* the spectacle of the masculine bond. It is the optimal display of masculine collectivity in America, since battle, as defined by American culture, is an exclusively male activity. War is the stage where men can perform, for themselves and their "enemies," it is the ostentation of bonding. (One of the most frequently celebrated acts of the war was of men who sacrificed or risked their lives to save other men during battle.[44])

Broyles argues that war is necessary to human life because it is part of a structure for meaning:

> The power of war, like the power of love, springs from man's heart. The one yields death, the other life. But life without death has no meaning; nor, at its deepest level, does love without war. . . . It is no accident that men love war, as love and war are at the core of man. . . . War, like death, is always with us, a constant companion, a secret sharer.[45]

Viewing war in the context of the masculine bond reveals its relation to a different structure of meaning—not love and power, but "man" and "woman," the gendered construction of reality. War displays not only bonding, but also the violence and destruction that can result from a failure to accept the definitions of that bond. But because that bond is itself a tenuous one, maintained only within the idealized and isolated frame of battle, the masculine bond needs only the slightest excuse to stage its performance, to reopen its theater, to display its willingness to enforce itself, needs only the provocation of difference, *in any form*—for any difference will hint at the difference that is gender—to exercise/exorcise its contradictory motto of "different but the same." And because each staging of the masculine bond risks and insures a reminder of difference in its assertion of itself, war as masculine bonding reproduces itself. As long as there is gender, there will be war.

## IV

The pattern of proposing collectivity as masculine bonding through the structuration of gender is not limited to Vietnam narratives but can be found in critical studies of Vietnam as well, underscoring the extent to which this ideology inhabits almost all current discussions of Vietnam, whether as voices of popular culture or academics. Three works are of particular interest for their focus and disciplines: John Wheeler's cultural study of the effect of the Vietnam

War on American society, *Touched with Fire: The Future of the Vietnam Generation* (1984); John Hellmann's *American Myth and the Legacy of Vietnam* (1986), an analysis of the fiction and nonfiction generated by the Vietnam war; and Philip Beidler's *American Literature and the Experience of Vietnam* (1982), a reading of Vietnam narratives in the context of American literary traditions. In each case, gender is the suppressed/expressed category on which the individual analysis depends. In each case, masculine bonding—the collectivity—is projected as a basis for the regeneration of society as a whole.

John Wheeler, in his defense of the value of the Vietnam War as cultural experience, argues for the nonsexual aspects of male homosociality in what he calls "commitment," the sense of mutual responsibility and fulfilling of one's promise that comes from serving in the military during wartime. Soldiers in battle have, according to Wheeler, experienced this commitment; as veterans, they are the best means for transmitting that sense of unity and commitment to Americans who, in Wheeler's view, have tragically forgotten it. For Wheeler, for instance, the U.S. military was keeping John Kennedy's promise to "pay any price, bear any burden." And the individual soldier was "honoring a commitment we made to serve as a member of the United States armed forces."[46] Although other people of his generation also made commitments, to the Peace Corps, to the civil rights movement, "I consider my commitment as a statement that there are things worth dying for. It is a masculine statement. I think it is *the* masculine statement. This is why war has tended to be viewed as a masculine enterprise" (p. 140). "Woman," on the other hand, "expresses the idea that there are things worth living for" (pp. 140–41). "In Vietnam," Wheeler concludes, "masculinity did not go out of fashion" (p. 141).

One of the stated goals of Wheeler's book is to revive collectivity in American life: "if we have the will, it is possible for us to identify fundamental divisions among us, assess whether they are unnecessary impediments to intimacy, to relationships, to unity. If we will, we can bridge these divisions" (p. 127). But in contrast to the cohesiveness of Wheeler's visions, his vocabulary of analysis and reason undercuts his proposed desires for unification. He assumes the existence of "fundamental divisions" that can be "bridged" but, presumably, not erased. That unity can occur only as a result of "will"—the enforcement of a point of view—places Wheeler firmly in the pattern of a Vietnam representation that is defined by and in relation to individual interests, specifically, the interests of the masculine in exclusion of women.

Like many Vietnam representations, Wheeler's analysis denies (other than gender) barriers. For example, in discussing the treatment of Vietnam veterans, he concludes: "The Vietnam veteran was the nigger of the 1970s." Wheeler defines "nigger" in such a way that it is no longer a racially specific term: "You create a nigger by depriving a person of part of his or her personhood. Ignoring that person or inflicting traumatic hurts is the traditional way to treat a nigger" (pp. 16–17). As a result, racial categories become meaningless in Wheeler's analysis. Wheeler abstracts the label of "nigger" so that his interest group—the

Vietnam veteran—can be served by it. More directly, by translating nigger to include other than blacks subject to racism in America, he is denying the existence of a separation, such as black and white, that could distract from the formation of his collective. Here we see the operation of Wheeler's "will," as he forms a "bridge" between black and white—"unnecessary impediments . . . to unity"—in order to serve his larger interests of collectivity. He is not working against racism by eradicating the structure that promotes the term but instead is expanding the category to create a collective of soldiers returning from the war. By maintaining the category of nigger while changing its definition, Wheeler can eliminate a level of difference that detracts from the masculine collective while retaining the operation of oppression by difference. Because we have already been told that it is these soldiers whose shared commitment can revive America, being a "nigger" takes on an inversely (and perversely) positive aura that conveniently disregards the connotations of racism in favor of the interests of commitment.

Wheeler's analysis, designed to redeem the Vietnam experience for an entire generation and oriented toward reaping its value for future generations, participates in the same pattern of gender difference and collectivity as the novels, films, and personal narratives. But while most Vietnam narratives collapse gender into sexuality for the purpose of making gender constructions seem "natural" and universal, Wheeler collapses sexuality into gender for the purpose of making gender difference seem a necessary aspect of social relations. Eradicating the precise biological difference of the capacity for reproduction, Wheeler argues that modern medical technology has made this level of difference obsolete: "A baby could be conceived without a father present. The baby could develop without a mother present. In a sense, penis and testicle, vagina and womb were machines replaceable by alternate technologies" (p. 85). By mechanizing the body, Wheeler brings it squarely into the realm of the performative, an arena in which all human bodies are part of the "green machine" that is the hierarchical structure of masculine bonding. Wheeler seems to be avoiding "sexist" distinctions between men and women (women, he says, can be "niggers" too) by abstracting their roles from sexual identification. But, in fact, he is making gender characteristics appear all the more cogent, dictated not by biology but by social necessity: "The technology of our bodies has always been integral to our lives together, but only part of our lives together. More important is that we face each other and *choose* to have relationships with each other. The real issue is commitment. . . . bonding is paramount" (p. 85). Wheeler thus uses reason to bridge the gaps between social differences. Having dismissed biological and racial differences as determining categories, he can introduce choice—"will"—as the path to social regeneration. Given the opportunity, he suggests, we will choose commitment.

Although Wheeler uses for sexuality the same strategy he established for race—abstraction as a means to collectivity—and seems to be leading toward the same conclusion—that differences should be "bridged" for the purpose of creating "unity"—his valorization of masculine commitment as a source for social regeneration reintroduces gender as it negates sexuality. Wheeler's definitions of commitment are exclusively gender related, based on whether one does (masculine) or does not (feminine) believe that "there are things worth dying for."

Although Wheeler's book lauds commitment as social bonding, it is clear that he excludes feminine commitment from his social vision. Feminine principles, according to Wheeler, not only threatened the commitments established by masculine bonds, but also destroyed the lives of the men who participated in them. Although soldiers fought according to their (country's) commitments, the protesters at home, exercising a feminine paradigm, did not (and here Wheeler reintegrates Nixon's characterization of protesters [see chapter 1]). Because of these protests, he reasons, American forces were constrained from fighting to their potential and, as a result, either lost lives directly or enabled them to be lost later by allowing the enemy to escape (across the border to Cambodia, for example). In this logic, a feminine principle prohibits the full exercising of the value of the commitment inherent in the masculine bond.

Feminine commitment—that there are "things worth living for"—proves destructive to a masculine commitment—that there are "things worth dying for." Because Wheeler's hopes for American society are based on a masculine model, he effectively dismisses feminine commitment from aiding in the construction of any American future and, like other Vietnam narratives, excludes women from the privileged circle of the masculine bond. By collapsing sexuality into gender, Wheeler is able to foreground a masculine society, formed by masculine values and principles, in which females have two options: either to align themselves with masculine interests through "choice" and "will" or to become sexually technologized to fulfill the needs of reproduction, "replaceable by alternate technologies."

John Hellmann's persuasive analysis of American myth and the way it was changed and challenged by the Vietnam War is, like the Vietnam narratives he discusses, asserting a regenerated myth of collectivity at the expense of an awareness of how gender structures that collectivity. Tracing the myth of American innocence and frontierism through Leatherstocking and Daniel Boone to the Green Berets, Hellmann argues that the encounter with Vietnam forced a reevaluation of the sufficiency of that myth for the modern world. The Vietnam narratives, he concludes,

> have presented a Southeast Asian landscape that overturns the meaning of the previously known landscapes of American myth. These narratives purge us, forcing the reader or viewer to reexperience, this time self-consciously, the tragic shattering of our old myths. This process may prepare the culture to accept a significant alteration of our view of ourselves and of our world, a new mythic interpretation of our historical experience that will intelligibly include the experience of Vietnam.[47]

Hellmann's utopian projection fails to analyze the gendered quality of those myths. Cultural interpretations of Vietnam may force, as Charles Reich said, "people . . . to question the other myths of the Corporate State,"[48] but, because the Vietnam war was itself dependent on gender for its structure, it did not or could not present gender as a myth to be questioned. As Hellmann's argument reveals, the character through and on which American myth depends was and is a specifically masculine one: Natty Bumpo, Daniel Boone, the Virginian. That character, reincarnated as John Wayne in *The Green Berets,* is at the center of "the romantic desire of Americans to escape their own machines, their own affluence, their own racism, their own alienation" (p. 88).

Hellmann speaks confidently of "our" views and "our" alienation, assuming a cohesive characterization for his speaking subject. But, as he shows, that subject is always and already masculine. It may speak of class, race, and technology, but it cannot speak of gender, cannot raise the question of women.[49] Hellmann assumes and accepts this masculine voice for his narrative of social change. The self "we" are to examine is only the self that masculinity projects, the self that is constructed by gender. In such a context, to speak of "our view of ourselves" and assume that this view encompasses all Americans is decidedly deceptive. Hellmann states that Vietnam narratives can "offer *Americans* only journeys away from *their* myth that ironically re-create it within *personal consciousness* while denying its larger cultural, historical validity" [italics added] (p. 169). In discussing Del Vecchio's *The 13th Valley,* Hellmann astutely recognizes collectivity in operation: "Each of the secondary characters making up the elite inner circle of Brooks' company embodies an aspect of the ideal American self-concept. . . . Del Vecchio has taken the one continuous theme of moral affirmation found in the American literary narratives of Vietnam . . . and transformed it into a mythic representation of the living American ideal" (pp. 132–33). That this "American ideal" can "live" only inside the "elite inner circle" of the masculine bond emphasizes the extent to which the "significant alteration of ourselves" that can be brought about through Vietnam narratives is a singly masculine one. In Hellman's work, the ideology of collectivity is reinforced as it pretends to establish a revived and restructured myth for America that reevaluates everything except the very framework within which that myth resides—the construction of gender.

Hellmann's argument is implicated in what Nina Baym has identified as "a restriction of literary creation to a sort of therapeutic act that can only be performed by men."[50] In this context though, it is not literary but social creation that is being set forth as a masculine activity, one that is "therapeutic" for the society as a whole. Whereas for Wheeler it was the Vietnam veteran himself who could regenerate society through his embodiment of commitment, for Hellmann, it is the literary narratives of Vietnam that can perform the same activity. Occupying again the positions of both participant and observer, soldier and reader, these studies predelimit responses to Vietnam representation (soldiers as emblems of commitment become representations of themselves). As products of the masculine point of view, the societies they narrate are not "significant alterations" at all.

Peter Marin, in discussing Vietnam veterans' loss of the myths of American society, "the myths that ordinarily protect people from the truth,"[51] implies that they are now closer to those truths, that they can in some way be the conveyers of those truths to the rest of society, just as, in its narratives, Vietnam is presented as the site for the speaking of that truth: "it was the home of lost causes, and forsaken beliefs, and unpopular names, and impossible loyalties."[52] Oliver Stone's *Platoon* offers perhaps the most poetic of these statements: "those of us who did make it have an obligation to build again, to teach others what we know and to try with what's left of our lives to find a goodness and meaning to this life." Hellmann's conclusion, that "from the landscape[53] of our Vietnam failure, we can find a new determination to brave the opening expanse" (p. 24), defends a naive nostalgia for the gendered story that is America. Studies like Hellmann's help reincorporate Vietnam into that image by subordinating its disruptions to a larger myth of progress presented within the narrative of gender.

Philip Beidler's eloquent *American Literature and the Experience of Vietnam* works as well to establish links between Vietnam literature and an American tradition. Likening the Vietnam War's best writers to Hemingway, Melville, Crane, Dos Passos, and Mailer, Beidler links them through what he calls "a primary process of sense-making"[54] that pervades the best American writing, the ability to construct meaning out of an otherwise chaotic and pointless experience. Establishing for Vietnam literature a canonical precedent, Beidler writes that "American writing about Vietnam . . . often turns out to be very much in context, so to speak, with regard to our national traditions of literature and popular-myth-making at large" (p. 19). So closely linked is Vietnam literature to its American literary heritage that "it seems almost as if our classic inheritance of native expression has prophesied much of what we know of Vietnam" (p. 19), from Ahab's monomaniacal obsessions with maps and calculations to Twain's Hank Morgan, whose easy confidence in progress and information makes his relationship to his Arthurian friends much like that of American advisors in Vietnam. In such company, the American literature of Vietnam stands not as exception to but as repetition of American literary strategies.

But Beidler's insightful recognition of the intimacy between not only the literature but also the events of Vietnam and the American cultural traditions that surrounded them is lost in his unwillingness to identify any causation in this schema. Subscribing to the patterns of blurring that are so typical of Vietnam representation, Beidler insists that "all the basic categories of meaning one might think of—facts and fictions, realities and imaginings, things remembered and things reconstituted in the shapes of collective myth—had to be reckoned in this case as simply and flatly interchangeable" (p. 31). More to the point, the Vietnam War itself is a feature of this blurring of causation.

> Now whether at a certain point Vietnam simply started looking like a second-rate *Catch-22* (and later on, *Slaughterhouse Five* and *Gravity's Rainbow*) mixed with some witless version of 'concept' TV gotten horribly out of hand, or whether *an inescapable process of cultural conditioning had dictated from the outset* that it could have hardly turned out to look like anything else, is probably by now something that is just not worth trying to figure out. *Like most things connected with the war, it just happened.* [italics added] (pp. 12–13)

Echoing Charles Anderson's "faceless and nameless forces" that govern class relations, Beidler's "inescapable process," while correctly identifying the cultural frame for war, applies to it an abstract autonomy that is neither identifiable nor alterable. An abstraction such as this enables Beidler to argue, in spite of all of his insistence on Vietnam's placement in a cultural tradition, that the Vietnam War had "self-generated rules" (p. 8), by which Beidler means the repeated phrases and labels that permeated American interaction with Vietnam: soldiers named "Snake," "Superfly," and "Space" in every outfit; new officers called "Pillsbury," "Shake 'n' Bake," or "Ready Whip"; refugee huts known as "Dogpatch" and firebases named "the Alamo," as well as a "Dodge City" that led to "Indian Country" (p. 8). But these repetitions were not generated by the war; they were cultural carryovers from advertising, television, movies, and comics. The abstraction of causation enables Beidler to posit a capacity for "self-generation" to the war that blurs the extent to which it is equally a product of mass cultural imagery and significations.

What Beidler's analysis finally makes clear is that this "self" that is generated by the war—the self that can be produced only by denying its connections to cultural formations and blurring questions of causation and relation—is a self generated not by the war but by the masculine point of view. Comparing Michael Herr's *Dispatches* with Gloria Emerson's *Winners and Losers*, Beidler praises Herr's ability to "allow the truth to tell itself" and disparages Emerson's intrusive polemicizing. "Where Herr depicts characters who were, for good or ill, simply what they were and nothing more, Emerson would seem to prefer caricatures. . . . Where Herr tells the story, Emerson is often too eager to supply the gloss" (p. 150).

While this might at first seem a simple preference for objective as opposed to subjective writing, Beidler reveals something important about Emerson's writing that alters such easy judgments. In spite of her polemic,

> Nearly everything Emerson sees, everything she senses and says about the experience of Vietnam, we now know to have been essentially correct. She is "right." The difficulty of *Winners and Losers* even as exposé or polemic is that this "right" or "true" vision of things seems so often to be much more of an imposition than a discovery. What the book tells us seems mainly to be what the author knew from the start (p. 150).

In discussing Herr's *Dispatches* in chapter 1 it became apparent that his "truth" as well is told through a polemic, one of a masculinity that is not so obtrusively identified in Vietnam literature and the culture that produced it. Only in a context where the masculine point of view is assumed as "natural" could Herr's writing be taken as any more objectively "true" and unintrusive than Emerson's. In spite of Emerson being as "right" as Herr, her "polemic" eliminates her from serious consideration because Herr's writing, as an echo of the masculine point of view, is taken to be transparent whereas Emerson's is not.[55]

Like Wheeler and Hellmann, Beidler concludes with a collective vision for American culture that can be fostered by Vietnam representation. Employing much the same language and assumptions as in his argument about Emerson, Beidler celebrates the "last heroism" of Vietnam writers in leading American culture to a "new architecture of consciousness," citing

> the emergence in Vietnam writing of what I have earlier described as a certain identifiable *centrality of vision,* an understanding that just as the "real" war itself so often proved a hopeless tangle of experiential fact and projected common myth, so a "true" literary comprehending of it would come only as a function of experiential remembrance *and* [italics in original] imaginative invention considered in some relationship of near-absolute reflexiveness. It would have to come of some *new architecture of consciousness* founded . . . on an awareness of the degree to which each had ultimately to be seen as implying and indeed quite probably entailing the sense-making possibilities of the other. [italics added] (p. 195)

This "centrality of vision" belonging to American writing about Vietnam can lead finally to a new set of cultural understandings, both about the war and the culture that produced it. More significant, Beidler insists that the war itself cannot be over until "we have made it so through a common effort of signification" (p. 202). In his terms, only by incorporating and centralizing the "vision" of Vietnam into cultural understanding can Vietnam ever be behind us as a nation.

But, of course, by incorporating this vision and promoting a "common effort of signification," the Vietnam War will not be over. On the contrary, its imagery and "truths" will become central parts of a new consciousness for America, one in which Vietnam is no longer a marginalized experience but will instead pervade all cultural formations and interpretations. What enables this shift toward centrality is the shared masculine point of view from which Vietnam representation is written and which is receiving renewed emphasis in contemporary American culture. In such a context, the inescapable process that dictates the way the war was fought and interpreted becomes an abstraction of this point of view as itself inescapable, one of the "faceless and nameless forces" that circumscribe the collectivity of Vietnam.

Beidler tells us, "the only kind of distance a GI could think about really, and stay close to sane, was something that could be related to the next step—one more yard sweated out, no mine, no booby trap, no sniper, no ambush" (p. 8). Like *Platoon*'s hand-held camera and close-up motif, the soldier's vision is immediate and personal. But Beidler's study, like Wheeler's, Hellmann's, and so many other Vietnam essays, finally steps off of this jungle trail and offers a more global perspective. As in *Platoon*'s closing scene, where the helicopter provides a distant look over a battlefield that we had previously seen only through the soldier's eye, these authors step back from their object of study. "The chopper," Stone says, is "now rising to meet God."[56] It is only through these abstracted godlike viewpoints and not those of the individual that the ideology of collectivity can be proposed and identified.

Charles Griswold's study of the Vietnam Veterans' Memorial in Washington, D.C., captures this positioning in the context of its cultural implications. Rather than examining, as others have done,[57] the design of the memorial or the names that have been inscribed on it, Griswold takes a view of the entire Mall and the relationship this monument holds to it. It is this perspective that enables Griswold to argue that the memorial functions as a "therapeutic reconciliation" that can draw together and unify the diverse aspects of the American self-image and its historical representation.

Seen as politically neutral, the monument can stand as a unifying force, one that has given rise to, in Griswold's eyes, a renewed patriotism. For him, the Vietnam Veteran's Memorial has accomplished "the goal of rekindling love of country and its ideals, as well as reconciliation with one's fellow citizens."[58] While not patriotic in the sense of endorsing the war, the memorial encourages a questioning of the war "*on the basis of* a firm sense of both the value of human life and the still higher value of the American principles so eloquently articulated by Washington and Lincoln" (p. 713). In attendance at the dedication ceremonies, Griswold, himself a Vietnam veteran, recalls that "At the conclusion of the ceremony he joined in the refrain of 'God Bless America'. Those words swept boldly through the chill air, expressing the belief that, in spite of everything, America remains fundamentally good" (p. 714). Reminiscent of the closing scene of Michael Cimino's *The Deer Hunter*, in which those wounded and scarred by Vietnam gather at a breakfast and spontaneously break into singing "God Bless America," this collectivity has the aura of a healing, a renewal, a "therapeutic reconciliation," one that can aid not only the veterans themselves but also all Americans who have participated in the sense of loss that accompanied the war.

But it is a collectivity enabled only by this distancing point of view, provided by the helicopter, the camera, or a bird's-eye view of the Washington Mall. It is not available to the individual or the immediate. And like Anderson's "faceless and nameless forces" and Beidler's "inescapable process," Griswold's collective regeneration is also enabled by an external force:

> That the author of the winning design of the VVM turned out to be a woman of oriental extraction too young to have experienced the Vietnam War itself looks like another instance of the unifying work of the "invisible hand" evident in the Mall as a whole. Even with respect to the designer of the VVM, the unex-

> pected has conspired to reconcile the seeming contraries of east and west, male and female, youth and experience. (p. 713)

Able to gather into the collective even those who did not participate in the war, this "invisible hand" has reconstructed a collective patriotism and renewed faith in America that is available to all citizens.

Like the external narrative position from which Caputo could narrate his own simultaneous experience as participant and observer, spectator and actor in the movie of Vietnam, the collectivity of Vietnam representation requires the distant positioning of a viewpoint above the experiential and immediate, one that can also exist in both frames. While Griswold is one of the members of the crowd that sings "God Bless America" at the dedication ceremonies, he is also the writer who studies the plans of the Mall from above and can reconcile the apparent tensions of the various monuments. The collectivity produced here, not by Griswold, but by the "invisible hand," depends on both the proposition of such a position and its maintenance as an illusion through the dual positioning of the narrator/participant. In such a scheme, the collective seems to be not the distant view but the gathering of the immediate, not the excluding but the encompassing, not the contrived but the natural.

Such is the characterization of the masculine point of view, the position from which collectivity as a product of gender can be narrated. Seeming to be produced by circumstances rather than producing them, to be participant rather than spectator, this point of view is the "invisible hand," the "faceless and nameless forces," the "inescapable process" that constitutes the narration and articulation of Vietnam representation. Only from the masculine point of view can such collectiveness be narrated, collectivities that finish, not simply with the integration of Vietnam, but with the regeneration of the belief that "America remains fundamentally good," revealing the extent to which the current regeneration of an American "good" is intimately linked to and dependent on the regeneration of the American masculine.

## Illocutionary Acts

Susan Brownmiller says of femininity that it "always demands more. It must constantly reassure its audience by a willing demonstration of difference."[59] In the context of Vietnam representation and the social and cultural matrixes for which it is an emblem, such excess cannot be limited to femininity but must be applied to masculinity as well.[60] The very plethora of Vietnam narratives, devouring and regenerating themselves, speaks of the overdetermination required of masculinity and its metaphors. It is not femininity but gender that is excess.

It is, then, not accidental that an ideology of collectivity (perhaps ideology itself) should be hinged on gender difference, for such myths equally demand excess, require constant and devotional reaffirmation. At a reunion of Vietnam veterans, journalist Joe Klein records what happens to a bonded group of Vietnam veterans that has not reaffirmed itself:

> They'd been intimate once, but they were strangers now . . . and their former intimacy made the estrangement all the more awkward. The others might pretend that time and distance didn't matter, that the foxhole bond still prevailed, but Steiner felt trapped in the defensive perimeter that had been recreated in Taylor's basement; the blizzard outside seemed as vast and claustrophobic as the jungle.[61]

It is only in the reassertion of the myths of collectivity that the collective exists, as does gender. And when, as in this case, those myths have not been successfully reaffirmed, the bond disappears.

Wheeler's directives about commitment are an example of such a reaffirmation; commitment, as Wheeler defines it, can never be satisfied (the soldier who has fought in one war may yet be asked to fight another). Commitment is what J. L. Austin calls an "illocutionary act," the "performance of an act *in* saying something as opposed to performance of an act *of* saying something."[62] In such cases, "the uttering of the words is, indeed, usually *a*, or even *the*, leading incident in the performance of the act" (p. 8). Such performances, because they constitute the act, must be continually repeated in order for the act to be achieved. And yet, because the act passes with the performance, it cannot exhaust itself, cannot finish.

War itself is excess, an act whose meaning is constituted only in its performance. This is why it must be reenacted. The Vietnam War, never officially declared and never finally "ended," is thus the ideal realization of the demands of excess instituted by gender. Refought in its representations—in novels, films, journalistic accounts, Senate hearings—each performance reiterates the structuration of gender that enables the war and its representations to take place.

While the masculine bond (and its framed gender construction) is the defining paradigm of Western warfare and its consequent social relations, the shape and direction of that bond are oriented by and through specific cultural moments. It takes place as a story in relation to particular social interests. The ideology of collectivity is, for example, an answer to concerns about institutional bureaucracy in American society. Loren Baritz, in his analysis of the Vietnam War, suggests that bureaucracy is now a "social institution." He answers Hector St. John de Crevecoeur's pre-Revolutionary question, "What is an American?" with "He is a bureaucrat."[63] In such a context, it is not difficult to understand the interest an ideology of collectivity might serve. As a member of a highly structured and hierarchically oriented society, it would be most appealing for an individual to accept images of a world in which the barriers between levels of the hierarchy are broken down. It is the contemporary pervasiveness of bureaucracy as an end in itself, often typified by the military, that defines collectivity as a specific interest and differentiates Vietnam representation from earlier war narratives.

A second interest that is linked closely to the ideology of collectivity is a response to feminism, a response that is discussed in more detail in chapter 4. Wheeler's argument for a renewed commitment, like Hellmann's for a revived American myth, depends on a pervasive masculism that can function to regenerate American society. Read through the "Nam Syndrome" and the technology of reproduction, men can now not only take the place of the feminine, but can overtake reproduction as well and eliminate women from their narratives. This is one explanation for the burgeoning popularity of Vietnam narratives, as they allow a space for an apparently final separation of masculine from feminine.

The war in Vietnam was an eruption of the gendered structure of American society that released the pressures of race and class change through reinforcing the lines of gender. As the Reagan administration and other political forums are rethinking those changes (affirmative action, quotas, the tax structure), gender is again being used as a framework within which those social reversions can be actualized. This framework is most subtle and effective because it carries the illusion of not itself being a source of stratification (the conservative claim is that gender difference is biological and therefore "natural"; the liberal is that feminism has eliminated most levels of sexual difference). But because gender has not been challenged at the general social level *as a structure,* it remains the easiest route of access to any reinvocation of hierarchization in contemporary American culture.

One of the characteristics of much contemporary popular narrative and imagery is that they function to disguise social hierarchies through the presentation of images of collectivity. (One of the most common of recent examples is the numerous beer commercials that celebrate divergent workers from different parts of the United States.) These images are most often portrayed in a framework that, while collapsing other forms of difference—racial, economic, ethnic, class, geographic, and national—retains the difference of gender. (As Dave Barry quips, "there are never any women in the part of America where beer commercials are made."[64]) A gendered framework enables the apparent collapse of difference by providing a stable environment for its articulation. (Films like *The Big Chill, The Breakfast Club,* and *St. Elmo's Fire,* whose narratives proceed by displacing economic difference with sexual difference are instances of this pattern; racial difference is scanned for these all-white casts in other ways, such as the Motown soundtrack for *The Big Chill.*) In such a context, Vietnam narratives become only one of the several ways in which the ideology of collectivity is being enacted in contemporary American culture. These narratives simply serve as one of the most straightforward means of gaining access to the fracture of gendered ideology because of their foregrounded logic of sexual difference.[65]

Vietnam representation makes clear that in U.S. culture the sphere of mass culture is not, as some have argued, the feminine but the gendered. Judith Williamson, for example, suggests that the arena of mass culture is women in the home, consumed as leisure in the "feminine" role within the family. Mass culture, says Williamson, focuses on this arena as the "subject matter of its representations."[66] Such representations function not only to place women but also to draw attention away from class differences by emphasizing sexual difference that seems to cut across class lines.

But Vietnam representations function also like images of the domestic, to draw attention away from difference—both racial and class—by working within the framework of the apparently clearly structured difference of gender. Class and race differences can be denied for the masculine through the presentation of gender as war. War is thus, for the masculine, the functional equivalent of the domestic for the feminine in mass culture. As representations of the domestic suggest a separation from the workplace through leisure, so representations of war offer a separation from the workplace through commitment. Both offer arenas in which the questions of class and racial difference can be subordinated to the presentation of gender.

In a different form, Rosalind Coward's studies of daytime radio programs in England suggest that "daytime radio works to validate the choices which women have made,"[67] specifically sexual desire, romance, and heterosexual relations. For these listeners, Coward argues, a collectivity has been invoked in which "sexual desire has been constructed as the daytime lowest common denominator. . . . The listener is lured by a promise; you are special . . . but your life and experiences are exactly the same as everyone else's" (p. 149). Vietnam narratives function to validate the choices men have made—"that there are things worth dying for." But these choices, becuase they depend on and construct a system of gender difference that underlies the operation of American social relations, function not only to satisfy individual men, but to reaffirm a masculine construction of reality as well.

Such constructions reiterate the dichotomy that has long been noted by feminist theorists between the public and the private realms of society, in which the masculine is associated almost exclusively with the public and the feminine with the private. Nancy Hartsock aptly traces this separation to the development of the *polis* in Greek society, "the community built to protect the warrior-heroes" from threats of the natural world, the world of women.[68] In such a context, it is quite logical that representation in contemporary mass culture should find both the arena of the domestic and of war to underscore gender constructions, as war stands in greatest extreme to the domestic in current representational schemes.

The chief difference that identifies the two arenas is the emphasis on the body. While "the masculine gender . . . requires the denial of the body and its importance" (p. 176), representations of the feminine foreground the body, whether as leisure or as pornography. In contrast, war, as noted in chapter 1, represses the body, subordinating it to the interests of the collective technology of the military. The public world of the *polis* is epitomized in this denial, and war becomes, not its failure, but its achievement. As Jean Franco suggests for the romance, that women are invited in its narratives to reenact the parts of themselves that are suppressed,[69] so in war narratives, men reenact the denial of their bodies in and through the collectivity of war.[70]

By presenting collectivity as a desired goal, Vietnam narratives, as a political strategy, disallow expressions of difference and work to restabilize a patriarchal

structure for social relations. This ideology functions then not only to respeak the voices of gender difference but to repress acknowledgment of other constructed difference as well. Vietnam representation in contemporary American society thus functions as an emblem for cultural representation at large as grounded in the narrative of gender. The specific productions of the ideology of collectivity that appear in Vietnam narratives are simply the most ingenuous, not the most extreme, versions of a general cultural narrative that denies the existence of hierachical difference by reaffirming the difference of gender.

# THREE

## FALSE LABORS
## Compensatory Reproduction and the Narration of Vietnam

### I

In Tom Mayer's short story "A Birth in the Delta," an Army platoon enters what appears to be a deserted village after an American airstrike. Inside one of the huts they find a pregnant woman lying on a cot, killed by shrapnel while in labor. Though her body is dead, her contractions continue. The troop's medic, Burns, decides to try to deliver the baby. First pressing on her abdomen to help the contractions and then finally trying to cut the baby out with his Navy K-bar knife, he succeeds only in delivering a baby that is as dead as its mother. Covering both baby and mother with a blanket, the troop leaves the village.

The misnamed "birth" in the Delta prompts two responses by the troop members. First, for several men, the scene reminds them of other incidents. Leyba, the radio man, thinks of a cow that wouldn't calve on his family's farm, and of his father, who "had not wanted to call the vet, had not wanted to have to pay."[1] The father tied one end of a rope to the calf's head and the other to his horse's saddle, then slapped the horse. "The calf had been jerked out, its neck broken, but the cow had recovered." Leyba "thought of suggesting something like that to Burns, but of course the mother was already dead, and there weren't any horses around" (p. 169). Prissholm, a new guy, is reminded of his fraternity initiation night, "when they had gang-banged the whore hired for the purpose, everyone very drunk, people sitting and standing in the bedroom watching" (p. 173). Nervous about his own performance, Prissholm, "when there had been no graceful way left to refuse," and "surprised at his own potency" (p. 174), completes his initiation by having sex with the prostitute.

The second response was disconcertion. Captain Harkness, whose "composure was one of the things Leyba hated about him most" (p. 167), became visibly disturbed by the birth. Leyba recalls: "It was the first time he could remember seeing a crack in [the captain's] composure, and he had seen him in and after four or five real firefights, seen him any number of times when anyone normal would have been shitting in his pants" (p. 167). Harkness himself knows he failed to act in his usual manner. Not only should he have done something with the woman's body so that it could not be used for enemy propaganda—"GI dogs murder pregnant woman, rip infant from womb" (p. 171)—but he should also have destroyed the large cache of rice stored there for enemy soldiers ("Next to getting confirmed kills, or weapons, capturing rice was about the best thing that could happen to a commander"). But "he had been so involved with the other thing" (p. 172) that he forgot to do either. At this moment he thinks, "coming back [to Vietnam] had been a mistake" (p. 172). Private Prissholm, in spite of his excessive thirst, forgot to fill his canteens from the earthen jars in the hut filled with clean drinking water; "he had been too absorbed" (p. 173). And Burns, "the good medic," who had earlier been immersed in his favorite dreams of how he would spend the money he'd make as a chiropractor after leaving the army, "was too tired to make his mind go the way he wanted it to, to force out the woman and the cutting and the slapping, the defeat" (p. 174).

Because the woman is dead at the time they find her, the task of giving birth to her child (the question of whether the child is to be born at all is never raised) falls to the members of the platoon, specifically its medic, Burns. Because Burns thought "her contractions were not forceful enough to do any good," he began himself "pushing on the women's [sic] abdomen" (p. 168). He then tries cutting the baby out. "His first incision was not big enough, the abdominal muscles clamped shut, he could not get hold of the baby" (p. 170). Finally, he pulls the baby out but is unable to bring it to life. "Burns kept slapping, could not think of what else to do, harder now, urgently, as if he could force life into it, but he produced no response" (p. 170).

This narrative shows us a man trying to deliver a baby without the aid of the baby's mother.[2] First pushing on her abdomen, then cutting the baby out, then slapping the baby—nothing can bring this baby to life, in spite of the fact that it was, before the attack, about to be born. As if resisting Burns's intervention, the mother's muscles tighten, trying to hold the baby in. Burns cannot, for all of his efforts, "force life into it."

"A Birth in the Delta" is about the tension between life and death in wartime, but it is a tension defined exclusively in terms of gender, echoing a key theme of Vietnam representation: women are associated with life and men with death. Burns, a member of a platoon whose task is to kill the enemy, cannot, in the midst of wartime, "force life into it." John Wheeler, a former Army captain and West Point graduate, states this gendered thesis most clearly:

> I consider my commitment [to the military and his country] as a statement that there are things worth dying for. It is a masculine statement. I think it is *the* masculine statement. This is why war has tended to be viewed as a masculine enterprise. . . . Woman expresses the idea that there are things worth living for.[3]

These gendered associations with life and death are most often articulated in Vietnam representation through the images of birth and death, with reproduction and birth epitomizing for this dichotomy the antithesis of the death of war. For William Broyles, Jr., "War was an initiation into the power of life and death. Women touch that power at the moment of birth; men on the edge of death. It is like lifting off the corner of the universe and peeking at what's underneath."[4] The philosophy of William Eastlake's *The Bamboo Bed* is clearest: wars are fought because men express their fears of death through competition and aggression, while women, who have no such fears because they touch life, are capable of love and sharing and therefore have no need for war. Appelfinger, the novel's self-made metaphysician, explains that "every soldier hears death ticking off inside him. . . . Not only every soldier . . . but every male human being. Not every female human being. They don't hear death ticking off inside them because they feel life ticking inside them . . . A female would rather fuck than fight."[5] Women, he suggests, "don't have to go to war to prove something" (p. 85).

War is, as Broyles declares, "for men, at some terrible level the closest thing to what childbirth is for women: the initiation into the power of life and death."[6] Following this logic, men who don't go to war "now have a sort of nostalgic longing for something they missed, some classic male experience, the way some women who didn't have children worry they missed something basic about being a woman" (p. 56).[7] Broyles's inversion here of gender and biology—that war is basic to the "male" and reproduction to "women"—marks the strategy of the presentation of war and reproduction in Vietnam representation. War is described as a biological necessity for the human male; without it, he is somehow only half alive. In the same way, reproduction is portrayed as requisite for the social well-being of the human female, something for which she will feel a nostalgia for having "missed." These questions suggest that biology and the social construction of gender are in fact inseparable, and to deny this is to risk an unfulfilled human character.

As Wheeler was to say of his service in Vietnam at MACV headquarters,

> The question which is naturally open is how a troop unit under my command would have fared, how I would have fared. The answer is, I don't know. Not having the answer was a loss. It was a thing to grieve over, to say goodbye to.
>
> I wonder if the heated debate among women about the time to set aside for child rearing is similar as an emotional issue.[8]

Here as elsewhere, Wheeler blurs categories. The question of how Wheeler would have fared in battle is comparable to women who did not bear children asking how they would have fared as parents; the comparable situation is not deciding *when* to have children, but *whether* to have them. By selecting for his example a group of men who are already in the military and a group of women who have, apparently, already decided to have children, Wheeler's example implies that decisions about war and reproduction have already been made. The fact that Wheeler's decision to take a battle command was taken from him by the military hierarchy allows him to infer that such choices, like the "choice" of reproduction, are somehow "natural" and out of the individual's control. By not allowing for the decision *not* to have children, Wheeler is eliminating from his analysis the very females whose experience would deny the equivalence of biology and gender, that is that to be female is to be a woman. In so doing, his analogy allows for the conclusion that war, like reproduction, is not a matter of choice but instead of necessity; one can decide only when, not whether.

Lionel Tiger's anthropological study of *Men in Groups*, published in 1969 during the height of the Vietnam war, endorses the framework of Broyles's and Wheeler's argument, inasmuch as war, or what Tiger calls "aggression,"[9] is a byproduct of selected features of human development that have become incorporated into our biological predispositions. While Tiger declares that "Bonding is a part of a subtle political process rather than a simple, clear, and specific event, such as reproduction" (p. 19), he asserts that male-male bonds, which lie at the heart of aggression and, for Vietnam writers, war itself, "are of the same biological order for defensive, food-gathering, and social-order-maintenance purposes as the male-female bond is for reproductive purposes" (p. 42). Equivalent to but distinct from each other, according to Tiger are the different behaviors that fall to male and female as a result of these biological determinants:

> Maleness is a concomitant of the sense of moment, of matters requiring rigour, hardness—the unvarying and unimpressionable prosecution of ends by means. (p. 87)

> "Female" implies tasks involving specific interactions of a personal or quasi-personal kind, while "male" implies activities on a larger scale, with potentially more impersonality, with more direct and active relevance to communal integrity and social dominance. (pp. 114–15)

Although Tiger tries not to claim that the male behavior is more significant to society than the female, and, in his conclusion, even deplores the violence that results from it, his vocabulary valorizes the activities of the male over those of the female: males are "more," their activities are "larger," with more "relevance to communal integrity." That Tiger devotes his discussion to bonds between males, addressing only in a footnote the question on "female aggregation" (p. xiv, n), itself suggests that bonds between males are implicitly more important to study than bonds between females.[10] To use Rosalind Coward's description: "Men's labour is seen as value-producing, integral to the life of society; women's as peripheral to productive relations, significant only for reproduction."[11]

Judith Hicks Stiehm offers a possible explanation for the perceived parallel between war and reproduction in the construction of gender:

> If a women's [sic] femininity, her uniqueness, lies in her capacity to bear children, she needs to demonstrate that capacity only once. That demonstration will be absolutely definitive: good for all time and for all audiences.

> Because proof of fatherhood is unsure, proof of manhood is more difficult. The only unique role men have had in society is a social one—that of warrior—a role that is risky, unpleasant, and often short in duration. During peacetime modern men lack a specific way of proving that they are men.[12]

But, as Tiger's argument states, such a split between a social and a biological identification and the consequences each entails underlies more than the subject of warfare. According to Nicole-Claude Mathieu, maternity is consistently interpreted as a biological role and paternity as a social one: "Whether it concerns the philosophy of history, social anthropology, sociology, or psychoanalysis, the common methodological fault remains the persistent treatment of the two sexes either separately or, in any case, *at different levels* of analysis—one sex being ascribed directly to the social, the other being considered principally as the *locus of mediation* between the natural and societal state."[13]

Mathieu's statements directly contradict and reveal the motivation of Broyles's equation of the male role in combat as "natural" and woman's role in reproduction as social. If, as Broyles and much Vietnam representation wants to claim, reproduction is a social and not only a biological activity, then it is possible for the masculine to appropriate this role to itself, to encompass the feminine position of reproduction within its own sphere of control. On the other hand, to the extent that women are limited in their roles by their biologically ascribed status, they will be unable to do the same, that is incorporate a masculine role. This blurring of the social and the biological in Vietnam representation takes place predominately through the matrix of reproduction and thereby enables the appropriation of gender by the masculine.

"A Birth in the Delta" recapitulates Mathieu's thesis in its exclusive identification of woman as biological mother and man as social father, at the same time that it allows for the appropriation of the process of reproduction to the masculine. Because the woman is dead from the time they find her, she has no other existence than as a (now dead) biological entity, whose "labors" are entirely physiological and separate from her will and control. She had, for this narrative and this audience of men, no life apart from that her body is involuntarily trying to give to her child. Burns's delivery of the child through Caesarean section underscores his social intervention in the birth process. In spite of the fact that "the top of the baby's head was showing" (p. 168), Burns decides to cut the woman's abdomen rather than try to continue her delivery of the baby, because "her contractions were not forceful enough to do any good, *he thought*" [italics added] (p. 168). Using a Navy K-bar knife and a zippo lighter for sterilization, Burns operates with the tools of social intervention, the tools emblematic of America's role in Vietnam: cutting and burning; what the army has done to the Vietnam countryside, it will do to her.[14] Neither birth is successful.

Because she is dead from the outset, the woman in "A Birth on the Delta" is effectively excluded from having a social existence as anything other than a biological mother. As Mathieu points out, a biological emphasis for women's identification

> unites the woman *with the child. . . . In the present state of analysis, the real social subject of maternity is the child, not the woman.* In focusing on the mother as the psychobiological *locus* for the child, there is every chance that the woman as a social subject will be forgotten: she is in fact thought of more as the object than as the subject of maternity.[15]

The emphasis throughout the story on the delivery of the child further eliminates the woman from consideration as anything other than an involuntary biological machine whose task is aided by American men, a move mimicking a general cultural effort to sever women as birth mothers from the children they bear. As Robyn Rowland points out, "Reproductive technologies are splitting women from the embryo/fetus," which is leading to a "representation of women as merely the capsules or containers for the fetus."[16] As a result of this separation, men, who by and large "man the governments, train the doctors, make birth-control devices, allocate research grants, decide on the availability of abortions, run the companies that will market the products, and make the money" (pp. 526–27), are able, through social intervention like Burns's, to enter into the birth process and gain control over its production.

The deliberate exclusion of the woman as a social being in "A Birth in the Delta" and the subsequent death of her child reveal the tensions surrounding the issues of birth and reproduction in the representation of war. The story of Vietnam cannot tolerate even the appearance of a woman giving birth, except when mediated by men. As Stiehm explains, there is good reason for this heightened anxiety: "Were women to enter combat, men would lose a crucial identity—warrior. *This is the only role now exclusively theirs*, the one that is as male-defining as child-bearing is female-defining" [italics added].[17] Recalling Hartsock's description of the birth of the *polis* as an extension of the warrior-role,[18] it is all too logical that the exclusion and socialization of reproduction should be not simply locally but historically linked to the role of the male as warrior. For this to be masculinity's only exclusively remaining space for identification marks the reason for the insistent resurgence in Vietnam representation of confrontations between reproduction and the masculine, confrontations that end with the exclusion of the woman/mother and the appropriation of the tasks of reproduction by the masculine.[19]

Women are given two characterizations in "A Birth in the Delta": the Vietnamese mother, now dead, and the prostitute who is gangbanged as Prissholm's fraternity initiation. In order to control the disruptive presence of women in the narration of war, neither woman is shown alive. The Vietnamese woman is literally dead, and the prostitute is never described in Prissholm's recollection as anything other than an inanimate object: "they" had gang-banged "the whore," while "people" (were there women in this audience?) were "standing in the bedroom watching" and Prissholm, "climbed on himself" to complete "the act" (pp. 173–74). Other than the noun the "whore," the woman (presumably, for it is never stated that the prostitute was female) is not again mentioned, even as pronoun.[20] "She" is effectively absented from the story, with the emphasis, as in the birth, on the responses and anxieties of men who come into contact with her. The men's participation is itself seemingly involuntary, as Burns, the only medic, is compelled to "work on her awhile" (p. 168) and Prissholm took his turn with the prostitute "when there had been no graceful way left to refuse" (p. 174).

Both characterizations—mother and whore—are, as Andrea Dworkin has argued, intimately linked. Analyzing the pornography of pregnancy, she insists that "the maternal does not exclude the whorish; rather, the maternal is included in the whorish as long as the male wants to use the woman."[21] More to the point for "A Birth in the Delta," since the woman is dead and can give no account of her own sexuality, "Pregnancy is confirmation that the woman has been fucked: it is confirmation that she is a cunt. . . . Her belly is proof that she has been used" (p. 222). Consequently, rather than portraying two divergent views of women in this story, we are reading the same, the mother and the whore both as objects of male socio-sexual domination. And though one is a case of reproduction and the other of deliberate nonreproduction (I will assume that the prostitute did not intend to get pregnant), Dworkin insists "there are not two sides: there is a continuum of phallic control. In the male system, reproductive and nonreproductive sex are both phallic sex" (p. 222). Even the attempted birth is, in the scheme Dworkin lays out, equally sexual, as Burns's Caesarean is a "surgical fuck" (p. 223).

In the logic of masculine identification, women as sexuality must be excluded from warfare, for they are reminders of the body and its possible death. As Hartsock argues, "because to be born means that one will die, reproduction and generation are either understood in terms of death or are appropriated by men in disembodied form."[22] The Vietnamese woman, as a direct reminder of birth/death, then *must* be killed, and the prostitute's apparent reassurance that sexuality can proceed without reproduction can occur only as she is disembodied and no longer a woman at all.

As the story records, the appearance of these women causes severe disruption for the men. Harkness acts entirely out of character so that he forgets usual routine and misses a chance for glory by failing to take the rice. Prissholm forgets even his raging thirst, and Burns cannot "make his mind go the way he wanted it to." Prissholm's solution is that "If he did not think about it, it would not touch him, and he'd be all right" (p. 173); Burns's is to take out his cache of grass and smoke a "bomber" (p. 174). The narrative's solution is to kill both the mother and the child.

"A Birth in the Delta" is an atypical story for Vietnam representation because it foregrounds as its subject the topic of reproduction.[23] For most Vietnam narration, that topic is suppressed, is embedded in metaphor, allusion, fantasy, denial. But it is there nonetheless. In fact, reproduction may be *the* repressed of Vietnam representation, the topic whose eruption orients the identification of women as the mother/whore whose appearance requires such violence to control, whose entrance into combat and the masculine collective demands death and silence. This demand is met in Vietnam representation in two ways, each an image of the other: through the identification of the feminine with reproduction and its subsequent rejection and replacement by the masculine, and through the abstraction and mechanization of reproduction and its appropriation by the masculine.

## II

What makes Michael run?

A moment that has plagued many filmviewers of Michael Cimino's *The Deer Hunter* (1979), part of what makes the film "infuriatingly obtuse" to some,[24] is the scene immediately following the wedding, when Michael, Nick, Stash, and John are escorting Stevie and his bride, Angela, out to their car. In the midst of frolicking camaraderie, Stash whispers something to Michael (Robert De Niro). Reacting with immediate and pained disbelief, Michael leaves his pals and runs off into the night, shedding his tuxedo as he goes.

Although Stash's secret message is never revealed, I think it can be reconstructed. At the opening of the film, we see Angela, standing before a mirror, wondering if anyone will notice her pregnancy beneath her wedding dress. From Stash's mother and from Stevie himself, we learn that he is not the father of this child; as Stevie confesses to Nick, "I never did it with her." Just before they drive off, Nick (Christopher Walken) reassures Stevie about the wedding night, taking on a confident and paternal role in relation to Stevie's virginity: "That's great, man. It really is." It is at this moment that Stash, looking at Stevie and Nick, whispers to Michael, concluding with, "You didn't know that about Angela, did you?" Michael can only repeat, "Bullshit. Bullshit."

What Stash told Michael, I suggest, is that Nick is the father of Angela's baby. (This would help to explain a later curious point, why Nick sends Stevie his winnings from the Russian roulette games, something that Stevie himself does not understand). Michael's reaction might then have several sources. It could be surprise that Nick, who has been dating Linda and has just proposed to her (and to whom Michael is attracted), would have had sex with another woman; but given later references to sexual relations with women, as well as the social context of expectations for masculine sexuality well established in the film, this alone should not provoke such an extreme reaction. More likely, Michael's response is to the fact that Nick would have violated Michael's code of ethics: the "one shot" that in hunting you can take at the deer, or, in the prison, the "one shot" they could take to save their lives. As a code for living, this "one shot" endorses a stiff morality that is circumscribed by discipline, endurance, purity, and responsibility for individual actions. Nick, by impregnating Angela and proposing to Linda, has violated this masculine code: as Michael concludes, "Two is pussy."

There is a clear hierarchy of behavior in terms of the code, a hierarchy that finally dictates how and if one survives Vietnam. Michael is, of course, the epitome of the code, acting not only as its spokesperson, but also as its model. He takes only one shot at the deer and kills it; he takes the one shot in prison when he kills the Vietnamese guard and leads the escape; he lives an ascetic existence, having nothing to do with women before going to Vietnam (he does not even kiss the bride); and only he is able, at the end of the film, to decide *not* to shoot the deer. Stevie is Michael's opposite, not even attempting the code. He does not go on the hunt and cannot take the shot in prison, panicking at the last second and firing over his head. He has the most complete association with women, succumbing to love and a woman's will by taking on the consequences of someone else's actions and marrying Angela. Nick violates the code by trying to have it both ways: he accepts his affiliation with Michael and the code (Nick is the only one Michael will hunt with) but violates the "one shot" agreement. He hunts, but does not get a deer; in the prison, he breaks down, but at Michael's insistence manages to take the shot; he proposes to Linda, marking his association with women, but does not make a definite commitment to her, saying he will marry her "if I come back"; unlike Michael, he dances at the wedding but, unlike Stevie, he does not get married. His position in this hierarchy explains why Nick, the most vital and attractive of the three friends, is the only one to die. One must either live all of the points of the code (Michael) or not attempt it at all (Stevie), but not attempt and fail; one must fulfill either the masculine or the feminine, but not both. (The system of gender that defines Vietnam does not include androgyny.) As Nick croons at the bar, this would be "too good to be true."

Michael, fulfiller of the code, returns from Vietnam a decorated hero. Stevie, whose self-knowledge accepts that he cannot meet the requirements of the code, returns from the war a paraplegic. His body enacts his relation to the code, as he comes back "half a man," but alive. Nick, whose temerity is to think he can bypass the code for his own desires, never returns from Vietnam, is lost in a land where codes seem to have come permanently undone. Significantly, he is killed, not as a "war hero," but as a drugged renegade at the mercy of vulturous gamblers. Vietnam, the tester of the code, will not grace Nick with its badge of honor, "death in battle," but instead condemns him to the ignominious death of its effluence. With its own sense of justice, the code sentences Nick to die a victim of his own violation. Willing to gamble with someone else's life (Angela's and the baby's)—as he tells Stevie about the pregnancy, "That's Angela's problem"—Nick now finds himself the object of other people's gambling. *The Deerhunter*'s Greek chorus—the thrillseekers of the gambling pits—throw money on Nick's life, waiting for the final penalty, the "one shot" that will reassert the logic—and the existence—of the code. Nick's death exercises the insistence of the code: it is the "one shot," the one bullet in the otherwise empty chamber, that is both the feared and the desired of the roulette game. While Michael upholds the phallocratic code, taking only one shot at the deer,

Nick, unable to fulfill the code as Michael does (he does not get a deer on their last hunting trip), remains perversely faithful to it.

## Broken Promises

Appalled by his closest friend's desecration of the morality of the code, Michael runs, stripping off the wedding clothes that mark his participation in the scheme of women. Alone and naked in the night, Michael hopes to regain his purity and resanctify the code. While the wedding couple drives off and other friends wander away, Nick follows Michael, finding him lying naked on a basketball court. Having sent Angela off, Nick and Michael are again free to reaffirm the masculine ties that mark their friendship. That bond is cemented when Nick pleads with Michael, "Don't leave me over there, Michael. Just don't leave me there."

This episode is an open sore at the heart of *The Deer Hunter*, an enigma in an otherwise embarrassingly straightforward film (as in the closing group chorus of "God Bless America," meant literally by Cimino but overinterpreted by uneasy filmviewers as ironic). The remaining narrative, for which the elaborate wedding scenes are a prelude, is motivated by this scene, in particular by the promise Michael makes. When Michael jumps into the river to save Stevie, who has fallen from the rescue helicopter, Nick is left alone. In the hospital, he seems disoriented, barely able to recall his own name. He begins to call Linda, but does not. It is after this that he first encounters the roulette gambling on the back streets of Saigon. Watching the players with disdain for their fear, he seizes the pistol and indifferently fires it at his own head; the wheel has begun to spin.

While a superficial reading of the film suggests that Nick enters the game because of the psychological trauma resulting from his experience in the prison, a reading of this scene through Michael's promise yields a different motivation. In particular, Nick's trauma is not that of the game but of Michael's broken promise. By leaping from the helicopter to Stevie, Michael has left Nick behind. When both Michael and Stevie go home, Nick is left to wander the streets of Saigon, another prison from which he cannot escape without Michael's help. It is for this reason that Nick cannot call Linda. When Michael failed to fulfill his part of the bond, all promises were invalidated, and Nick's commitment to Linda—to anything—seemed meaningless.

It is Michael's promise that prompts his return to Vietnam to retrieve Nick. The promise as well indirectly causes Nick's death. When Michael returns and finds Nick in the gambling pits, Nick looks at him with indifference, without recognition. Although Michael believes this to be the effect of the drugs, it is equally a consequence of the alienated promise. For Nick, he is no longer "Michael." When Michael sits down to play the game, believing this to be the only way he can rescue Nick, he is bringing together the place of the promise and the "one shot" code. Michael thinks only of his promise and his bond to Nick ("I love you. You're my friend"). Nick, seeing the promise betrayed and the bond broken, thinks only of the "one shot" ("One shot, right?") and, putting the gun to his temple, pulls the trigger and dies.

It is significant for this film that, when the masculine promise and the "one shot" code meet, it is the bond that determines meaning. It is the bond that in fact provides a structure for meaning. Just as the structure of gender provides the frame for the expression of the ideology of collectivity, the masculine bond, a product of gender, here stands as the frame for the delineation of the "one shot" code. As the ostensible content of the film, the foregrounded "one shot" code seems to provide closure for *The Deer Hunter,* as the hunting scenes, shot with panoramic expansiveness and backed by a mythic sound track, take on a transcedental aura that calls attention to itself as primary meaning. But it is the masculine bond that in fact determines/overdetermines the film, by its insistent and anxious exclusion of the feminine.

The film opens with shots of a masculine territory—the steel mill—and the men leaving work together. They go to a bar where only men are present. Although the first half of the film is devoted to the wedding, it is framed by the masculine moments of the steel mill and the hunting expedition. The film closes on the gathering in John's bar after Nick's funeral. Michael has finally fulfilled his promise and not left Nick "over there." With all of the men present who opened the film except Nick, who is present as the reason for their meeting, the film comes full circle on its masculine imagery.

Although Linda and Angela are present at the last breakfast, their positions are subordinated to the masculine interests. Angela speaks only one inconsequential line, "It's a gray day." Linda begins the singing of "God Bless America" that swells into a collective reaffirmation. The singing is Linda's effort to enter into the bond shared by Michael and Nick. The only way she can participate in their bond is through the ostensible reason for Nick's death—"America"—and the cause that he and Michael shared.

Like Wheeler's assertion that the hope for America's regeneration is through the masculine bond of men who made and kept commitments, Cimino's ending reinforces a hope for an American collectivity through promises kept by men to each other. Only through these bonds can women, otherwise alienated from masculine promises, enter into the collective of "America." Cimino, like Wheeler, is holding out for us an image, not of the "one shot" code that Michael finally abandons when he decides not to shoot the deer, but of an affirmation of unity through the achievement of masculine bonds and the fulfillment of their promises.

## "You Didn't Know That about Angela, Did You?"

When Michael hears about the pregnancy, he runs, trying to escape the evidence that the masculine bonds that define his world—that tell his story—have been disrupted by a different kind of bond, the fact of reproduction. Although Michael's promise to Nick determines the second half of the film and impels the action of the narrative, the wedding promise that Stevie makes to

Angela for the baby compels the scenes that constitute the first half of the film. These two promises, placed back to back, constitute the film's narration and the tension that it attempts to resolve.

But the mechanism for the promises differs from the first to the second section. The scenes of Vietnam, both of the war and the later gambling setting, are replete with action, from the opening shots of Michael torching the Vietnamese soldier to the Russian roulette games and escape from prison to the relationship between Michael and Linda to Michael's return to Vietnam and Nick's death. And that action operates with the logic of the promise behind it, motivating its complex progression and achievement. But the wedding scene is of a different sort. Fluid, slow-moving, and focused on multiple characters, the first half of the film operates in a style opposite the second. Associative rather than linear, collective rather than individualized, ponderous rather than rapid, the film shifts its tone, pace, and character with the voicing of the masculine promise. Both structurally and thematically the Vietnam scenes reject the wedding, reject, in the film's phrasing, the feminine in favor of the masculine.

The wedding day is, in the language of *The Deer Hunter*, the arena of women. It is the place where women gather to decorate the church and orchestrate the food, where bridesmaids rustle their dresses with importance, where Stevie's mother can drag him from the bar by his ear to prepare for the ceremony (the parallel scene in the second half, now masculine, is Michael dragging Stevie from the hospital). It is the place where a bond is formed between men and women, not only Stevie and Angela, but Linda and Nick as well. It is the place where a pregnancy can compel a promise. Vietnam is, in contrast, the arena of men, not only as they fight in battle, but also as they risk their lives for each other. Vietnam is the place where promises to women are forgotten and only the masculine bond remains.

Framed by the imagery of masculinity and structured by its bonds, the narrative of *The Deer Hunter* tells the story, not of the war in Vietnam, but the war of gender. The feminine scenes of the wedding are explored in such detail in order to reject them wholeheartedly. What had been established at the wedding has been dismissed by the close of the film. Stevie and Angela's marriage is tenuous at best. Linda's proposed marriage to Nick is never discussed, and no firm relationship to Michael is established. The women who were found primarily in groups during the wedding are now separated, frightened, and alone. When Michael goes to see Angela, he finds her in retreat in her bed as her blond-haired son (both Angela and Stevie have brown hair, compared to Nick's lighter color) looks on. He discovers Linda sheltered in a small room at the back of the grocery store, marking packages and crying. Even at Nick's funeral breakfast, Angela and Linda sit apart from each other and do not exchange words or glances.

Assigning both women to places of confinement in the second half of the film (in the back of the store, the back of the house), in direct contrast to their more central, open, and social roles during the wedding scenes, marks the congruity of their treatment in the film. Both women fulfill the characterizations established in "A Birth in the Delta," as mother/whore. Angela is, of course, immediately established as mother figure with her first appearance (like the Vietnamese mother, she is, in effect, not alive, does not speak). But because she is wearing a wedding dress, she is also, as the film will later make even clearer, a whore, not a virgin at her wedding. Cimino represents this in the drop of wine Angela spills on her white wedding dress; in spilling this wine and bringing bad luck on the wedding couple, Cimino makes Angela responsible for Stevie's later suffering—not because she spilled the wine but because she tried to blur the boundaries between virgin and whore. And Linda, who, we may suppose, is a virgin (and is the blond-haired antithesis of Angela's darkness) when she agrees to marry Nick, shifts her affections quickly to Michael on his return, her first thought being to alter a sweater that she was knitting for Nick so that it will fit Michael. With these rapidly changing allegiances, she is also whore, mothering Michael with sweaters and seductive comforts that could prevent him from fulfilling his promise. As Linda's father says about women before he slaps her, "They're all bitches."

What initially brought the women together—the wedding promise—has been rejected in favor of what instead brings men together—the promise of the masculine bond. This pattern succeeds as well in rejecting the false bond of the feminine. During the wedding celebration, Michael, Nick and Stash spot a Green Beret drinking at the VFW bar. When they approach him to ask about the war, wanting to assert their bond with him, his only reply is "Fuck it." In the film's logic, this rejection of the bond would occur during the feminine scenes. By overturning these feminine locations (the VFW has been tainted by the presence of women), the film can overturn their statements as well. Vietnam is thus not the subject of *The Deer Hunter* but merely the occasion for announcing the primacy of the bonds between men.

The first half of *The Deer Hunter* revolves then around the promise of reproduction, and the second is motivated by that which denies reproduction, the promise of the masculine bond. The structure of the film rotates around Nick, the one figure who links these two experiences. Although Michael's code and strength of character dominate the film, they are clearly not its central force. It is instead Nick, who is less disciplined, more flexible, and clearly more attractive (not only to Linda, but also to the camera that lingers on his image throughout the film), whose position motivates the progress of the narrative. And it is Nick's ambivalent connection to the fact of reproduction that makes him so attractive to a narrative whose design is to clarify just that ambivalence.

Nick embodies the suppressed and yet insistent reminder of sexual difference that underlies Vietnam narratives. His is the point at which gender is made manifest because he is a part of both the masculine and the feminine promise. His own sexuality mimics the ambivalence of his position. He is, on the one hand, fulfilling the demands of masculinity by going to fight in a war (in contrast to John, whose "bad knee" prevented him from going) and yet, on the other, linking himself to the feminine through Angela and Linda. His own actions portray both the masculine and the feminine. Although he works at the mills and is going to war, during the after-work bar scene, Nick dances and sings with obvious feminine movements while Michael sits on a barstool, watching; Nick is also associated more with women at the wedding, dancing, kissing, joking, while Michael again stands at the door to the dancehall, immobile, watching; and finally, during the prison scene, Nick breaks down and cries, while Michael remains firm, watching for the moment to escape.

Nick's position in relation to the oppositional structure of the masculine and feminine in *The Deer Hunter* might seem at first to be a deconstruction of that polarity offered by the film. Resting in neither the masculine nor feminine worlds, Nick's character and function in the narrative take on the quality of what might appear to be what Derrida calls the "sexual otherwise,"[25] the point at which gender distinctions no longer determine meaning. But the overt presentation and punishment of Nick's role in the film suggests that such androgynous positions are not only destructive but must themselves be destroyed. Rather than deconstructing gender oppositions, Nick's ambivalence and death assure their continuation.

Nick's feminine position in relation to Michael is so pronounced that it prompted Robin Wood to propose a reading of *The Deer Hunter* in which the tension of the film is not that of reproduction but of homosexuality. In his reading of the film, "Nick both is *and knows himself to be* in love with Mike and Mike reciprocates the love but can't admit it, even to himself."[26] Nick's fixation on the Russian roulette game is then a displacement of the moment at which he and Mike were most closely bonded, "a monstrously perverted enactment of the union he has always desired" (p. 296). As a result, when Mike comes back to rescue Nick, Nick is prepared for a revelation of their love, especially when Mike begins by saying, "I love you." But when Mike follows this with "You're my *friend*," Nick is disillusioned. When Mike refrains his "one shot" code, Nick, "has recognized that Mike offers nothing but a return to repression" (p. 296–97) and he kills himself.

Wood closes with a plea for a resolution of the tension between the masculine and feminine that takes on an almost transcendental tone: "The problem [of the repression of bisexuality and the oppression of women] . . . can only be resolved when the boundaries of gender construction become so blurred that men can move with ease, and without inhibition, into identification with a female position" (p. 291). Wood's reading of the film accepts Nick's sexual description as a positive feature of *The Deer Hunter*'s portrayal of gender, one in which homosexuality would function as a deconstructive move toward the sexual otherwise. But Nick's ambivalent relation to the promises of masculinity and femininity does not constitute a moving beyond the categories of gender, merely a blurring of them, another maneuver to avoid the threat of reproduction.

## III

The flaw in Wood's "solution" lies at the heart of his misreading of *The Deer Hunter* and also, more important, is the nexus for Vietnam narrative's response to reproduction. Wood's description of a changed and improved gender construction is one in which "men can move with ease, and without inhibition, into identification with the female position." In several ways this design matches the plan and interests of Vietnam representation at large.[27]

(1) *Equating biology with gender:* Wood's formula elides "female" with "women," suggesting that "men" can inhabit the "female" position. But as Toril Moi summarizes, "It has long been an established practice among most feminists to use 'feminine' (and 'masculine') to represent *social constructs* (patterns of sexuality and behaviour imposed by cultural and social norms), and to reserve 'female' and 'male' for the purely biological aspects of sexual difference."[28] By eliding "men" and "female" Wood is confusing the status of gender as a social construction and thus clouding its role as an element of narrative. In Vietnam narrative, it is important that the constructed position of the masculine should be equated with the biological position of the female in order to make the masculine itself appear to be both "natural" and necessary. And it is, again, this move that enables the appropriation of reproduction (biology) by the masculine (social). Narratives of Vietnam inscribe this hypothesis by equating the socially constructed activities of men in war with the biologically constructed activities of the female in reproduction.

(2) *Becoming the other:* Men move to inhabit the "female position" through the mechanism of identification, making oneself into another. This means that one knows the other well enough—even, it is suggested, better than they know themselves—to be able to speak and act for them. To inhabit another's position is to take over that person's interests while still maintaining one's own, to speak for the other through the self. It is not out of keeping with Wood's argument, and is in complete alignment with the narratives of Vietnam, that it should be the man who inhabits the "female position," speaking for her and taking over her space. As we shall see, this taking over the space of women is most often enacted in Vietnam narratives through men taking over the role of reproduction.

(3) *Masculine point of view:* Most important both for Wood's reading of *The Deer Hunter* and for a study of Vietnam narratives is that Wood depicts this desired change in gender structures from the point of view of the masculine. It is men who should gain ease and lose inhibition, men who should be able to identify with women, and men whose interests should be the goal of any move to alter the construction and operation of gender.[29] Because he does not interrogate this point of view Wood accepts unquestioningly the male-male relationship as the center of meaning in *The Deer Hunter.* He, like the films and narratives of Vietnam, represses the matrix of reproduction in favor of the

masculine bond. His reading continues to whisper Stash's secret, to suppress reproduction, and to acknowledge only the promises between men as determinate of meaning.

Wood's desire to "blur" the lines of gender is the hidden secret of Vietnam narratives: to confuse the categories of gender by asserting the masculine colonization of the territory of reproduction. Such confusion defuses possible challenges to the construction of gender by making it appear as if the categories of gender are themselves flexible and available to individual change. In addition, blurring becomes, like Nick's dancing in the bar scene, a spectacle of its own. By drawing attention to itself as a set of images, this spectacle diverts investigation of the gendered framework that supports its representation. Rather than challenging this spectacle, the blurring of gender categories reinforces it by allowing the masculine not only to portray itself, but to take on the portrayal of the feminine as well through the imagery and metaphors of reproduction. Threatened by recent social assaults on the delineation of gender, the spectacle of masculinity responds, first by reasserting its determination of gender by claiming for itself reproduction as privilege and, second, by blurring this reassertion with the appearance of vulnerability and change.

One of the few Vietnam novels written by a man from a woman's viewpoint, Donald Pfarrer's *Neverlight* exemplifies these three operations whereby the masculine appropriates the feminine through the matrix of reproduction. The novel tells the story of Richard Vail, a naval artillery officer who returns to Vietnam after he has been wounded, and his wife, Katherine, who lives in a remote mountain cabin with their daughter during his absence. The bulk of the novel is devoted to Katherine's struggle both with Richard's decision to return to his unit even though he has been released from active duty and Richard's subsequent death in battle.

In the presentation of gender in Vietnam narratives the masculine identification with/of the feminine is portrayed through sexuality and reproduction, the points at which biological difference most threatens the masculine assumption of the female. While making love before his return to Vietnam, Richard Vail, for example, displays this assumption: "The man who came to her that night out of these changes was the disciplined, all-knowing man. He knew her body, soul, and psyche with a knowledge so thorough that she wondered where it came from, since it exceeded her own."[30] Richard, the "all-knowing man," has the capacity to be the two of them, whereas she is not sufficiently herself (his knowledge "exceeded her own"). In Vietnam, Richard continues to take on Katherine's position, at this point through the imagery of reproduction. While trying to sleep one night on patrol, he reenacts Katherine's posture after the birth of their daughter: "Katherine nursed her baby in this posture, lying full length on her side, for two days while she was weak. He brought her the baby and she drew it to herself, presenting the breast, and when it was taken closing her eyes." (p. 147) Richard then closes his eyes and falls immediately asleep.

That Richard should know Katherine's body better than she, that he can successfully mimic her pose during nursing—these are the signs that the masculine can assume "with ease, and without inhibition, the position of the female." In a novel that is told from a woman's viewpoint, it is suggestive that the relation between man and woman should be established in favor of the man knowing, deciding, and meaning for the two of them. *Neverlight* insures what most Vietnam narratives imply: that the voice of the feminine is not a determining one, except as it is spoken by and through the masculine. (Just as Burns delivers the dead baby of a silenced woman.) Although these novels allow for a relational character of gender in order to maintain a certain functional flexibility of gender identifications, this relation can occur only in one direction—the feminine is given meaning only in relation to the masculine. Reproduction and war are thus made metonymic equivalents of the feminine relation to the masculine in Vietnam representation, suggesting that reproduction has no meaning except in relation to war.

When Richard decides to return to Vietnam, he does not try to explain his decision. Believing that he is telling her she could not understand his situation (the motif of exclusion), Katherine retaliates by invoking a parallel experience to match his: "I have never been ambushed, thank god, and you, thank god, have never had a miscarriage at five months" (p. 74). Like the equation of men with female, the linking of war and reproduction elides the social with the biological: war is as "natural" for the male as reproduction is for the female. An ambush is simply a "miscarriage" of the usual process of war, a break in the chain of actions.

Reinforcing the association of life with the feminine and death with the masculine made by Wheeler and Broyles, Katherine is concerned with the question of life, while her husband is troubled by the question of commitment and duty. She writes to him in Vietnam: "Dick, I only ask, is life sacred? I write this to you because you are my friend and husband and also out of fear, in a way, because, forgive me, you seem to be willing to kill. If you can take life, how can it be sacred" (p. 241)? Richard is killed shortly after he receives this letter. When Katherine later opens a box containing his belongings, she finds his writing pad with an unfinished letter, containing only the words, "Dear Kit—Yes—" (p. 284). Believing this to be his response to her last question, she contemplates her own position. Troubled that she only posed the question of the sacredness of life and did not assert it, she concludes:

> I evaded my own self-contradiction, because I too am willing to kill. Not that I ever could, except perhaps in defense of Richard or Terry. But willing in that I believe in the just war. He thinks this one is just and I do not. . . . I had no warrant to taunt him with the sanctity of life. If Richard was inconsistent, so was I. We held life sacred, and we admitted war into our moral universe." (p. 286–87)

Katherine's "I" that asks, "Is life sacred?" becomes, through her process of reasoning, a "we" that can admit war, that can hold the position of *both* life and death. She first posits her own statement, then thinks *as Richard would think,* then thinks as the two of them together. Importantly, Richard is dead when she examines this question, enabling her to speak for him—to become him, to bridge the gap between life and death, between her voice and his—without contradiction. Richard's death—apparently a separation of the bond between husband and wife—has instead broken the boundary of death—penetrated its "veil"—and enabled him to think through Katherine. Now as "we" they speak for the combined masculine and feminine, erasing the "self"-contradiction of separation and replacing it with a boundless identity that encompasses life and death in one voice.

The choice of establishing this unity through a woman narrator would seem to undercut the suggestion that appropriation occurs from a masculine point of view. It is, after all, Katherine who survives, Katherine who speaks Richard's answer and reaches "their" conclusion. But the question here is not so much who speaks (Katherine or Richard) as whose voice is speaking (the feminine or the masculine). Jessica Benjamin, in discussing the role of continuity and discontinuity in gender identity, offers a concept that can explain Katherine's position, what she calls "rational violence," "the controlled, ritualized form of violence which is expressed in sexual fantasy life and in some carefully institutionalized sexual practices."[31] Following Evelyn Fox Keller's description of the male child's experience of differentiation as one of opposition and objectification and the rational frame of mind that is associated with this experience, Benjamin suggests that certain forms of sexual fantasy, particularly sado-masochistic forms of erotic domination, are vehicles for the expression of this rationality. In the erotic relationship then, the traditional role assigned the woman is one of "breaking continuity, of risking death," whereas that of the man is to "uphold[s] the boundaries of reason for her by keeping his violence within ritual limits" (p. 50).

In *Neverlight,* while Richard risks death by going back to Vietnam, Katherine controls the expression of that risk through her reason and through the maintenance of ritual limits as logic. While Richard is in Vietnam, she reads philosophy, studies Greek, and comes to pride herself on her powers of logic. When she finds Richard's unfinished letter, she approaches it rationally, reflecting: "'Certainly if you place the word "Yes" beside the question they appear to connect,' she said, still in her skeptical vein, 'but what you're seeing is simply the physical proximity you yourself created. I could write, "Is the earth flat?" and put it in the same place—and by the same procedure I would have a professional geologist [Richard's training] saying it was'" (p. 286). Katherine imposes this reason onto the otherwise confusing and disorienting realm of death—the decontextualized "yes"—by providing Richard's answer, continuing a conversation that can take place only by placing it within the bounds of logic, creating a voice out of silence. The "yes" that Richard seems to send to her from death itself has no meaning outside of Katherine's use of "rational violence." While Richard breaks the "continuity" of their lives by cutting off conversation in death, Katherine "upholds the boundaries of reason . . . by keeping *his* violence within ritual limits" (italics added). Katherine re-places the unfamiliar within the bounds of the known by speaking Richard's voice, no longer from the realm of death but now from the realm of the masculine.

As Richard once knew Katherine better than she knew herself, in death he still "knows" better than Katherine, this time not simply the body of a woman in addition to the body of a man, but the world of woman as well as the world of man, both life and death, both "commitment" and the sense that "there are things worth living for." Having fulfilled his commitment by fighting in Vietnam, he can now hear "Is life sacred?" and answer "Yes." With Richard dead, Katherine takes on his role, answering her question as he would answer it, no longer herself but the "we" that is their union. The narrative succeeds in thus blurring the lines between the masculine and the feminine, so that what was "I" becomes "s/he" and then "we." The apparent exchange of roles—Richard envisions himself in the position of Katherine nursing their child and Katherine uses logic to answer her own question as Richard would have answered—suggests an inversion of gender roles. But, as Benjamin's analysis allows us to see, although these characters contemplate their individual identities in the spectacle of the opposite gender, their positions as voices of gender reinforce rather than contradict the constructions of gender as a whole. As Richard comes to speak through Katherine's voice, she has enabled him to occupy "with ease, and without inhibition, the position of the female." *Neverlight* narrates the etiolation of the position of the female and its habitation by the voice of the masculine through "rational violence," reaching beyond death itself.

Such narrations and the spectacles they construct are presented in Vietnam representation through the point of view of the masculine. In relation to the matrix of reproduction, this is most often accomplished, as in the presentation of the masculine bond as preface to collectivity analyzed in chapter 2, by the strategy of reaffirming the existence and stability of gender constructions before gender roles are exchanged through reproduction. The apparent breaking of gender boundaries that occurs when men "occupy with ease, and without inhibition, the position of the female" is simultaneously a spectacle to distract from the reaffirmation of gender boundaries and a controlling of gender movement through the reinstitution of rational violence. In this way, the apparent occupation of the feminine position by the masculine is not seen as a challenge to constructions of gender but instead an appropriation of them. As Zoe Sofia phrases it, "masculinist production depend[s] upon the prior cannibalization of women, and the emulation of female qualities."[32] Men do not *become* women in these narratives, they occupy them.

James Webb, Marine Corps veteran wounded twice in Vietnam and later Assistant Secretary of Defense, confirms these constructions of gender in writing about his experience "when my son was born." Defining himself first as firmly occupying the position of the masculine—"I was raised from my mother's milk to be a man"[33]—Webb briefly recites his "manly" abilities: as physical laborer, marksman, boxer, soldier. As he explains, "There was no pain that I could not endure" (p. 8). And then his son is born. "But the capstone came when my son was born: The doctors let me inside the delivery room and, in so doing, opened up a world for the most part kept from men. . . . They helped me see my children, however awkwardly, as their mother does every day (p. 8). Webb here moves to occupy the position of the feminine, "however awkwardly," as he comes to see, through the permission of the doctors, the world through the feminine. Importantly, he does not see "my children" as his "wife" sees them, but as "their mother." He is aided in this not by her but by her doctors, thereby eliminating the woman herself from the birth and inserting himself into her position as "their mother." Because he nowhere quotes her responses to the child's birth, he speaks for her in the essay, assuming her voice, appropriating her view of her children. His wife then becomes merely a functionary through which he moves in order to appropriate his children and their birth. As he later concludes, "for the first time, I looked at life as women always have" (p. 10).

What is most intriguing though is to find, in a brief mention, that Webb has another child, a daughter born before this son. But the intensity of his experience with the birth of his son was markedly different from the birth of his daughter. This might be simply explained by the fact of witnessing his son's birth and not his daughter's. But as Webb himself analyzes the situation: "This is not a testimonial for the Lamaze technique or for the recent trend that allows fathers inside the delivery room. The availability of either or both, while nice, does not translate into automatic understanding" (p. 8). What marks the difference, we can only conclude, between Webb's feelings toward the birth of his son and the birth of his daughter is their sex. It is finally the presence of a masculine bond that enables Webb to "understand" as a woman can, that enables him to give birth to his son.

The exclusion of mothers and daughters from both birth and death in Vietnam narrative excises them from the significant gender relations surrounding the questions of life and death. In *Neverlight,* Katherine's merging with Richard takes place within the frame of a war that declares gender difference in Katherine's exclusion from battle. She is thus excluded from confronting the question, "Is life sacred?" in any way except through Richard's experience and answer. Although she admits that she might kill, her personal encounter with death is when she and her daughter see a deer that has recently been killed by a hunter. As with the death of her husband, she has been excluded from the event, as she and her daughter only view the deer after its death and do not kill it themselves. James Webb's identification with his wife's experience of childbirth is prefaced by his admission that he has an older daughter for whom he has not felt this same bond. Thus, only after we are reminded that daughters are different from sons—are excluded from the moments at which life and death intersect—can the masculine move to "break" gender boundaries.

What Vietnam narration reveals is that such boundary crossings are not transgressions but confirmations: the masculine can move into the "female position" by occupying that position, not altering its own. Conversely, women do not exchange positions with the masculine but are excised from exchange altogether. Katherine Vail recuperates the meaning of life by taking on her husband's voice, not affirming her own; James Webb's wife is, at the moment of giving birth, extracted from it, her voice silenced by his narrative; the woman in "A Birth in the Delta" dies before she can even speak. There is not then an exchange of gender roles, but an elimination of them, so that all that exists, all that speaks at the ends of these narratives is the voice of the masculine point of view, the voice that has succeeded in occupying, "with ease, and without inhibition, the position of the female."

In one of the lengthiest dialogues of *Rambo: First Blood, Part II*, Rambo speculates to Co Bao, his Vietnamese contact (Co, in Vietnamese, means "Miss"), that he was picked for this rescue mission because he is "expendable." When Co asks him to clarify this term, he explains: "It's like if you're invited to a party and you don't show up, it doesn't matter." Later, when Rambo has rescued a POW and saved Co's life, she declares, "Rambo, you not expendable!" This is the anxiety that Vietnam representation sets out to relieve through the masculine appropriation of reproduction—that the male is "expendable" in the reproductive process. As Webb confesses: "Men are essentially interlopers in the life process. They are indispensable to creation, but only as something of a catalyst" (p. 8). By appropriating the position of the feminine and the process of reproduction, the masculine can assert its significance in the life/death opposition.

Like Judith Stiehm's suggestion that the masculine needs continually to prove itself because it does not possess the proof of reproduction, Mary O'Brien's theory of patriarchy lays the groundwork for an explanation of Rambo's anxiety. In her thesis, the female participation in reproductive labor marks a direct experience of contintuity—temporal, biological, social. For the male, conversely, the reproductive process is an alienated one, as his experience is indirect and dicontinuous, mediated in its uncertainty by the female. As a result, the male establishes other forms of continuity, and it is these that constitute patriarchy.

> Male reproductive consciousness is a consciousness of discontinuity. . . . The alienation of his seed separates him from natural genetic continuity, which he therefore knows only as idea. To give this idea substance, man needs praxis, a way of unifying what he knows as real with an actual wordly reality. Men must therefore make, and have made, artificial modes of continuity.[34]

These "artificial" forms of continuity take the form of political systems, appropriation of children through legal control of the mother, and so on.

> The problem of continuity over time has developed in western societies as a political problem, a quest for an 'order' of procession which transcends individ-

> ual life spans in some self-regenerating way. Principles of continuity appeal either to cyclical time, and appear in all organic theories of the state, to an idealized form of continuity, such as the notion of eternity, which are a component of theocratic formulations, or to a practical insistance of stable continuity, such as an economic order or a hereditary monarchy. (p. 62)

For all of the problems with O'Brien's thesis,[35] she nonetheless pinpoints a key moment of tension for the masculine/feminine opposition, and that is the question of continuity and control. Because the male experiences no direct continuity in the reproductive process, he may construct ways in which he can control that process so that his role is least discontinuous. The optimum strategy is to control the process of reproduction itself. The function of Vietnam representation is to enact that control, not simply by legislating reproduction, but by appropriating it for the masculine.

What Vietnam representation has at its service for accomplishing this task that was unavailable to earlier representations of warfare is, discussed in chapter 1, the "blossoming" of technology. It is then not coincidental that one of the mechanisms for responding to the perception of male exclusion from reproduction should be through technological means. John Wheeler's response to male expendability is, for example, to argue that the technology of reproduction has now made the female expendable as well: "A baby could be conceived without a father present. The baby could develop without a mother present. In a sense, penis and testicle, vagina and womb were machines replaceable by alternate technologies."[36]

Vietnam representation here captures a larger cultural movement toward the appropriation of reproduction through technology.[37] In keeping with O'Brien's thesis, Gena Corea notes that modern technologies like artificial insemination, sperm-washing, sex-determination techniques, amniocentesis, surrogate mothering, along with projected completion of projects for artificial wombs "are transforming the experience of motherhood and placing it under the control of men. Woman's claim to maternity is being loosened; man's claim to paternity strengthened. Moreover, these techniques are creating for women the same kind of discontinuous reproductive experience men now have."[38] In essence, she argues, "Through these technologies, man is increasingly creating a continuous reproductive experience for himself and a discontinuous one for women" (p. 9).

The primary purpose for such appropriation, according to Corea, is generated by the tension in the boundary between life and death foregrounded in war narrative: to conquer the barrier of death through the creation of immortality by continuous self-production. Epitomized in projects like cloning and artificial wombs is what Corea describes as "the patriarchal urge to give birth to oneself, to be one's own mother, and to live forever," so that "the desire to control birth through the reproductive technologies, then, is also a desire to control death" (pp. 262–63).

By inserting themselves into the birth process—whether through Webb's entrance into the delivery room via the doctors or through Burns's attempted delivery by Caesarean of the dead Vietnamese woman's baby—Vietnam's narrators endeavor to gain control over the moment of reproduction through technology and to thereby control death. In doing so, they must, as do Webb and Burns, eliminate women from the birth process—from war—altogether. This battle with death is thus not a cooperative but a competitive one, one that, as Robyn Rowland suggests, centers on power itself:

> Because women, even in patriarchal culture, have always retained without question the power and responsibilities of reproduction, the new technologies have disturbing implications for our lives. For many women—past, present, and future—child-bearing represents the major power base they have from which to negotiate the terms of their existence.[39]

Consequently, for Rowland, "with the possibilities offered by technology [men] are storming the last bastion [of women's power] and taking control of conception, foetal development, and birth."[40] In such terms, the insistent exclusion of women from war, coupled with the foregrounding of technology in Vietnam narration, marks the cultural force of these representations—to respond to the anxieties of the boundary between life and death by repressing and repossessing those who have been traditionally assigned the social, cultural, and biological power over that realm. The technologization of the male body seen in *Rambo* therefore describes the perfect shape in which to summarize all of these responses: the masculine gives birth to itself as a technologized body that not only defies death but incorporates—embodies—the very means by which death itself is to be conquered. Reproductive technologies are thus the very means by which Vietnam representation performs its narration and produces its "self."

In a war that is credited for introducing the greatest display of technology to the process of battle, it should thus seem no accident that Wheeler's answer to expendability should take the shape of the war itself. We can recall here Loren Baritz's identification of technology as one of the key defining features of the Vietnam experience: "The war in Vietnam caused an explosion in the research and development of the technology of war."[41] In describing the frame of mind behind such an explosion, Baritz concludes: "The technological mentality designs standardized means to achieve predetermined results. . . . *In a technological society authority is located in the process itself*" (italics added) (pp. 32–33). By invoking technology as the solution to biological exclusivity, Wheeler and narrations like his thus reinforce authority as process rather than as goal, returning again to Lyotard's shift "from the ends of action to its means."[42]

To focus on means rather than ends in this context is to highlight the process of reproduction over its results. For this reason Vietnam narratives invoke as the parallel experience to war the birth process and not the relation with the child. Katherine Vail discusses miscarriage; James Webb, the delivery room; William

Broyles, Jr., the "battle" between sperm and egg; John Wheeler, the decision to have children. The experience of the Vietnam veteran is even likened to that of abortion, as Peter Marin recalls "a woman friend" responding to his description of veterans' feelings by saying, "That's how I felt having my abortions, after the abortions."[43] "Mothering" is thus reduced in the logic of Vietnam's gendered structure and reproductive technology to a biological act alone, one that can be easily appropriated by technology, one in which bonds between the masculine and technology—the technologized body—are foregrounded over and above bonds between the feminine and the child.

This shift from ends to means and its consequent emphasis on the implementation of technology explains why the baby of "A Birth in the Delta," even though it is a boy, must die. The focus of the story must be, not on a successful birth of a child, which would draw attention back to biological reproduction, but on the successful linking of the masculine and technology. This is the "birth" that is being produced and celebrated in the narration of Vietnam.

## IV

The dichotomies that frame Vietnam representation are examined in the work of Georges Bataille: life/death, masculine/feminine, self/loss of self. Specifically, Bataille focuses on the moment of transgression, the crossing of the boundaries between these oppositions in ways that seem suggestive for understanding Vietnam narration. Bataille identifies the opposition between life and death as a tension between the independent self and the loss of self, between discontinuity and continuity. As Freud explained, it is only in death that the self can regain the sense of infantile oneness that it loses with maturation and differentiation.

For Bataille, this tension stages itself in the body. The erotic act is the occasion for the transgression of the boundaries between life and death, since the violation of the boundaries of the individual body is a breaking through the boundaries between life and death. But because the violating body remains intact while the violated experiences discontinuity, the act of transgression is simultaneously an act of confirmation that boundaries exist and can be maintained, if only through force and violence. These acts of transgression traditionally take place, according to Bataille, with the masculine as violator and the feminine as violated, thus, as in Benjamin's framework, it is the man who maintains boundaries and the woman who breaks them.

It might then seem at first that Bataille's paradigm is openly contradicted by the Vietnam War and the masculine position it represents, since in Vietnam representation the masculine is presented as epitomizing, not the bounded, but the transgressive, confronting and crossing the boundary of life/death. It is, for instance, the masculine that most often trangresses the boundary of death, as in the character of Richard Vail; it is the masculine that dissolves its self in the unbounded collectivity of combat; and it is the masculine that most often willingly violates the integrity of the body in injury or death and becomes the violated. The displays of technology discussed earlier are only one aspect of the excess that characterizes the transgressive position, as, most clearly, are the soldiers' deaths themselves. More than any other American war, Vietnam provided the context for challenging death outside of the arena of rational productivity; no ground was gained, no causes were won, no specified ends were achieved. And, for the individual soldier, the war was primarily irrational, only a disruption and not a confirmation of boundaries, an experience that could not be recuperated as "reason" or "product."

But a focus on the issue of reproduction alters such a first impression both of Bataille's schema and the paradigm of violation in Vietnam representation, revealing finally that they are one and the same. Let me refer here to Susan Suleiman's summary of Bataille's opposition between the transgressive and the normative. The transgressive experience, she summarizes, allows for the destabilization of the limits of the self, the simultaneous pleasure at crossing and anxiety at realizing boundaries, free play, the excessive, what Bataille calls "nonproductive expenditure".[44] The normative, however, reaffirms stability, "rationalized exchange and productivity," or what Suleiman calls "reproductivity," "purposeful action, or work" (p. 120). As Suleiman's phrasing indicates, reproduction is perceived, not as the transgressive, but as the normative, the purposeful, a product of and for exchange.

By appropriating reproduction to the position of the masculine, Vietnam narrative succeeds in rewriting the irrational as the rational, the abnormal as the normal, the discontinuous as the continuous, the nonproductive as the productive, war as "natural." In so doing, Vietnam narrative legitimizes transgression as productive, rationalizes excess, and attempts to gather control over both its boundaries and their breaking. But such legitimation belongs only to the masculine, signifying reproduction only from the masculine point of view. Female reproduction is, on the other hand, relegated to the arena of the "merely" biological, so that its narrative begins, like "A Birth in the Delta," with the death of the mother, the single transgression that the masculine position of war must deny. In such terms, female reproduction takes on the character of the limited (bound to biology), the parochial (appointing only physical and not social production), and the selfish, whereas masculine reproduction attends the unbounded, the universal, and the community of comradeship.

To quote Wheeler, "*self-giving was the essence of life in the war zone*."[45] In this paradigm, women are portrayed as self-withholding as opposed to men's self-giving. In *Uncommon Valor,* Mrs. Wilkes, while trying to stop her husband from going to Vietnam, phrases her objections in reference to herself, not to him. "Look," she tells Col. Rhodes, "why don't you just do me a favor and go away. . . . You have no right to be here. It's taken me ten years to get that goddamn war out of his head! . . . Where were *you* all the days he just sat for hours staring at the walls?" And *Mission M.I.A.*'s Angela Fisher finishes her plea for Phil Houser to stay home by saying, "Don't you care how I feel about this?"[46] Sarah Galimore, whose husband goes on the same mission, tells him, "Nothin's worth more to me than you" and reminds him that their daughter, Natalie, "needs you, Joe" (p. 115). To return to Tiger: "'Female' implies tasks involving specific interactions of a personal or quasi-personal kind, while 'male' implies activities on a larger scale, with potentially more impersonality."

Bataille's own strict religious upbringing, he confesses, was designed to repress the recognition "that the mother's body is *also* that of a woman."[47] By appropriating to itself the labor of reproduction, the masculine can effectively sever any connection between the mother-as-child-rearer and the woman-as-sexual-being who first conceived the child. Interjecting itself into reproduction at the moment of birth, the masculine can maintain the connection between the woman (with whom he procreates) and the mother (with whom he does not) while denying that these women are the same. It is for this reason that Burns delivers the baby by Caesarean, even though "the top of the baby's head was showing." A vaginal delivery would have forced recognition that the site of procreation and birth are one and the same, that, in the terms prescribed by "A Birth in the Delta," mother and whore are one. It is for this reason that Webb celebrates the entrance of men into the delivery room: by participating in his son's birth, he can repress his wife's role in reproduction. It is for this reason that Michael intervenes in Stevie and Angela's marriage, separating the woman who was (Nick's) whore from the mother of the now-emasculated Stevie ('s child).

And it is for this reason that Vietnam narration interposes itself at the point of (re)production in "A Birth in the Delta." There, the apparently mislabeled "birth" of the title, of the mother's child that does not take place, is replaced by the birth of the masculine subject, apart from the mother, *self-delivered* by the hands of its own medic. As Corea explains, "the patriarchal urge to give birth to oneself, to be one's own mother,"[48] is "an acting out of that myth [of single parenthood by the father]. Fathers can be, or appear to be, the sole parent" (p. 292). Such parenting here is accomplished by Burns's medical intervention in the birth, the moment at which he becomes solely responsible for "delivering" a newborn subject, only here that subject is not a baby but the masculine itself. Only after the "birth" do we read these characters—Captain Harkness, Prissholm, and Burns—all of whom had been only labels—captain, "new guy," medic—as subjects, men who have anxieties, doubts, personalities. The disruption that each experiences—Harkness forgets the rice, Prissholm his canteen, and Burns his fantasies—is his own individual birth trauma, his own labor, to produce himself. What might first appear to be a somewhat positive experience for each—the disruption of the military veneer and confrontation of individual anxieties—turns instead into the production of the masculine character within the context of war.

Far more significant to the (re)production of the masculine is that its character can be produced during war, so that the arena of the masculine and the masculine character can be joined together and not separated as they might be if that character were to continue to be associated only with "home" or "career" or "fraternity." The bonds of other masculinities are here drawn together and redefined to encompass these diverse personalities. In "A Birth in the Delta," the masculine subject *as subject* is (re)produced. Out of the denied sexuality of the mother—the hidden vagina—is rewritten ther subjectivity of the masculine, born of the now appropriated vagina—the "delta" of Vietnam.

The only other moment women are allowed into the narrative is Prissholm's meeting with the whore: the encounter with the Vietnamese mother "was like his fraternity initiation," "another unreal event, another threat to his imperiled sanity" that "he must not dwell on" (p. 173). The introduction of the whore might seem at first to be a denial of the death of the mother, a reappearance of the feminine to betray the production of the masculine. But this narrative gives us in the whore only a nonproductive female, a scenario from which reproduction has been deleted. Why? Because the role of the reproducer has now been taken on by the masculine—Burns—and no longer "belongs to" the feminine, has been disassociated from the female body altogether. Reproduction has not disappeared but has been transferred, from the feminine to the masculine. The appearance of the whore is not denial but confirmation that the masculine has indeed appropriated reproduction to/of itself.

"A Birth in the Delta," in its opening insistence on the death of the mother, seems to fall in line with the suggestions made by the French feminists, Luce Irigaray in particular,[49] that it is the mother in every woman that the male child works to repress, not, as Bataille and Freud say, the sexual woman in the mother. But what Vietnam reproduction reveals is that these activities are one and the same, that the repressed is not the mother *or* the whore, but the mother/whore from reproduction itself, from social continuity, from social reproduction, from control, from gender. As Donna Stanton suggests in her critique of the French feminists' use of the maternal metaphor, it "does not produce revelations so much as revalorizations or relodgings of topoi, images, and myths embedded in binary phallologic."[50] These "revalorizations" work through the strategy of inverting gender categories in Vietnam representation to reinscribe the position of women—whether mothers or whores—as the merely biological, the selfish and therefore non-self-producing, and, with the introduction of technology, the expendable.

Both the positions of arguing the repression of the mother (Irigaray) and the repression of the woman in the mother (Bataille) mimic the operations of capitalism as a mode of operation for patriarchy. Borrowing terms from Giles Deleuze and Felix Guattari, Klaus Theweleit suggests that capitalism is a constant process of deterritorialization—dissolving codes, laws, boundaries, interpretations, discovering new raw materials and sources of labor—and reterritorialization—reconstituting new boundaries as bases for the stabilization and incorporation of markets and resources.

> Capitalism brought about a comprehensive deterritorialization; in the course of its evolution, it dissolved every previous order and code (religious, scientific,

> philosophical), altering their functions and rendering them obsolete. It opened up new worlds, made new areas accessible, created new avenues for the deployment of human bodies, thoughts, and feelings, even for escaping from the existing order.[51]

But, succeeding this process of deterritorialization,

> Like every dominant force that wishes to remain dominant, feudal capitalism (followed by bourgeois capitalism and the bourgeois state) took up the task of blocking new possibilities, obscuring their existence, chaining them up, redirecting streams for their own benefit, "codifying" them in a way that served dominant interests, yet allowed subject peoples to retain the illusion of newfound freedom. (p. 270)

Theweleit's paradigm for capitalism provides a frame most clearly for the interpretation of Bataille but can be applied as well to many of the concepts of French feminism. The postulation of transgressive and normative modes of behavior corresponds precisely to the deterritorialization and reterritorialization phases of capitalism. The transgressive valorizes the stage of breaking down boundaries in the process of discovering new market arenas and the normative typifies the stage of stabilization and rearticulation of codes under capitalism. What Bataille celebrates as the transgressive belongs as well to the maternal in Irigaray's and Julia Kristeva's language, to its undifferentiated and changing character, its breaking of bounds, its inability to be captured by codes. Whether speaking of the repression of the sexual woman or the mother, both are replicating positions taken by the stage of deterritorialization in the operation of capitalism, foregrounding it over the stages of recodification and reterritorialization.

What Theweleit applies to his discussion of capitalism can better be articulated through an analysis of patriarchy. As Theweleit himself goes on to argue about the desire that he sees channeled through capitalism, "in all European literature (and literature influenced by it), desire, if it flows at all, flows in a certain sense *through women*" (p. 272). Hartsock insightfully argues that masculine experience provides the framework within which capitalism is expressed, not the other way around:

> the epistemology and society constructed by men, suffering from the effects of abstract masculinity, have a great deal in common with the society and ideology imposed by commodity exchange. The separation and opposition of social and natural worlds, of abstract and concrete, of permanence and change, the effort to define only the former of each pair as important, the reliance on a series of counterfactual assumptions—all this is shared with the exchange abstraction.[52]

In short, the epistemology promoted by masculinity suggests a competitive and oppositional frame within which commodity exchange is produced.

In such terms, the valorization of deterritorialization—Bataille's transgressions, Irigaray's unboundedness, Broyles's celebration of "a love that needs no reasons, that transcends race and personality and education"[53]—reinscribes an aspect of the process of patriarchal appropriation that is not an end in itself but a prelude to "reterritorialization" and is not a challenge to it. And it is the point of reproduction—the shift from deterritorializing (breaking the bounds of the mother's body) to reterritorializing (separation of mother and child)—that marks the transition between these two stages, the point at which the mother and the boy become vulnerable to repression by the man/father.[54] Vietnam representation, as the arena for the production of the man/father/masculine/capitalism, must repress this moment in order to repress the acknowledgment that it was ever anything other than its "self," that any possible alternatives to its mode of (re)production exist. For this reason Vietnam representation presents as one of its primary impulsions the effort to appropriate the operation of reproduction, to control the moment of its own "birth" and, simultaneously, the production of its own death.

By enabling itself to occupy "with ease, and without inhibition, the position of the female" through the appropriation of reproduction and the repression of the feminine as mother/whore, the masculine in Vietnam representation can appear to produce its "self," can appear both to determine the boundaries of that self and to transgress them at moments of its own choosing, to make gender seem flexible and subject to individual rather than social construction. The death of the laboring mother as a result of technological intervention signifies the alliance established between the masculine and the technological body, the alliance that "fathered" Rambo, invited James Webb into the delivery room, and prompted Burns to "deliver" the Vietnamese woman's baby. Becoming both seamless and boundless through the spectacle of excess that is Vietnam, the technologized masculine body can appear invulnerable to death. By appropriating to itself the process of reproduction, that body can appear to live forever.

# FOUR

# "DO WE GET TO WIN THIS TIME?" Reviving the Masculine

> For when we immerse our heads in the water, the old man is buried as in a tomb below, and wholly sunk forever; then as we raise them again, the new man rises in its stead.
>
> John Chrysostom[1]

The argument of this chapter is a simple one: established as victims—of their government, the war, the Vietnamese, American protesters, and the women's movement—Vietnam veterans are portrayed in contemporary American culture as emblems of an unjustly discriminated masculinity. Through this image of the veteran, American manhood is revived, regenerated principally by a rejection of the feminine and sexuality; reborn and purified, the veteran takes his place as an experienced leader and spokesperson for a conjointly revived morality and social politics that will regenerate America itself. But while this program is fairly simple, its operation is complex, intersecting with feminism, the civil rights movement, militarism, international relations, law, economic stratifications, and more. There is not an aspect of American society that is not now being shaped by the impetus of a revived masculine imagery and ethics. The task of this chapter is to explore how this project works in and through representations of the Vietnam War. It remains to later efforts to articulate the multiple and intricate ways in which the emblem of Vietnam is being stamped across American culture.[2]

## I

A. D. Horne's *The Wounded Generation* (1981) is a collection of excerpted comments on the Vietnam War accompanied by a central section recording a symposium between veterans, journalists, novelists, draft resisters, and others. During that symposium, Lucian Truscott, former writer for the *Village Voice*, talks about the "deep division between men and women in this country . . . [that] centers around the war":

> I can recall back in those days, having short hair and being at West Point, you were damned if you did and damned if you didn't. Every woman you ever went out with thought you were going to be completely fucked up if you did go to Vietnam, on the one hand. But then there was always an undercurrent that if you didn't go to Vietnam then there's going to be something wrong with you as a man, because we all know that civilizations have constantly over the course of history called upon people to go and fight wars whenever wars have come along. And I think the fact that women were not confronted with this decision that everybody had to make that was a guy back then, and were left free during those years to pursue the kinds of careers that make 49 percent of these women now part of the work force and to increase the number of their enrollments in law schools and whatever, I think that that's an extraordinary result of this war.[3]

Truscott's confused and rambling commentary picks up a few minutes later in a discussion of the "black rages" veterans often have, as he responds to Philip Caputo's recollection of an uncontrolled outburst of rage he once experienced: "Every guy I know—*guys who went to Vietnam and even guys who didn't go to Vietnam*—in the Army went through the same ups and downs and black rages. I would just note that while all this was going on and all these people were feeling rages, the women's movement had picked 'rage' as their favorite word" [italics added] (p. 113).

The leap that Truscott makes between the rage felt by "every guy I know" and the women's movement suggests two things. First that the rage expressed by the women's movement was somehow illegitimate when compared to that felt by veterans.[4] While men who shared the experience of the Army all felt these almost unexplained rages, women "*picked* 'rage' as their favorite word" [italics added]. What for men is an expression of real feeling is thus for women a choice of vocabulary, rather like that of choosing a favorite color. Rage becomes a word women, unlike the men for whom rage was sensed as an uncontrollably immediate emotion, could "pick" as if in leisure, not necessity. Second, and more important, Truscott's leap hints at what is perhaps the real source of this "rage" felt by him and "every guy I know," the women's movement itself, the changes that enabled women "to pursue the kinds of careers that make 49 percent of [them] now part of the work force and to increase the number of their enrollments in law schools and whatever." Truscott's erratic leaping from "civilizations" to "rage" reveals the underlying connection behind his and other veterans' confusion about the war—that they seem to have lost their place to women, the place of warrior, the place of wage-earner, the place of professional, the place of men.

John Wheeler's analysis of the "Vietnam generation" comes to much the same conclusion, in a similar pattern of reasoning. Truscott begins with the uncertain expectations women placed on men and moves immediately to women's achievements while those same men were at war. Wheeler, after defining what he perceives to be the key masculine and feminine statements—that there are things worth dying and living for, respectively—moves as well to the women's movement:

> Barbed wire is conventionally used as an obstacle in defending the perimeter around a fighting base. It was first used on a wide scale in World War I. In wars ever since there have been men who fell, wounded, slain, voluntarily or involuntarily, across the barbs, forming a bridge for buddies. . . . There is a certain sense in which the women's movement sped to fulfillment across the backs of the American men in Vietnam. But for our presence in battle, their protest would have died. . . . But for our fires and our dying, there would have been no revolution. No story for TV. No sense of defilement. No overweening sense of righteousness and anger and unmasculinity.[5]

Thus, for Wheeler, the Vietnam veteran has fallen, "voluntarily or involuntarily," across the barbed wire of the perimeter of social change. Across this bridge women have climbed, literally stepping on their fallen "buddies" to reach, according to Wheeler, their own goals at the expense of the men whose bodies lay beneath them.

A staging of Wheeler's scenario yields a battle in which women and Vietnam veterans fight, not for opposing interests of a gendered battle, but on the same side, against the same enemies. The consequences of this depiction are several. First, it seems the Vietnam veteran is saying to women, as Luke says to Bob Hyde in *Coming Home*, "I'm not the enemy." The Vietnam soldier and veteran cannot, then, because they are "on the same side," represent or reiterate the oppressions women are fighting against. Second, the "enemy" is, as a result, made nonspecific and ambivalent. For the many women whose feminism grew out of or along with their resistance to the war in Vietnam,[6] Wheeler's logistics are problematic. What enemy did they share with the soldier in Vietnam—the North Vietnamese? the U.S. government? The systematic oppression of women by patriarchal structures is not recognized here as an "enemy." Third, whatever enemy was being fought, in whatever battle, men were there first. The Vietnam soldier threw his body, "voluntarily or involuntarily," over the barbed wire so that women could come after him. In such terms, the women's movement is not really by women at all but is a consequence of masculine struggle. Fourth, the women's movement did not have the ability to sustain itself but had to feed off of the media and "fires" and death started by the Vietnam soldier. The "righteousness and anger"—the "rage"—expressed by women were not generated by women's conditions at all, but by the "fires" of men. And last, women could accomplish their goals—their "49 percent . . . of the work force . . . and whatever"—only via the unmanning of men, only at the price of "unmasculinity." Wheeler stages his strongest irony here, showing that the women's movement could capitalize on "unmasculinity" only by climbing over the backs of those who were most masculine, the soldiers who had made the commitment that "there were things worth dying for."

It is in women's treatment of men that Wheeler and Truscott find women exhibiting their greatest duplicity. For Wheeler,

> Part of the price of women's progress has been a new double standard. The double standard operates against men. Under it, America has learned to celebrate both the femininity *and* the professional accomplishments of women. The duplicity is that men are not affirmed in their masculinity, but only in their professional lives. (p. 142)

Truscott sees things more baldly. For him, men have simply learned to oppress themselves:

> When we were growing up, macho was when you were playing football, when they hiked the ball if you knocked over the other guy and he went down and you were still on your feet, the coach kicked you in the ass and said, "Hey, baby, that was macho!" Now these guys go out and run 20 miles, which is absolute masochistic self-punishment, and they brag about it. And that's macho! They're not knocking the other guy down, they're knocking themselves down. . . . It used to be cool to hit the other guy and now you're supposed to hurt yourself.[7]

The "unmasculinity" popularized with the women's movement has led then, not to the growth of men's personalities released from the constraints of traditional definitions of masculinity, but to their repression, to men hurting themselves, denying themselves, "voluntarily or involuntarily," and to women having it all.

Truscott, Wheeler, and other Vietnam veterans conclude that women's gains since the sixties have been made at the expense, specifically of the Vietnam veteran, but generally of masculinity itself. *Time* magazine's special issue in 1985 on Vietnam concurs, suggesting that the "damage to American faith in government and authority . . . had a sometimes chaotically liberating effect, breaking old molds and freeing the imagination to create new forms, new movements (environmentalism, say, or feminism)."[8] But this "liberation" came again at the expense of the veteran and of masculinity: "Viet Nam changed American notions about the virtues of masculinity and feminity. In the 60s, during the great violence of the war, masculine power came to be subtly discredited in many circles as oafish and destructive. . . . Femininity was the garden of life, masculinity the landscape of death" (p. 24). As Wheeler concludes, "men and the idea of manhood pay[ed] a material amount of the upfront cost of making women equal."[9]

In these scenarios, the Vietnam veteran is taken to be the emblem of a more widely based victimization of "man and the idea of manhood," in which men, veterans in particular, paid the price of women's equality, both in their careers and in their self-definition. And Wheeler's discussion makes clear that this is not an equality at all, but an inversion, that "the women's movement sped to fulfillment across the backs of the American men in Vietnam" and produced a situation in which women can have both femininity and careers while men, the very men who risked their lives for women during the war, cannot.

Thus much recent Vietnam representation is geared toward establishing the veteran as victim for the purpose of displaying a presumed discrimination by women against men. And, presumably, as the veteran has suffered, so have American men as a whole. In these terms, women have made their gains toward equality at the expense of men, particularly of the veteran who was absented from the competitive race for jobs, education, prestige. But even those men who were not in the war suffered as well, because what the women's movement challenged most directly was not individual men themselves but the idea of masculinity. So while particular veterans may indeed have lost places in businesses and colleges, American men lost their "place" en masse when their manhood was put in jeopardy.

Yet what men really lost, as Judith Hicks Stiehm points out, was not their equal status but their privilege:

> [cadets] (and many other) young white men do feel that they must compete with women and minorities, and that having to compete represents a loss to them, even if that loss is only one of privilege. This loss is especially felt when young white men compare themselves to their fathers and older brothers.[10]

The loss of the luxury of not having to compete is seen by these men as the most severe consequence of feminism and civil rights. And as Stiehm makes clear, that loss has meaning only within the frame of masculine bonding itself, "when young white men compare themselves to their fathers and older brothers." Within the community of American manhood, men are seen to have had something taken away from them, to have been deprived, to have been discriminated against. As Samuel Osherson's study of fathers and sons declares: "For all that feminism has contributed to our culture, it has also brought with it a subtle idealization of women and a more subtle denigration or misunderstanding of men."[11]

This sense of discrimination is articulated by Wheeler when he declares that "the Vietnam veteran was the nigger of the 1970s." Wheeler's definition of "nigger" here is telling: "You create a nigger by depriving a person of part of his or her personhood. Ignoring that person or inflicting traumatic hurts is the traditional way to treat a nigger."[12] Removing "nigger" from its racist origins and its identification of "a Negro or member of any dark-skinned people,"[13] Wheeler manufactures an all-purpose term of discrimination that can be applied to whites and blacks, men and women alike: "In this metaphorical sense, woman was the nigger of the 1960s. The black was the nigger of the 1950s."[14] The historical shifts can occur because "as the hurt dissipates, and ignoring turns into recognition, your time as a nigger begins to end" (p. 17).[15]

As in the masculine bonding of Vietnam discussed in chapter 2, race here is elided as a significant category for the veteran/soldier. Thus, the position of "nigger" is open to occupation by any group that is "deprived . . . of part of his or her personhood." And, as we have seen, the loss of privilege associated with the production of the "unmasculine" is sensed by American men as a deprivation of their "personhood," of part of what makes them men. Consequently, this deprivation is not depicted as a necessary alteration in the relations of gender but as a discrimination, as the production of a "nigger." By applying a chronology to his historical constructions of "niggers," Wheeler implies that the oppression of these other "niggers" has ended. Neither blacks nor women are "niggers" any longer, putting them in a position of privilege in relation to the "nigger of the 1970s," the Vietnam veteran.

## II

The Vietnam War provided the context in which American males could most clearly be identified as victims of a wide range of factors, most of them articulated in the personal narratives of veterans. This list is long and diverse.

The clearest example of American soldiers as victims comes with the depiction of the nearly six hundred American POWs held prisoner by the North Vietnamese. Soldiers were seen to be subjected to mental and physical torture, conditions of near starvation, harrassment, isolation, and deprivation. These soldiers' narrations of beatings, humiliation, and illness at the hands of the North Vietnamese serve, for the American public at large, as distinctive evidence of the victimization of a segment of the American population.[16] To the extent that the war in Vietnam is seen to be the cause of a general disillusionment with American government and ideals, POWs are taken to be emblematic of the American public as a whole, victims of a war it never understood. As *Newsweek's* lead story of its special issue "The Legacy of Vietnam" states, "We're Still Prisoners of War."[17] Fears about the estimated twenty-five hundred MIAs possibly still being kept in camps create anxieties about the continuation of such victimization. In Wheeler's terms, the North Vietnamese "created" "niggers" out of the American POW.

Yet another way in which Vietnam soldiers/veterans were seen as victims was in treatment they received by the American public on their return from war. Ron Kovic's *Born on the Fourth of July*, an account of Kovic's Vietnam service and paralysis from a gunshot wound, recalls his first exposure to the American public's reaction to Vietnam and its veterans: "I was in Vietnam when I first heard about the thousands of people protesting the war in the streets of America. I didn't want to believe it at first—people protesting against *us* when we were putting our lives on the line for our country. . . . How could they do this to us?"[18] Asked to be grand marshall for a Memorial Day parade after his return, Kovic experiences firsthand the response of the American public. Expecting the rousing cheers he had heard as a child at earlier parades, Kovic is stunned when he and another veteran receive only stares and dis-ease. He becomes convinced that the crowds do not know who they are, for if they did,

> they'd have been flooding into the streets, stomping their feet and screaming and cheering. . . . They'd have been swelling into the streets, trying to shake their hands just like in the movies, when the boys had come home from the other wars. . . . If they really knew who they were, he thought, they'd be roaring and clapping and shouting. (pp. 103–104)

But instead, "he couldn't help but feel like he was some kind of animal in a zoo or that he and Eddie were on display in some trophy case" (p. 104). Rejected by the very people whom they were defending, Vietnam veterans feel they were deprived of the reintegrating homecoming given soldiers from earlier wars and made scapegoats of the country's discomfort with the war and its outcome.

Vietnam soldiers/veterans were also seen to be victims, not only of the people they were defending, but of the very government who sent them to war in the first place. In addition to criticizing what appeared to them an often confused and misguided government policy, veterans' accounts speak most forcefully to the government's failure to make an all-out commitment to winning the war once the decision had been made to engage in it. Two comments are representative, both from soldiers in the Army's Charlie Company serving in Vietnam during 1967–69. David Brown:

> They might have won anyway . . . if they hadn't been bound down like Gulliver in Lilliput by the rules and the tactical restraints of a limited war. *A nine-to-five-war*. . . ; they could have used all that power to blow the whole country to hell, but instead they kept bumping around on little nickle-and-dime, hit-and-run operations.[19]

And Frank Goins:

> *It could have been over within six months. . . . Easy. We could have took the 57,000 troops that got killed and put them all in a line behind tanks and APCs instead and just started them at one end and walked across the country.* (p. 102)

By refusing to use its technological superiority, these veterans reason, the U.S. Government willingly sacrificed its own soldiers' lives and bodies for limited warfare.

Vietnam soldiers are seen as well as victims of an inequitable draft. Early on it provided deferments for primarily college-educated and middle- and upper-class draftees, and later it enabled systematic preferences to be given those who were middle and upper class and white, leaving a disproportionate amount of combat fighting to blacks, southerners, Hispanics, and the urban lower class. As Ruben Treviso puts it, "The draft boards chose those individuals who were most vulnerable. . . . Unlike middle America, many of the poor and minorities did not have money for frivolous-type deferments."[20] Of blacks in the military during the Vietnam era, 55 percent served in Vietnam, as opposed to 47 percent of whites, primarily because more blacks entered the military through the draft than whites (28 percent versus 24 percent) and more draftees served in combat. In the state of New Mexico in 1970, Hispanics made up 27 percent of the population, but 69 percent of those drafted and 44 percent of combat deaths. When it came to serving in heavy combat, minorities were disproportionately represented. 48 percent of Hispanics and 34 percent of blacks as opposed to 29 percent of whites served in heavy combat. One of every two Hispanics who went to Vietnam served in a combat unit; one of every five was killed in action; one of every three was wounded in action. Educational level was an even more important factor. Of those serving in Vietnam with less than a high school education, 49 percent were in heavy combat, whereas of those with college educations, only 15 percent served in heavy combat.[21] Whereas at the end of World War II, blacks made up 12 percent of all combat troops, by the start of the Vietnam War blacks composed 21 percent of combat troops so that in 1965, 24 percent of all Army combat deaths were blacks.[22] As General S. L. A. Marshall commented: "In the average rifle company, the strength was 50% composed of Negroes, Southwestern Mexicans, Puerto Ricans, Guamanians, Nisei, and so on. but a real cross-section of American youth? Almost never" (p. 10).

Perhaps the most distressing form of victimization came for American soldiers in their sense that they were betrayed by the very people for whom they were fighting—the Vietnamese. As Sgt. Phillip L. Woodall wrote in a letter home:

> [My platoon leader died] fighting for a people who have no concern for the war, people he did not understand, [who] knew where the enemy were, where the booby traps were hidden, yet gave no support. People that he would give portions of his food to yet would try to sell him a Coke for $1. . . . This country is no gain that I can see, Dad. We're fighting, dying, for a people who resent our being over here.[23]

Many veterans recount their realizations that the Vietnamese who seemed most to serve them—hootch maids, barbers, washerwomen, prostitutes—turned out to be spies for the NLF. As Michael Herr wrote, "the VC got work inside all the camps as shoeshine boys and laundresses and honey-dippers, they'd starch your fatigues and burn your shit and then go home and mortar your area."[24] In John Wayne and Ray Kellog's *Green Berets* (1968), Sergeant Muldoon catches a member of the Strike Force, a special team of Vietnamese who work with the American military to "kill all stinking Commie," pacing off the grounds of their base camp for mortaring. Loren Baritz summarizes what many soldiers saw as "the open hostility of some South Vietnamese, the people they had come to defend," throwing grenades into troop trucks, turning American food over to guerillas, giving information on troop strength to the NLF, and so on.[25] In narrative after narrative, American soldiers speak of the people whom they were defending as, at best, indifferent to their survival and, at worst, a threat to it.

To compound matters, soldiers felt that they could not count on those they were fighting with, the Army of the Republic of Vietnam. Again and again these soldiers are spoken of as cowardly, disorganized, unmotivated, and poorly trained. The American television-viewing public saw firsthand what seemed to be incontrovertible evidence of the cowardice of ARVN when, after announcing his policy of "Vietnamization," President Nixon launched the secret invasion of Cambodia. Sent on a major operation with nothing but American air support, the ARVN troops were ambushed. Fleeing from North Vietnamese troops, American cameras captured ARVN soldiers clinging to American helicopter skids and apparently faking wounds in order to be evacuated (p. 202).

The widespread belief in South Vietnamese corruption added to the general sense that American soldiers had of being betrayed by their ally. An example is in one of the U.S.'s most favored plans for defeating the Viet Cong, the strategic hamlet program, in which entire villages were relocated in order to isolate the Viet Cong and deprive them of both food and recruits. In addition to being forcibly removed from their ancestral lands, peasants were often "forced to construct [the hamlets] by corrupt officials who had pocketed a percentage of the money allocated for the projects."[26] Edward Brady, Combat Operations and Intelligence Advisor for the United States Military Assistance Command in Vietnam in the late sixties, recalls that ARVN command positions were bought and sold, a practice laid principally at the door of the wives of the General Staff members. He recalls that mistresses of general officers often supported themselves through selling their influence to obtain military posts for male relatives.[27]

The final and apparently clearest evidence of a victimization of Vietnam soldiers/veterans is in the growing evidence for the physical destruction caused by the exposure of thousands of U.S. troops to Agent Orange. Yet officially unestablished by government studies, some link exists between exposure to Agent Orange and the numerous cases of cancer, skin disease, birth defects, and other disorders experienced by these soldiers and their families. Innocent of the possible effects of such exposure, soldiers did not even become aware of their danger until years after the war was over, so that their bodies continue to be literal evidence of a victimization by U.S. government war policies. The 1986 television film, *Unnatural Causes* (dir. Lamont Johnson) presents this victimization in its clearest narrative form. William V. Taylor, a veteran whose body began producing tumors several years after his service in Vietnam, felt this victimization most clearly:

> For the first time in Taylor's experience, Vietnam veterans were being portrayed on television as something other than dupes or murderers; for the first time, they were being regarded with sympathy, instead of indifference or disdain. They were victims, entitled (as their opponents had been, ten years

> earlier) to all the dignity victimization seems to confer in the media. He saw the change in attitude—the interest, the concern, the *respect*—among his friends, and felt rather important as a result.[28]

As Taylor's response indicates, an alteration has occurred in recent years in American popular attitudes toward the Vietnam War and the people who fought in it, one that has solidified the image of the veteran as a victim of this and other factors, many part of the war itself, but many also products of American responses to that war and its warriors. Even during the years when the Vietnam War was still unpopular, in the late 1970s, many representations led toward a perception of the soldier as sympathetic victim. Films like *The Boys in Company C* (1978) urged us to sympathize with the young men who entered the war naively or unwillingly and who, in the later controversial metaphor of *The Deer Hunter,* lost all control over their own lives, thoughts, and futures in the confusing and indiscriminate Russian roulette game that was Vietnam.

In the years following the war, the plight of the veteran became more apparent—the increasing visibility of numbers of injured or disabled veterans returning from the wars to their homes (according to hearings before the Committee on Veterans' Affairs conducted in February, March, and May 1980, over half a million veterans were receiving disability compensation from the Vietnam War as of 1980[29]); the declaration by President Carter of Vietnam Veterans' Week, from May 28 to June 3, 1979; the popularization of knowledge about Post-Traumatic Stress Syndrome (estimated to afflict anywhere from 500,000 to 700,000 Vietnam veterans); and the publicization of the rise in deaths and child deformities linked to Agent Orange. Through all of these highly visible representations, American audiences were increasingly encouraged to see the Vietnam veteran as a victim.

*Time* magazine concluded in 1985 that "the most important change in American attitudes toward the war in the past few years has been the public acceptance of those who fought. The Viet Nam veteran, after a long struggle, has acquired a considerable respect . . . that he deserves."[30] And on Memorial Day, 1984, President Reagan presided over the burial of the Unknown Soldier from Vietnam at Arlington National Cemetery. Signaling his "pardon" of the Vietnam veteran, Reagan declared: "We may not know his name, but we know his courage. He is the heart, the spirit, and the soul of America."[31] Laying the "old man" of Vietnam officially to rest—the individual, named soldier who had been rejected, spat on, and denied—Reagan has authorized the entrance of the "new man," the emblematic soldier whose unknown identity lays him open to a renaming by those who signify him, a renaming that retrieves him from his marginalized position and places him at the "heart of America." A 1980 Veterans Administration study of American attitudes toward Vietnam-era veterans offers testimony to this changing perception. As its authors conclude, "one detects an increasing sense of sympathy for these veterans among the public as a whole. . . . Public sentiment that 'veterans of the Vietnam war were made suckers, having to risk their lives in the wrong war in the wrong place at the wrong time' has significantly increased between 1971 (49%) and today [1979] (64%)."[32] Similar responses were given to the statement, "Veterans who served in Vietnam are part of a war that went bad": in 1971, 62 percent agreed, and in 1979, the figure rose to 81 percent (p. 87). As the authors of the report conclude: "if anything, negative attitudes toward the war are associated with higher levels of sympathy toward these veterans" (p. 85).

Receiving greatest sympathy from the American public is the American POW. With responses on a scale from 1 to 10, a 1979 Lou Harris survey asked people to rate their feelings toward different groups of people. The category "veterans who were captured and held prisoner in Vietnam" received 10s across the board, and veterans who served in Vietnam during the war received an average of 9.8, somewhat above veterans of World War II or Korea (9.6). In contrast, "our military leaders" rated only a 6.3 (behind doctors, a 7.9), and "United States Congressmen and Senators" warranted a 5.2., only slightly higher than "people who demonstrated against the war in Vietnam," who were given an average of 5.0. (Lowest on the scale were "oil company executives," who scored a 2.9) (p. 88). Because Vietnam veterans, esepcially POWs, rate very high in their reception of public sympathy (significantly higher than government officials), it is efficient use of cultural perception for recent Vietnam narratives to have featured both rescues of POWs and rejections of indifferent and deceptive government representatives as their primary themes.

This shift in public opinion has been so severe that political scientist Jean Bethke Elshtain can conclude, "Vietnam is even now in the process of being reconstructed as a story of universal victimization—of Vietnamese by us; of our soldiers by the war—and by us when we didn't welcome them home; of our nation by the war at home and *the* war; of wives and girlfriends by disturbed veterans; of nurses by the war and later nonrecognition of *their* victims."[33] Although this sense of "universal victimization" is now operating in American culture, Vietnam representation in general speaks, not to the situations of nurses or even of the Vietnamese (the numbers of narratives that actually include Vietnamese people as other than stereotypes is extremely small[34]), but to the men who fought there, in particular to white men. In spite of the fact that 9.3 percent of Vietnam-era soldiers were black and disproportionately higher numbers of blacks served in heavy combat, that approximately 5 percent were Hispanics and 3.2 percent were women,[35] most media and film attention has focused on the white male. The stars of recent films like *Missing in Action I* (1984) and *Missing in Action 2* (1985) and *First Blood* (1982), *Rambo: First Blood, Part II* (1985),[36] and *Rambo III* (1988) are white males.[37] Even the black veteran in *Uncommon Valor* (1985), a decorated helicopter pilot, is an outsider, not a member of the original LRRP team that has been reassembled to rescue one of their members in a POW camp, and in *Missing in Action 2* the only POW to defect to the Vietnamese cause is black.

This must make us question the social function of this recent shift in cultural attitudes toward the Vietnam veteran as more than a simple cultural apologetic for mistreatment of American soldiers and guilt over an uncertain war experience. If, in spite of the facts of war service, only certain veterans are being chosen as emblems of this cultural shift, then the production of the Vietnam veteran as victim must be further interrogated. More important, we must examine the consequences of the production of victimization in these emblems, specifically, the images and constructions generated by the scenario of victimization. A look at two of Vietnam representations' most popular films, *First Blood* and *Rambo: First Blood, Part II*, shows that the proposition of victimization, once established in films like *First Blood*, is being used to bolster a call for the regeneration of these victims—particularly white men—for a restitution of their "rights" and a return of their identity. It is, as *Time* magazine declares, "a very literal and significant transaction . . . [that] suggests that in the American imagination, the Viet Nam veteran, erstwhile psychotic, cripple and loser, has been given back his manhood."[38]

## III

In *First Blood*, John Rambo returns from Vietnam where he served on a Special Forces team and escaped from a POW camp in which he was severely tortured (within the opening minutes of the film, we see the numerous scars on his back from this torture). Having lost all but one of the men in his unit, Rambo hitchhikes to the town of Hope, Oregon, where he has finally traced the one remaining member of his team, Delmar Berry, but is told by Berry's mother that he died the year before of Agent Orange. Alone, rejected, purposeless, Rambo goes into the town of Hope, only to be "escorted" out by Sheriff Teasle, who sees Rambo as an undesirable hippie who doesn't belong in his town. Not willing to be told what to do, Rambo returns to town, where he is arrested by Teasle. When the sheriff's men strip, hose down, and shave Rambo by force, he experiences flashbacks of the torture he suffered at the hands of the Vietnamese in the POW camp. Breaking out of the jail, Rambo begins a one-man war against the town, in which he succeeds in destroying much of the town's property and injuring (not killing) most of its police officers and national guard.

Finally, trapped inside a gun shop, surrounded by police cars and the burning flames of his rampage, Rambo is confronted by his former teacher and mentor, Colonel Trautman. Facing Trautman, the only man who can understand his plight, Rambo breaks down. Collapsing in Trautman's arms, Rambo cries tears of loss for his dead buddies and of frustration for his treatment on returning from the war. Once in charge of "million dollar equipment," Rambo is now unable to even hold down a job at a car wash. And the job that he has been trained to do and at which he excels—killing—is disallowed. But "You don't just turn it off," he cries. Winning medals and praise for the job he did in Vietnam, Rambo comes home to find only rejection, scorn, and prejudice from the country whose ideals he fought to defend. Trautman finally escorts the broken Rambo out of the gunshop under his own trenchcoat, his arm around Rambo's shoulders. As the police handcuff Rambo and take him off to prison, the camera freezes on his pacified image, now controlled, not only by the military (Trautman) and the government (the police), but by the camera as well, frozen in his confusion.

From the film's outset, Rambo is produced as a victim, first of his Vietnamese torturers, then of the war that took his buddies away, then of an autocratic sheriff who doesn't like Rambo's looks and thinks he's inappropriate for his town, and, finally, of the very military apparatus he fought for when he is trailed by the National Guard. In addition, Rambo's friend, Delmar Berry, was a victim of Agent Orange contamination. And, as Rambo tells Trautman, he was himself a victim of his government's policy, for though he and his friends fought well and in his mind could have won the war, "Somebody wouldn't let us win." Rambo comes to stand as emblem of the multiple avenues of victimization available to Vietnam representation. The close of the film freezes Rambo's status as victim. For all of his expertise, desire to be reintegrated and pacifism (Rambo only fights when goaded and, importantly, he *kills no one* in this first film, though it is very clear he could have done so with ease), he does not step out of his role as victim. Instead, he steps only into the arms of Colonel Trautman and the waiting police.

But in 1985 the confused and lonely veteran of *First Blood* became the triumphant hero of *Rambo: First Blood, Part II* (dir. George P. Cosmatos). As Harry Haines puts it, "*Rambo* proclaims a regeneration of pride in the Vietnam veteran and . . . hails him as a warrior hero."[39] Rejected and persecuted by his government in *First Blood*, Rambo is finally taken into custody by the police to be punished for stepping outside of the law. But in *Rambo*, after pinning down a government representative and threatening to "find" him if he doesn't expedite the rescue of American POWs, Rambo, now strong and self-reliant (bare-chested instead of hidden beneath Trautman's raincoat), strides into the sunset toward Thailand. Whereas in *First Blood* Rambo accepts the government's demands for order and reintegration by surrendering and going to prison, in *Rambo* he refuses assimilation (walking away from a presidential pardon), institutes his own law ("Find 'em [the POWS]. Or I'll find you"), and sets forth his own conditions for reintegration: "For our country to love us as much as we love it!" The fires that illuminated the end of *First Blood* have been washed into the pastel shades of a setting sun, and the divisive fighting going on "outside your front door" has given way to the unified closing song of the "Home of the brave," where "we'll never fall" because "the strength of our nation belongs to us all."

*Rambo: First Blood, Part II* begins with Rambo in a prison labor camp, where he is forced to break rocks in a hot sun that is reflected off the mirrored sunglasses of the prison guards. In the film's ethical balance, Rambo is completing his penance for destroying property in *First Blood* by "serving time" in the purposeless destruction of useless property. Colonel Trautman, who rescued Rambo from his first victimization, now arrives to retrieve him from his second—victimization by a state institution that is punishing Rambo for its own failures to deal properly either with him or the war in which he fought. Trautman offers Rambo a possible presidential pardon if he can complete an unnamed "mission," suggesting that Reagan, whose photograph appears in several key shots of the film, unlike the government he represents, understands the value of the veteran and wants to "pardon" his errors and mistreatments, in some ways himself stepping outside of the law, much as Rambo must do to rescue the POWs. (Reagan's repeated photographic appearance suggests as well that he would endorse the devictimization of the white male if Rambo succeeds.) Rambo pointedly asks Trautman, "Do we get to win this time?" Trautman's reply records the shift in the narration of victimization that has taken place between this film and its predecessor: "This time, it's up to you."

Rambo is released to attempt a Special Operations mission that will try to find American POWs left in Vietnam, to find prisoners being held and tortured by the government of Vietnam, just as Rambo, in similar though less severe terms, has been released from a prison where he was held by his own government. His task is not only to achieve his own "pardon," but that of his victimized buddies as well, showing that he is to be seen, not as an exception in his treatment but as the rule. And this time, unlike in *First Blood*, Rambo does win, defeating not only the Vietnamese who guard the POW camp from which he rescues five POWs, but the Russian soldiers who advise them as well. And, perhaps more to the point, he defeats his own government, retrieving the very men the government has denied for years.

Rambo's worst "enemy" in the film is not the Vietnamese or even the Russians, but Marshall Murdock, a Washington bureaucrat who was sent to supervise Rambo's mission and finally, when it appears that evidence of POWs does exist contrary to his own government's policy statements, tries to sabotage Rambo's mission. Murdock's pronouncement on the POWs makes the victimization of POWs and veterans clear; to him and the government he represents, they are worthless: "Do you think somebody's going to stand up on the floor of the United States Senate and ask for a couple billion dollars for a couple of forgotten ghosts?" Trautman's reply fixes the film's response: "Men, goddamn it! *Our* men!" When Trautman accuses Murdock of just "trying to cover his ass," Murdock makes his function clear, that it is not his ass, but "a nation's!" So the POWs and, by analogy, veterans as a whole, are being made to pay the price, again with their lives, for a misguided and misdirected government policy about the Vietnam war.

But Rambo and the film that displays him confront this victimization directly, not only by insisting that there are still POWs, but also by showing their continued valor, heroism, and patriotism. Although their country has betrayed them, they have retained, to use Wheeler's terms, their "ability to make a commitment." Rambo's final speech instantiates the reversal that *Rambo* has inscribed. When Trautman asks what he wants, Rambo speaks not only for himself but for all veterans: "I want what they want, and what every other guy who came over here and spilt his guts and gave everything he had wants—For our country to love us as much as we love it!" In the economy of *Rambo*, veterans are not asking then for "special treatment," only for the fulfillment of a bargain, to be paid fairly for their work and sacrifice. And, as Rambo's brutally enunicated words to Murdock make clear, *Rambo* reiterates the government's debt in this agreement. Unlike the government's "mission" in Vietnam, Rambo can grittily declare for himself, "Mission accomplished!" The failure of Vietnam, to echo Richard Halloran's paen to the U.S. soldier, owed not to the individual soldier/veteran, but to the government that sent him to war in the first place. *Rambo* blares into thousands of movie theaters and homes the message that not only did the soldier/veteran perform his job well, but he can still accomplish his "mission," one for which he has never been adequately paid.

Thus, from *First Blood* to *Rambo* the character of the veteran has shifted dramatically. No longer a confused and tearfully inarticulate misfit, he is now a determined and demanding leader; no longer destroying property in a blaze of revenge, he rescues other forgotten heroes, bringing them home as well; no longer under the protection of the military or subject to the law, he now strides independently out to a brilliant landscape that awaits the institution of his own law; no longer a victim, he is a hero, reviving for a disillusioned nation the very ideas of heroism itself; no longer feminized, he has "been given back his manhood."[40] *First Blood* and *Rambo: First Blood, Part II* set the poles for the alteration in the image of the veteran that has transpired in recent years, an alteration in which the image of the victimized soldier/veteran/American male has been regenerated into an image of strength and revived masculinity.

## IV

While offering a message of victory in Rambo's extravagantly successful mission,[41] *Rambo* reinforces the theme of regeneration through a simple and repetitive symbolic program: purification through fire and rebirth through immersion in water. As a common feature not only of *Rambo* but of other recent Vietnam films as well, the symbolic significance of this imagery is crucial to understanding the power of these narratives to renew the image of the American male, "reborn" from the waters that have purified him of his tainted past images. Mircea Eliade's explanation indicates the force of this imagery: "In whatever religious complex we find them, the waters invariably retain their function: they disintegrate, abolish forms, 'wash away sins': they are at once purifying and regenerating."[42]

The most explicit of these images appears in *Missing in Action* when Colonel Braddock (Chuck Norris) appears to have been defeated by Vietnamese guards in his effort to free American POWs being transferred from one camp to another.[43] Riding in a high-speed assault raft, Braddock is thrown from the boat when it is hit by a Vietnamese bazooka and explodes in flames. With the boat overturned and no sign of Braddock or his accomplice above water, the Vietnamese soldiers begin laughing among themselves at the ease with which they have defeated the Americans (again). But, as with Rambo, this time there is a new soldier, a "new man," who is not so easily defeated or humiliated. In a slow motion straight-on shot, Braddock is shown rising out of the river, droplets of water creating an aura around him, firing his M-16. As the triumphant music reaches its climax, Braddock kills the laughing Vietnamese soldiers and rescues the POWs. The slow-motion camera (only one of two uses of this technique in an otherwise mundane cinematography) draws our attention to this as mythic action and underscores its significance for the audience.

Rambo endorses this imagery by rising from the waters no fewer than four times in *Rambo*. In the first of two important scenes, Rambo is immersed in the waters of a river as he leaps from an exploding boat. Both his guide, Co Bao, and a rescued POW watch the waters tensely, believing that Rambo was killed, but he bursts from the river to their cheers and the rising strains of an exultant background score. And later, in a still more miraculous resurrection, Rambo dives into a pool at the bottom of a waterfall, escaping from a napalm bomb dropped by a Russian helicopter. The waters explode into flames, and the door-gunner shatters the water's surface with multiple, seemingly unsurvivable rounds. But as the helicopter lowers to the water's surface to find the body, Rambo leaps from the water, throws the door-gunner overboard, and lands on the helicopter.

These scenes, like the one in *Missing in Action*, link the regeneration through water to the defeated veteran—to the victim. Braddock is being laughed at by the confidently conquering Vietnamese; Rambo has been betrayed by Vietnamese pirates who have sold knowledge of his whereabouts to a Vietnamese patrol boat, and later, after excruciating torture, he is brutally bombarded by the overwhelming technological superiority of the Russians. In each case, the veteran was submerged long enough to be believed dead; in each case, the presumed "victors" look arrogantly pleased by this confirmation of the weakness of their American opponent; and in each case, the "old man" gives way to the "new man," the revived American male.

Klaus Theweleit's complex reading of Fascist literature establishes the link beween this kind of purification and the constructions of masculinity. Thus, we can read in these films not simply the rebirth of a victimized character, but the simultaneous regeneration of masculinity itself in contemporary American cultural productions. Theweleit locates the regenerative imagery of water in the ascendent bourgeois self-image of the eighteenth century as a signifier of "the bourgeoisie's 'moral superiority' over the absolutist nobility."[44] As a result of this moral fixation, water's purifying powers came to be associated closely with sexual purity, an image vital to the self-perception of what Theweleit calls the "soldier male" in Fascist Germany.

> Water was precisely the substance that possessed adequate redemptive qualities. No other substance could make people feel "reborn" after such a brief immersion. Water acquired the function of providing healthy competition for true "rebirths," those that involved real orgasms. (p. 422)

Theweleit traces the release of waters prominent in Fascist literature—floods, streams, rivers, burst dams—to its function as sublimated "release" of sexual energies. In an uncontrolled state, it is a release to be feared, possibly overrunning the soldier male and drowning him. What is preferred are controlled streams of water in which the soldier male can immerse himself to be reborn. As Theweleit shows again and again, intimately connected to these fears are women, especially women of the lower class, for women are reminders of that sexuality from which purifying water has rescued the soldier male.

> In the guise of the promised ocean, the "infinite vagina," water not only hides the reality of women, but flows forth against the ("dirty") sexuality of the women of oppressed classes and strata: that is, "proletarian" women. At the same time, splashing out of the sink and on to the bodies of bourgeois men, water became the new religion of Asexuality. . . . Water guarantees that the desires of these men are clean, that their unconsciouses are pure. (p. 421)

In these terms, the taint of impure sexuality is identified with "dirty" women, women who must be rejected in order for the soldier male to maintain his purity and energy.

Both Braddock and Rambo are radically disassociated from women in *Missing In Action* and *Rambo: First Blood, Part II*. Ms. Fitzgerald, an assistant to the State Department accompanying Senator Powers on his fact-finding mission to Vietnam, thinks Braddock initially rude and uncivil, trying more to disrupt than to further negotiations about POWs. She confesses that her job is to "keep an eye" on him while they are in Ho Chi Minh City. Believing that he is coming to her room for a nightcap and suggesting that he is being forward when he starts immediately to undress, Fitzgerald is dumbfounded to find Braddock redressing in nightgear and sneaking out of her hotel room. Anxiously awaiting his return, Fitzgerald, now dressed in low-cut black negligee, sees Braddock sneaking back into the hotel moments before a military patrol that pursues him for killing Vietnamese general Trang. Braddock enters Fitzgerald's room, grabs her, strips off her negligee and throws her on the bed. As Braddock jumps under the covers with her and soldiers burst down the door to her room, she swears that Braddock has been with her all night. The next morning, with a decided change in attitude toward Braddock, even displaying some jealousy about whom he is traveling to Bangkok to see, Fitzgerald wishes him a wistful good-bye at the airport, telling him, "I'm sorry you have to leave." Fitzgerald appears again in the film only at the end, when, seated with the government negotiators who have just accepted the Vietnamese statement that "there are no American POWs in the Republic of Vietnam," she is witness to Braddock bursting into the negotiating room with one POW under his arm and several behind him.

Rambo's contact for his POW rescue mission is, to his surprise, a Vietnamese woman, Co Bao, daughter of an ARVN intelligence officer killed during the war. She is tough, resourceful, and a capable fighter, though she cautions Rambo to "follow orders" when he goes in to the POW camp (he is only supposed to take pictures as evidence of POWs, not rescue them, an intertextual reference to Rambo's own victimization as frozen by the cameras at the end of *First Blood*, an act *Rambo* will not repeat). And although Rambo must first rescue her when she is caught by a Vietnamese guard, she later rescues him from his Russian torturers, showing no inequality in terms of their abilities to work together. But Co's rescue is somewhat different than Rambo's. Whereas he saves her by coming up on her captor from behind and overpowering him, she uses a decidedly feminine deception to rescue him. After sneaking into the camp dressed as a prostitute, she kills the captain she has gone in to have sex with and then goes to Rambo's aid. When they escape from the camp chased by dozens of Vietnamese and Russian soldiers, Co is killed by an unexpected bullet, only moments after Rambo has agreed to take her to Thailand with him after the mission is over. After burying her body, Rambo places her necklace around his own neck.

Fitzgerald and Co, for all of their differences of character and role in these films, share a number of features important to the accomplishment of masculine regeneration. First, both initially side with "order," with their respective governments' rules (Co's are clearly the U.S.'s not the Vietnamese government's) against the veterans. Fitzgerald chastises Braddock for being rude and Co urges Rambo to do only what he has been assigned. But both also shift their allegiances to the veterans' cause—the rescue of the POWs. Fitzgerald helps Braddock with his alibi and Co assists Rambo in his first rescue attempt of a POW. Second, both women are quickly attracted to the veterans: Fitzgerald says she will miss Braddock while he is gone and Co pleads with Rambo to take her with him to Thailand. And while Braddock (questionably) and Rambo (clearly) are attracted in turn, neither initiates a bonding; this must come from the women. As if negating Rambo's interest, the more powerful ethics of the narration kill Co immediately after Rambo agrees to take her with him. Third, neither woman has anything to do with the actual rescue of the POWs. Fitzgerald seems to side still with the government negotiating teams that believe there are no camps, and Co is killed before Rambo's final rescue attempt that actually achieves the release of the POWs.

But a more important shared feature, one that returns to Theweleit's tie between purifying waters and sexuality, is that both women are eliminated from the plots almost immediately after sexual encounters. (Although Fitzgerald is still alive, she does not speak again in the film after her good-bye to Braddock.) No evidence exists for an actual sexual liaison between Braddock and Fitzgerald, but her milder, fonder, and more sensual attitude the morning following Braddock's leap into her bed (she is dressed now in a frilled dress and not a suit) suggests that they have had sex. More austere in its reinforcement of the purity of the soldier male, *Rambo* rejects Co, not after she slept with Rambo, but with the Vietnamese captain whom she killed in order to rescue Rambo. The behavior of these women is distinct from that of their male counterparts, neither of whom expresses sexual desire or appears interested in establishing bonds with women. Braddock is nothing less than brutal in his treatment of Fitzgerald, stripping her and throwing her to her bed before leaping in after her. And although Rambo is clearly interested in Co in some way, he expresses no sexual desire for her.

After signs of their sexuality have been displayed, both women are forcefully eliminated from the narrative, both now somehow tainted and unfit to accompany these men any longer. It is as if Braddock and Rambo can accomplish their "missions" only by severing themselves from women and the sexuality they represent. In order to be regenerated and to reestablish both the POWs and their masculinity in the face of a disbelieving and hostile audience, Braddock and Rambo must be sexually pure, their masculinity unsullied by any suggestions of femininity, domesticity, order, or the body.[45]

In keeping with Theweleit's linkage of purification and masculinity, both Braddock and Rambo are regenerated after their dissociation from now "dirty" women. In order for these men to achieve their goals—the rescue of POWs/the rescue of American masculinity—they must sever their ties to women and sexuality. They must depend instead only on the male bonds (apparently desexualized) that precede and succeed the appearance of the women (Braddock knew Tuck, the man who provides boats and equipment for him and accompanies him on the mission, during the war; Rambo, although he did not know these POWs personally, is linked to them, as is Braddock, by having been himself in a prison camp). Women are, as has been seen in so many cases, excluded from these bonds. But what makes this distinction unique is its causal link to the mythology of regeneration of a victimized manhood. In order for the POWs to "come home," the bonds of masculinity must be reaffirmed and severed from women, sexuality, and the body. More to the point, these regenerative bonds are confirmed, not simply by the exclusion of women but at their expense as well. Women are forced in these representations (Fitzgerald literally) to bear the burden of masculine victimization through their "dirty" sexuality, becoming the repositories of discarded traits that do not fit the character of the "new man" being reborn in Vietnam.

## V

Several features of Vietnam representation make it an optimal arena for a regeneration of American manhood. First, because combat in American culture and representation is a stage peopled almost exclusively by male characters, the

Vietnam war provides a more stable environment within which to restore a masculinity whose dominance is being consistently challenged in terms of its relation to/positioning of women; to return to a genre/gender[46] in which women's position seems historically, socially, and economically stable invites a reorganization of masculinity on its own terms.[47] Second, because American manhood seemed itself to be on trial, with soldiers fighting and frequently being killed by women, children, and an often poorly equipped and nutritionally depressed enemy, it is important to revive the image of American strength through Vietnam, the place where it was, apparently, "lost." (This need goes a long way toward explaining the outdated invulnerability of Vietnam film heroes, who battle entire towns and scores of soldiers and come away unscathed, as well as Rambo's resounding defeat in *Rambo: First Blood, Part II* of Russian soldiers who are, presumably, stronger and better trained.) Third, because Vietnam, though undeclared, was the first war that America lost, a regeneration of the men who fought in that war accomplishes in some ways a reclamation of the war itself, so that Vietnam is reappropriated as a satisfactory encounter (for example, the "honor" of supporting a commitment was upheld, a lesson learned for future conflicts, Thailand and other Southeast Asian countries "saved" from similar fates, and so on).[48] In this way, the interests of American masculinity can be aligned with the interests of the nation as a whole. And finally, because of the American mythography of masculine bonding in wartime that disregards such barriers as class, race, and demography, war provides the logical ground for seeing Vietnam veterans as emblematic of the condition of all American men, not just those who went to war.

But at the same time that these wholesale regenerations of masculinity are being proffered through the Vietnam War and its soldiers, the social revisionism proposed in these films is linked to but not exclusively identified with other kinds of social thematics currently in operation in American culture: among others militarism, patriotism, individualism, and recuperation of America's international image. When the dynamics of films like *Rambo* are examined, it becomes clear that the primary impetus driving these narratives is the regeneration of masculinity, not, as would seem at first to be the case, a militaristic or patriotic fanfare.

That the regeneration of masculinity is the primary operation of contemporary dominant U.S. culture through which other ideological matrixes are being refurbished is made most clear in the frequent suggestions by veterans and nonveterans alike that those who fought in Vietnam can act as spokespersons for American culture, able to lead others to insights, conclusions, and behaviors needed in order to further the development of American society. In such terms, a regenerated masculinity becomes not simply an aspect but the primary project of regenerating American culture as a whole.

John Wheeler argues that the Vietnam War and the veterans who can tell us about it are the key to understanding both the present and future of American society. Citing current issues of American politics at work in El Salvador,

Nicaragua, Afghanistan, Poland, Iran, Lebanon, and Southeast Asia, Wheeler notes the extent to which they are influenced by attitudes toward Vietnam and concludes, "The great issues in our time will be impenetrable if we do not sort out how our passage in the Vietnam War years is shaping each of us."[49] And crucial to understanding these years is listening to the veteran: "Learning from Vietnam will proceed, if at all, only when our country can fully acknowledge the integrity of service and the embodiment of cherished values represented in the soldiers sent to Vietnam" (p. 29).

Wheeler sees these values as epitomized in veterans' abilities to make and keep promises and their capacity to return to America as a whole its sense of commitment and to its citizens their willingness to keep their promises. As he asks,

> Back on earth, in the late eighties and early nineties, another question arises: as the women who are wives in our generation age, which marriage commitments will endure? Which men will keep their promise? Well, which men kept their promise in other fields of social life? Will that make a difference? How true will be the man who wore the uniform or the man who went to jail rather than fight, compared to other men? (p. 143)

In light of the strategies of regeneration identified in *Rambo* and *Missing in Action*, it is not accidental that Wheeler should phrase his questions of commitment in terms of women, particularly married women, since it is these women as opposed to "dirty" women to whom men of commitment will make promises. And the veteran's relationship to American society as a whole is emblematized here in the image of marriage, as the country, the soldier's wife, best knows which men can keep promises.

Even a feminist political scientist like Jean Bethke Elshtain acknowledges this position of the veteran in his ability to act as a guide to American citizens. Her valorization of the Vietnam veterans' experience as guide to others is all the more intriguing in light of the fact that she clearly is not reinforcing the masculinity that Wheeler sees associated with the veterans' position. Her study, *Women and War*, calls for "a *way of being* in the world that promotes civic identity and connection, even—at times, especially—if the form it takes is to reject the politics of the day"[50] and seeks "exemplary figures" who can "help us get our own bearings in times of social conflict, not as characters to imitate but as persons whose struggles teach us much about our own" (p. 248). Her earlier discussion of Vietnam veterans seems to suggest that they can be such "exemplary figures":

> Not surprisingly, given the themes that dominate contemporary American culture, the Vietnam vets' struggle for self-definition emerges as a form of individual and collective *therapy*, a public and private discourse. Their needs can be structured to speak publicly to those whose lives were not cracked open violently, helping them to approach those who have been internal "others"—not just women but the majority of males of their age group. (p. 220)

They can do this, Elshtain's reading suggests, because they have been in the position of the "other," of the victim. This victimization accounts, according to Elshtain, for the increasing numbers of personal narratives by women who served in Vietnam, "because male fighters in that war have been represented, and have represented themselves, as *victims* above all—an identity to which women are interior" (p. 213). Out of this victimization, Vietnam veterans can speak to American culture and provide a therapeutic relief for its social ills, "help[ing] us to get our own bearings."

Lucian Truscott reinforces this therapeutic relationship between veteran and society while demarcating the lines between men who fought in the war and men who did not: "I think there's more personal rebuilding going on, and more success at it, among Vietnam veterans than there is among the 18 million guys who didn't go."[51] In these terms, veterans hold a privileged position not available to other men, one that enables them to speak from the position of victimization and move from there to a large-scale social regeneration based on their exclusive experiences. As George Swiers phrases it,

> There must come, through national discussion, a reckoning for Vietnam. And, very clearly, it is the war's veterans, those with insight born of deep personal tragedy, who must cry out the loudest. For it is mainly they, abandoned first on one front and then another, who have the capacity to return hope to the process.[52]

The portrayal of Vietnam veterans in popular television programs is only one indication of their promotion as spokespersons for this "rebuilding." There are, for example, numerous television law enforcers who are veterans—"Miami Vice"'s Sonny Crockett, "T. J. Hooker"'s Vince Romano, Magnum P.I., Matt Helm, and the gentlemen of "Rip Tide" and "The A Team." Much like Rambo, these characters often display a willingness to break rules, to violate standards, to operate on their own, and to base decisions on their own judgments and values rather than those of the institutions they enforce. Most insistent in its presentation of veterans as leaders is the 1986 television serial, "Amerika," in which the hero (Kris Kristofferson), who shows the way to an America that must be revived in the face of a Russian occupation (a Soviet feminization of the United States), is a veteran of Vietnam. Each of these programs suggests in some way that the veteran's experience in Vietnam has made him not only more capable but also more astute and compassionate and that the system of values he has internalized from the war is far more valid than those articulated by the society at large, which should, theoretically, be following the lead of the veteran in "rebuilding" its own laws. From these values and abilities the veteran is able to achieve what few other men can, "Mission accomplished!"

Wheeler states the mission of the veteran most clearly: "We've got to convince the other 57 million people in our generation of what it is we [veterans] have to offer and get somebody to give us a chance to *start carrying out our mission*" [italics added].[53] As Rambo, Braddock, Mr. T, and the released POWs signify, there is no doubt that these veterans, having kept one commitment, are fully capable of keeping another. But as the mythology of regeneration discussed earlier makes clear, the veterans' "mission" is intimately and inextricably linked to the restructuring of masculinity as well, so that the veteran's position as "rebuilder," as therapeutic guide, cannot be severed from his position as victimized and regenerated man. This then is their mission—the mission Rambo was released from prison to fulfill, the mission for which President Reagan will pardon him, the mission that Rambo, unlike the weaker men such as Murdock who did not fight in this war and cannot keep promises, is able to accomplish—the mission not simply to revive men who can keep promises but to revive the promise of masculinity itself.

## VI

After postulating the Vietnam veteran's role as therapist, Elshtain asks "whether the current accessibility of the 'Vietnam experience' in and through the language of victimization, estrangement, therapy, and healing will, over time, narrow the gender gap,"[54] and Wheeler claims that "The single most creative outcome of the turbulence of the war years is the emerging equality and partnership of woman and man throughout the culture."[55] Both of these statements would seem to counter the conclusion that Vietnam representation is leading to an increasing affirmation of masculinity in opposition to women and the feminine and would suggest instead that these representations are leading to possibilities of gender balance and compromise more than exclusion. A look at two of Vietnam representation's most recent films—Oliver Stone's *Platoon* (1986) and Francis Ford Coppola's *Gardens of Stone* (1987)—explain why Elshtain's and Wheeler's hopes are illusory passages of a renewed patriarachal ideology. Not moving toward a narrowing of the gender gap, these films indicate a shift in the late 1980s from Rambo's muscular masculinity to the position delineated in chapter 3 in relation to reproduction, one in which the new masculine affirms itself as incorporating, not accepting, the feminine.

*Platoon* presents as its ostensible thematic the confrontation between good and evil, a confrontation that gets quickly rephrased into a struggle between the more masculine Sergeant Barnes—battle-scarred, tough, insensitive, valuing information more than life, and wanting to win the war—and the more feminine Sergeant Elias—nurturing, emotional, eroticized, valuing life, and believing that "We're gonna lose this war." Caught in between their influence is young Chris Taylor, who sees Barnes and Elias "fighting for the possession of my soul." In the seemingly ambivalent ending of the film, in which both Elias and Barnes are killed, the film's primary question remains, as Richard Corliss asks, "Who won?"[56]

After their confrontation at the village, where Elias halts a potential My Lai massacre led by Barnes's unrelenting drive to find and kill the enemy, Barnes pursues and kills Elias in the jungle, eliminating him from his war. Although Taylor believes that Elias was murdered by Barnes, he cannot prove it and so must leave Barnes alone. But when they meet again at the end of a devastating battle in which most of their platoon is killed and their base is overrun by attacking Vietnamese soldiers, Barnes turns to battle Taylor as well. Eyes lit with animal fury, Barnes is about to kill Taylor when an air strike hits and both are knocked unconscious. When they awaken, Taylor finds Barnes crawling in the jungle, wounded but still alive. Barnes orders Taylor to get him a medic; Taylor instead raises his rifle and, in response to Barnes's hoarse "Do it," kills him. Of this dual murder, Corliss queries:

> But can Chris or the audience take moral satisfaction in this deed? Which "father" has he followed? Has Chris become like Elias, back from the grave to avenge his own murder? "You have to fight evil if you are going to be a good man," Stone says. "That's why Chris killed Barnes. Because Barnes deserved killing." Or has he emulated his enemy? Has he become Barnes in order to kill him? . . . A good man, and a murderer? (p. 59)

This apparent contradiction can be interpreted, not by reading the film through its presented moral or ethical viewpoints, which yield finally only ambivalence and confusion, but through the frame of its gendered characterizations. When Taylor kills Barnes, it would seem as if he has firmly repudiated the masculine character Barnes carries in *Platoon*, perhaps even in favor of Elias's more feminine one. But the fact that Elias has also been eliminated prevents any such simple reconciliation. Taylor has, in killing the man who killed Elias, absorbed both of their characters into his. As he says at the film's close, "Elias is in me and so is Barnes. . . . I felt like a child born of these two fathers." Why is this not the narrowing of the gender gap desired by Elshtain or Wheeler's balanced equality between men and women? Why is it not the androgyny many feminist critics call for and celebrate?[57]

A look at the manner of the two killings begins to provide an answer. When Barnes kills Elias, it is a deliberate and not accidental or even impassioned killing. Elias looks directly at Barnes, smiles, drops his rifle, and seems not to believe that Barnes will really shoot him. After a moment of hesitation, Barnes calmly raises his rifle and fires. Taylor's murder of Barnes is similar. If he had killed Barnes the previous night during the rage of battle and in self-defense, it would have been possible to see Barnes's death differently. But Taylor, like Barnes, raises his rifle with all deliberation after Barnes indicates as well that he thinks Taylor will not fire, almost taunting him by saying, "Do it." The shooting of Barnes is one that Taylor performs openly, without emotion, compassion, or hesitation. It is, as Corliss writes, that Taylor had to "become Barnes in order to kill him," or, as Rhah says, "Only Barnes can kill Barnes." His survival, though it may occur in the shadow of Elias's image, must replicate Barnes's actions.

Taking the law into his own hands in the style of television's Vietnam veterans, Chris Taylor's character at the close of *Platoon* rests firmly in the masculine realm. Although his motivations may be affected by the feminine, it is through the masculine that he survives. Much like Rambo's acknowledgement of Co's character in wearing her necklace, Chris Taylor's feminine character is a mere ornament to his masculine body.

And from this body he speaks the message of the Vietnam veteran in a voice that echoes Wheeler's. Taylor's concluding monologue reiterates the therapeutic, almost messianic role of the veteran in relation to American society: "Those of us who did make it have an obligation to build again, to teach others what we know and to try with what's left of our lives to find a goodness and meaning to this life." But what Taylor's final character forces us to realize about that "goodness and meaning" is that it is inscribed within these gender constructions. The "battle between good and evil" that is the film's ostensible subject gets rewritten as the struggle of masculinity to produce its self anew, now rejecting its simpler, older image—Barnes—and presenting the newer man who has appropriated the feminine to himself. Consequently, *Platoon's* presentation of good and evil is circumscribed by the masculine point of view, so that its ethics and moral vision are not "universal" but driven by the masculine. Its restitution of "goodness and meaning to this life" can occur only through the masculine; its prophetic voice is man's.

Coppola's *Gardens of Stone*, like *Platoon* an apparently antiwar film and thus seeming to go against the Ramboesque imagery of much Vietnam representation, repeats *Platoon's* construction of the "new man" as incorporating the feminine and then establishing the masculine point of view as a position from which to teach meaning to society as a whole. But whereas *Platoon* shows us the birth of the son as new man, *Gardens of Stone* portrays the father.

Although the war is still being fought, *Gardens of Stone*'s main character is already a veteran, having served two tours of duty in Vietnam and been promoted to the Old Guard regiment that is the nation's honor guard. Clel Hazard (James Caan) is Rambo's opposite. Although equally devoted to his country, he is in doubt about the validity of this war, thinking it's a "screw-up." He is cultured, enjoying classical music and fine wines; an expert on Persian rugs; a gourmet chef; sensitive and patient with women, respecting their independence; willing to accept opposing political views, proposing to a writer for the *Washington Post* who is firmly against the war and has been arrested in demonstrations; and willing to do things by the book, not breaking rules as Rambo does. It would seem then that his character would openly contradict the kind of regeneration *Rambo* accomplishes, shifting instead toward that more androgynous character that balances masculine and feminine.

But in spite of Clel's closeness with "Sam" Davies, the *Post* reporter, his firmest and most meaningful bonds, and clearly the most delighting scenes of the film, are still masculine. He and Homer "Goody" Williams (James Earl Jones), a black sergeant major, have been through Vietnam together and now serve together in the Old Guard. As their toast at the dinner party with Betty Rae Williams and Sam Davies declares: "Here's to those like us." "Damn few left." The toast is repeated at the wedding of young Jack Willow, son of their Army friend. Both are moments when women seem to be gaining some status in these men's lives, and both toasts serve as exclusionary signals confirming the primacy of masculine bonds. And even though Clel may not agree with the way the war is being fought, he is still bonded to the Army itself, speaking of it as if it were his true family: "I care about the U.S. Army. It's the only one I got."

Clel becomes Willow's surrogate father in this film, taking the place of Willow's real father, unseen throughout the film, who finally dies of a heart attack. Signifying Willow's inherited participation in the bond, young Jack wants his father to be buried at Arlington. Clel places on the father's casket one of his own medals that Willow, Sr., never got, noting Clel's supremacy to Willow's father and exchange of roles with him at the burial.

But Clel is father to more than Willow. His surrogate fathering of Jack Willow becomes emblematic of the relationship he feels to his troops as a whole, wanting to teach them things that might help them survive Vietnam, things they cannot learn from anyone but a veteran. In order to accomplish this, he takes on the "worst job in the Army," playing the part of the enemy Vietnamese soldiers during maneuvers. Clel, who respects the Vietnamese and their tenacity—they fight with arrows against American technology—echoes William Broyles's bonding with the Vietnamese enemy in favor of men who never fought in the war. Here soldiering crosses barriers between men that would otherwise be impassable. Clel and his "sons" become the Vietnamese for a short time and defeat the entire battalion. When higher ranking officers are embarrassed, only Goody, who has "been there," can find him and persuade him to stop.

Clel's fathering gains its greatest force in the film in that the women around him do not have children. His becomes the only avenue for reproduction in *Gardens of Stone*, fathers producing sons without the intervention of mothers (as Chris Taylor is "born of two fathers" in *Platoon*). Sam Davies tells Clel early in their relationship that she is unable to have children. Although Clel does have a child with his first wife, now in a mental institution, their child is a daughter whom Clel never sees. She and the wife, who divorced Clel when he decided to go back to Vietnam for his second tour, are quickly dismissed from the film's narrative, and Clel's relationship with a now sterile woman replaces his personal familial focus. And with Willow dead, Rachel, his widow, is also childless. Even Betty Rae Williams is caught in this characterization through a joke that Willow makes early in the film, before he meets her. During an inspection of the barracks in which young troops are asked sexually explicit questions in order to discomfort and embarrass them, Goody asks Willow, "How do worms copulate?" When Willow replies "Asexual reproduction," Goody asks, "Who first came up with that idea?" Willow's reply, "Your wife, sir?" implicates her as well. The only images of reproduction associated with women in this film are then of sterility or asexuality, in sharp contrast to the fathering Clel performs for his numerous troops.

This thematic of fathering deflects the otherwise antiwar impulses of the film, constructing it instead as an affirmation of masculine bonding and parenting in the face of a sterile world. Crucial here is the film's structure. Opening with shots of the graves and a burial at Arlington, the sound track records helicopter blades rotating while voices talk of going down to pick up wounded after a firefight. Then, during the burial scene, which we later find out is Willow's, Willow's voiceover recites a letter he wrote to Clel from Vietnam: "I'm here. But it's all wrong. I knew it would be blood and guts and death. . . . I don't think I have the answers anymore. Only the questions." At this point, the film moves back in time to Willow's arrival at Fort Meyers in 1968 before he met Clel and went to Vietnam.

Opening on a note that suggests disillusionment with the war and its death, the camera panning over the countless graves of Arlington, the film returns to this scene at its close, importantly repeating the identical burial we have witnessed at the film's opening. Yet now the context has changed. Not only do we know the characters of the scene, we have also lost Willow's voiceover and his questioning. Instead, Clel speaks, saying of Willow, "I know him. And I won't forget him." The questioning voice of disorientation and meaninglessness has been replaced by the voice of the answering father, whose inability to "forget" his son insures a continuity and meaning that the film's early narration lacked.

Significantly, Clel has decided to return to Vietnam, not because he believes in the war any more than he did, but because he feels that he can teach these young men things that will help them survive. Blaming himself for Willow's death, he laments, "What a sorry goddamn excuse for a man I am," as if not fulfilling this role as cultural father makes him less of a man. His return to Vietnam is clearly motivated by this father-son bonding, not by any political or social ethic portrayed in the film. In fact, the film's apolitical nature insures the masculine thematic, leaving, as did *Platoon*, only the circle of masculinity as determination of meaning in this film. The questions that Willow cannot answer in the opening are framed within the film to be answered by Clel Hazard, a veteran of Vietnam who has remembered his manhood and his responsibility as patriarch to "teach them what we know."

Both *Platoon* and *Gardens of Stone* show the next stage in the regeneration of American masculinity that is taking place through the character of the Vietnam soldier/veteran. Early on the veteran was shown as weakened, confused, and marginalized, as in *First Blood*. His character then shifted to the reborn and purified veteran of *Rambo: First Blood, Part II* and *Missing in Action*, a man whose experience and knowledge of Vietnam led him, not to helplessness, but to a superiority; this man is able to accomplish things, like the rescue of POWs, that men who did not fight in Vietnam are incapable of. Although Rambo walks off into Thailand at the end of his second film, his presidential pardon signifies a reintegration that *First Blood* denied.[58] Finally, this most recent stage of films like *Platoon* and *Gardens of Stone* narrates the veteran, not only as a superior individual, but as a superior leader for society as a whole. His is a voice that can heal wounds, provide direction, offer commitments, and fulfill promises. Vietnam veterans have traversed in these few years (1982–87) from child to adolescent to father, from outsider to leader, from destructive rebel to wise patriarch, from feminine to masculine. They carry with them, not the women's movement that "sped to fulfillment across [their] backs," but, as the freeze frame ending of *Missing In Action* displays, the returning POWs, the discriminated and now revived symbols of American masculinity.

Both *Platoon* and *Gardens of Stone* end on a salute. Before his rise in the helicopter that takes him out of Vietnam and brings him back to the world, Chris Taylor gives a final salute. Although he has been watching his buddies who survived, he is not looking at them when he salutes; his eyes shift to the side. He salutes an indeterminate soldier, perhaps his final goodbye to Elias, perhaps to his friends who died in the firefight, perhaps to Vietnam itself. And Clel Hazard closes *Gardens of Stone* with a salute to Willow and the graves at Arlington. It is as if both men, now off to deliver their messages and teachings to the rest of the world, are offering a final note of comradeship, duty, and connection to the men who fell before them, to those they will not "forget," to those who died pointlessly in this battle of gender and whose bodies now pave the way back to the manhood they fell to defend. The salute is the sign of a respect earned and a promise made, a promise to make the deaths of these men worthwhile, a promise to restore the manhood lost in Vietnam.

# FIVE

## "ACT BEFORE THE FIGHTING BREAKS OUT" The Feminization of Loss

The last chapter explored what I have elsewhere called the cultural "debriding" of the Vietnam veteran[1]—the successive removal of "dead tissue" in order to "reveal" the "healthy" body that lies beneath—for the purpose of regenerating the images and constructions of masculinity in contemporary American dominant cultural representations. A major part of that process was the gradual sloughing from that image its associations with and subjection to the feminine, so that Rambo and Colonel Braddock rejected femininity in all of its forms (including the sexual) and Clel Hazard and Chris Taylor appropriated it into the masculine field of reference. Given the dialectical and mutually defining nature of gender constructions, those associations with the feminine originally attached to the veteran could not have disappeared from these narratives but must instead have been deposited elsewhere. This chapter locates those deposits and explores their interrelationship with the promotion and definition of masculinity in contemporary American culture.

Separated from the veteran, the shifting positions and identifications of the feminine in Vietnam representation lead to the portrayal of the feminine as a multiple characterization, one primarily associated in recent years with the United States government. In contrast to this feminine character is established a centralized masculine unity, one that operates single-mindedly to accomplish what the feminine cannot—"winning" the war. This chapter explores the ways in which the multiplicity of the feminine in Vietnam representation can be used as a means for analyzing the operation of U.S. late capitalist culture and addresses the possible consequences of such constructions for current feminist theories and strategies.

### I

The litmus test for determining inscriptions of the feminine in Vietnam representation is blame for loss of the war. Numerous culprits have been identified throughout the years since it became apparent that America was losing the war in Vietnam. Early on, most of that blame was placed on the individual combat soldier who was seen not to measure up to the soldiers who had fought in previous wars. Because they served one-year tours and not the "duration"; because they had what were perceived as luxuries unavailable to former soldiers—ice cream, beer, maids, R & R to Hawaii, Australia, or Hong Kong;[2] because they had sophisticated technology to employ against an apparently ill-supplied and poorly trained enemy, the American soldiers in Vietnam, in the eyes of many of America's veterans from other wars, should have been able to win their war with ease.

Even those who disapproved of the war blamed soldiers for fighting in it, believing either that they should have decided not to fight or that they were "baby-killers" and somehow enjoyed it. As Lucian Truscott phrases it, soldiers were being "discriminated against"[3] because of the public focus on their individual activities rather than on the larger issues behind the war's operations. When demonstrators would come up to West Point, "the closest uniforms around" (p. 111), Truscott criticized them for not going over to "the Harvard Business School, where they were being trained to go down and sell war stocks, war profiteering" (p. 111). Films like *Coming Home* finally found the soldier blaming himself for his activities. As Luke laments in the closing scenes, "There are a lot of things I did over there that I'm not very proud of."

But in subsequent years blame for loss of the war began to shift. Whereas Luke would blame himself and pinpoint his adversary in the Marine recruiting officer who speaks before him to a high school audience of young men, Rambo, only two years later, would repel much of this blame from himself and place it instead on the shoulders of a vaguely defined and unspecified "somebody." In his final breakdown in *First Blood*, Rambo cries out with frustration to Trautman, "I do what I have to do to win, but somebody won't let us win." Contrary to earlier characterizations, he and his fellow soldiers *did* do their job in Vietnam. If the war was lost, this interpretation reads, it was not because the individual solider failed to do his job.[4] But at this point, although Rambo can begin to discard some of the blame for the war's loss, he cannot yet name another source. For him, it is still only a "somebody" who would not "let" the soldiers do their job. Loss belongs here clearly to that "somebody" and not to Rambo or his fellow soldiers.

The following year, 1983, Peter Goldman and Tony Fuller's anthology of personal narratives by Vietnam veterans makes a first effort to label this position more specifically. Their collection, *Charlie Company*, is subtitled, "What Vietnam Did To Us." In addition to participating in the establishment of the veteran-as-victim mythology, their subtitle now locates blame for the veterans' suffering in "Vietnam." Throughout the book, Vietnam takes the confused shape of the war itself, of the untrustworthy nature of Vietnamese allies, of the enemy's strategies and deceptions, even of the unfamiliar terrain (as one soldier remarked, "It wasn't Tennessee"[5]). But in spite of the move toward identifying

Vietnam as itself at fault, the phrase, "What Vietnam Did To Us," still focuses on the war as an interpersonal relationship in which the soldier has been victimized by the war and its circumstances. The move from Rambo's "somebody" is indistinct and diffuse.

In sharp contrast, by 1984 and 1985, with the production of *Missing in Action* and *Rambo: First Blood, Part II*, blame for loss of the war is now clearly defined. "Vietnam" mediated the translation of blame from the soldier to the United States, specifically to the government, with senators, bureaucrats, and CIA agents all assisting in the project of negotiation and public relations that now explains how the war was lost. In this scenario, the individual soldier has been completely exonerated for the loss of the war, with Rambo and Braddock successfully and courageously defeating the best the enemy has to offer, be they Vietnamese or Russians. Each of these heroes is set apart as an emblem of the American fighting soldier, one who can return to Vietnam and now, able to fight without constraints, win their war. As Peter Travers said in his review of these recent Vietnam films, "This time we win."[6] What lost this war, this most recent interpretation reads, was not the soldier but those who prevented the soldier from doing his job. And whereas *First Blood* left the culprit for this loss unnamed as "somebody," *Rambo* is precise about the enemy. Although tortured by both Vietnamese and Russians, Rambo's most cheered line in the film is not his accusation of these enemies, but his promise to Marshall Murdock, a Washington bureaucrat, when he finds out that Murdock deliberately aborted the mission that could have rescued Rambo and a POW: "Murdock, I'm coming to get you."

Blame for loss of the war is the consistent index of a shifting category in Vietnam representation. What marks this category and enables it to remain stable while still being occupied by multiple features is the representation of the feminine, principally the stereotypical characteristics associated with the feminine in dominant U.S. culture—weakness, indecisiveness, dependence, emotion, nonviolence, negotiation, unpredictability, deception. Each of the inhabitants of blame in turn takes on and then repels some of these qualities.

In *Coming Home*, Luke, initially an angry, violent, and resentful veteran, becomes sensitive, nurturing, nonviolent, and expressive of emotions by the film's close. His physical weakness—he is paralyzed and in a wheelchair—is foregrounded throughout the film as a nonthreatening posture in sharp contrast to the stiff-backed soldiers who still believe in the war. And although his actions toward the end of the film, particularly chaining himself to the fence of a recruiting base to prevent others from entering the war, indicate a strength and decisiveness, this strength is clearly a nonviolent and passive one (he is carried from the gate by soldiers) in contrast to his own violent anger in the beginning of the film. The price of his release from the hospital was his gradual containment of this anger and violence, now effectively neutralized (feminized/castrated.)[7] And Luke's increasingly feminine—some would say feminist—

characteristics parallel his growing expression of blame for his activities in the war, so that by the final scene he is both confessing his guilt and crying.

In speaking of "Vietnam" as occupier of the position of loss, different negative feminine qualities are foregrounded, particularly the perceptions noted by so many veterans of a deceptiveness, indecisiveness, and weakness. Michael Herr's *Dispatches* said of Vietnam that "reading [maps of Vietnam] was like trying to read the faces of the Vietnamese, and that was like trying to read the wind."[8] An unpredictable and deceptive ally in the South Vietnamese, a treacherous enemy in the North Vietnamese who did not seem to fight by the same rules of warfare as had applied in previous wars, even a duplicitous and hypocritical populace—all combine in veterans' accounts to depict "Vietnam." And, as Doc declared in *The 13th Valley*, these are characteristics shared by the Vietnamese with women: "Women. They all the time doin somethin jus so you can't expect why. They's like the dinks. If you expects them in the valleys they's gonna be on the hills and if you expects them on the hill they's gonna be in the valley. Women like that. They figure out what you expects then they do just the opposite."[9] "Vietnam" is typified in American veterans' accounts by this elusiveness, deceit, and treachery.

But since 1983, with the production of Ted Kotcheff's *Uncommon Valor* and *Missing in Action* in the following year, the signifier of loss has shifted again, this time to be named specifically as the United States government. And again it is the qualities of the feminine, now thoroughly repelled by the soldier, that belong to the government. As the following discussion shows, the tactic of negotiation with the current government of Vietnam, specifically in reference to the return of extant POWs or the remains of MIAs, is perceived and depicted as feminine and in stark contrast to the more direct, muscular, and effective actions of the veterans/soldiers.

On the most straightforward level, the affiliation of women characters with the government marks the occupation of the feminine position associated with loss in Vietnam representation. *Missing In Action*'s Fitzgerald is a representative of the State Department accompanying Senator Maxwell Porter on a fact-finding and negotiating mission about the POWs. Although initially presented as aggressive, articulate, intelligent, and well informed, she capitulates to Braddock's forceful overpowering of both her body and character. As noted in the previous chapter, when he physically strips and throws her to her bed, she becomes nothing more than an "alibi" to him. Effectively subordinated to his physical force, her assertive character is shown to be no more than an "excuse" for a typical woman underneath, one who succumbs to Braddock sensually and expresses jealousy and longing at his departure.

The women of *Uncommon Valor* represent three different aspects of the feminine repeated throughout Vietnam narratives and all finally rejected by the veterans of the successful POW rescue mission: (1) alienation from the bonds formed by soldiers during war, (2) neglect and repression of the memories and men of Vietnam, and (3) the economic devaluation of the war and its participants.

Jason Rhode's wife, Helen, typifies the inability of women—even the wives and mothers of military men—to comprehend the intimacy and tenor of masculine bonds, especially those between father and son as soldiers. In the first sequence of the film, Jason recalls a time when young Frank, frightened by a thunderstorm, came dressed in a baseball uniform to his parents' bedroom. Jason held out his hand to his son while Helen slept. Remembering this episode, Jason holds out his hand again to his now missing son and cries, while again, Helen sleeps, ignorant of both the bond that was formed and the pain of its separation. She is not simply indifferent to but is entirely unaware of the bonds that exist between soliders and between father and son.

More active and thus more threatening than Helen Rhodes (who never speaks a line during the film) is Mrs. Wilkes, distinguished from the more supportive Helen Rhodes by the filmscript's omission of her first name. Mrs. Wilkes tries forcefully to prevent her husband from accompanying Rhodes on his mission. Telling him first, "Listen, my husband doesn't want to talk to you," she then implores, as if of the war itself, "Look, why don't you just do me a favor and go away?" She complains to Rhodes, "It's taken me ten years to get that goddamn war out of his head." But displaying how clearly this excision is her effort and not her husband's, Rhodes looks around at the twisted metal sculpture Wilkes has produced and responds, "Looks to me like it's still in his head pretty strong." She finally attempts physically to stop Rhodes from entering the studio where her husband has been hiding. Pushing her aside with only somewhat less force than that used by Braddock on Fitzgerald, Rhodes attacks Wilkes directly, shouting, "What did you send your wife out here for? Don't you have the guts to come out here and talk to me yourself?" Tearfully watching as her husband comes out to talk to Rhodes, Mrs. Wilkes is powerless in the face of the bonds that exist between these men and the memories they share of the war.

Referring explicitly to the psychological state of her husband—"It's taken me ten years to get that goddamn war out of his head"—Mrs. Wilkes represents efforts to repress emotional and mental memories of the war. While Helen Rhodes simply was unaware of the very physical bonds that exist between soldiers, Mrs. Wilkes takes an active role in attempting to destroy those bonds. But her speeches make clear that these efforts are primarily in her own interest and not her husband's. When she tells Rhodes "do *me* a favor and go away" and emphasizes her efforts in altering her husband's memory—"It's taken *me* ten years"—she underscores the extent to which these desires are hers, imposed onto her silent and tormented husband, forced to express the pain of his memories on inanimate metal because his wife wants him to forget them [italics added]. And, as Rhodes points out, those memories have only been temporarily repressed, not changed. All it takes is the presence of other soldiers to revive them.

Mrs. "Charts," the least of the wives, is identified only by her husband's nickname, showing the distance that separates her from her husband; she is not even in possession of his real name or, consequently, of his real character. Unlike Mrs. Wilkes, she is basically indifferent to her husband. When Rhodes arrives, she is preparing to go to "happy hour" at a local bar. Dressed in pink, combing her blond curls, she tells Rhodes, "You know, maybe you *should* take him back to Vietnam. He sure as hell doesn't give a damn about anything around here." She stays only long enough to ask Rhodes, "If he did go, how much would he be paid?" When she leaves, Charts removes the sunglasses that she told us he has not taken off for six years and looks at Rhodes.

Not trying to repress Charts's memories of the war, Mrs. Charts seems stupidly indifferent to them except in the basest economic terms. More concerned about her own "happiness" than her husband's peace of mind, she cares only about how much money his war experience can gain for them, not what the experience has done to him. His distance from her is marked by the dark glasses through which he must look at her and she him. Only another soldier can see directly into the eyes of the veteran and understand. Mrs. Charts looks only at their wallets.

John Clark Pratt's *The Laotian Fragments* (1974) offers two female characters who add dimension to these depictions of women as emblems of government positions in Vietnam representation. Mary, wife of Major William Blake, seems most simply to stand for women's exclusion from any understanding of war and its bonds. As her husband writes to her:

> It's funny, but being at war gives one a chance to think—about his family, his home, his ideals, his values (no, my love, I'm not going to engage in what you call my "big-word generality")—*but why not, you bitch, you'll never try and understand anyway about my sense of duty.* [Italics added][10]

But more than this exclusion is Mary's own resistance to believing in the reality of the war itself. When she writes to Blake asking for a divorce, she explains: "I know how it looks—husband away at war and all that—but I can't really bring myself to believe that you are at war, just on another one of your trips. It certainly doesn't seem like a war here" (p. 55). She literally and figuratively divorces herself from the war and the men who fight it because it "doesn't seem like a war here," from her point of view, displaying her refusal to see the war from the point of view of the soldier who fights it, to whom it seems very like a war.

While in Vietnam, Blake meets Valerie Horowitz, daughter of the head CIA official in Saigon. Sleeping with so many of the Air Force pilots that it is said she should be their "personnel officer," Valerie approaches Blake through explicitly sexual terms:

> Here's poor little me, the daughter of the Big Chief—I'm not so bad, am I?—and there's a constant flow of neat young men coming every day—the best America has to offer—except they all look alike. Steely blue-eyed and dedicated. The faces never change—only their cock size. . . . But someday there'll be one who's not really married and I'll just woo the shit out of him and he'll take me away from all this and there won't be any bad memories because nobody will ever be able to talk about it. (p. 61)

Blake doesn't have sex with Valerie, although he's told by someone who does that "Valerie's a lousy piece of ass—plays with herself while you're screwing her. Poor girl" (p. 70).

Each of these characterizations of women signifies a different aspect of the U.S. government and its attitudes toward and treatment of the Vietnam solider/veteran as depicted in these narratives. Making explicit contacts with the State Department, the CIA, the military, and Congress, implicit threads are connected as well to the general government evaluation of the soldier/veteran's worth and value, as well as to attitudes of the American public that are seen to have affected government policy and action both in Vietnam and toward the veteran. Combined, these images create a picture of a government that not only failed to win the war but also failed in its responsibility to returning veterans. Chief among the characteristics of failure is the depiction of the government's negotiating posture toward the governments of both South Vietnam and the Republic of Vietnam. This posture is perceived as weak, passive, easily deceived (and yet capable of deceiving veterans), nonaggressive (read primarily as a failure to use aggression when appropriate rather than a decisive action itself), and, most important, ignoring or deliberately repressing the interests of the soldier/POW/veteran.

Fitzgerald's position in *Missing in Action* as spokesperson for the State Department and "alibi" for Braddock leads directly into her use as emblem for the government she represents. Her own assertive character, shown by Braddock's forcefulness to be a cover for a more stereotypically sensual and emotional feminine personality, indicates a government that is structured the same: an exterior of tough talk masks a basically weak and capitulative interior. All of the negotiating positions and determinations soon give way, for example, to Vietnamese denials that there are any POWs in Vietnam. Senator Maxwell Porter, chief U.S. negotiator, is fully prepared at the end of the film to return to the U.S. with this Vietnamese denial and not press for any further information. It is only Braddock's last minute arrival with one POW under his arm and several more behind him that shows the inaccuracy of Vietnamese statements and the inadequacy of American negotiations.

But *Missing In Action* provides a twist on the feminine, for Porter and Fitzgerald are bested by Vietnamese negotiators who are themselves characterized as feminine. It at first appears to be contradictory that a feminine negotiating position would itself be defeated by yet another feminine character, but *Missing In Action* employs this confrontation to underscore both the multiplicity of feminine possibilities for failure and the ascendancy of the unitary masculine over all of these types. Colonel Trang, chief Vietnamese negotiator, is, for example, characterized as quiet, deceptive, nonaggressive, and fearful. Trang's most feminine moment is, not uncoincidentally, in his bedroom. Braddock sneaks into Trang's house and finds him sleeping under ethereal white mosquito netting, sleeping in white silk pajamas beneath pink satin covers. Holding a knife at Trang's throat (the feminine male can only be treated with violence, not eroticism, by the American masculine),[11] Braddock threatens to kill him if he does not tell where the POWs are. Although Trang lies, he finally reveals the camp when Braddock presses the knife into his flesh. When Braddock leaves, Trang pulls a pistol from beneath his pillow and fires; Braddock then kills Trang with his hurled knife.

This feminine imagery, surrounded by the deceptively inverted threats of a sleeping femininity, is, like Fitzgerald and the government she represents, equally defeated by Braddock's forceful action. Both are silenced by Braddock's physical appearance and material insistence (he produces the POWs). His victories suggest that an equally forceful treatment of the government by the military would have brought about a similarly satisfactory and successful conclusion to both the war and the plight of the POWs. Rather than quietly acceding to the negotiating posture, Braddock's character suggests its literal overpowering, accomplished (both for Fitzgerald and Trang) through clearly sexual terms. And by immediately preceding Fitzgerald's scene with Trang's, the implied threat of death if she does not capitulate is maintained. Staging the scenes with Trang and Fitzgerald in bedrooms, along with the sexuality that is implied there, rewrites the encounter of force and submission—of masculine and feminine—as rape (both heterosexual and homosexual). Braddock puts his knife to Trang's throat and strips Fitzgerald as an insistence of the distinction of the masculine to accomplish its goals.

The dual characterization of the feminine—as negotiating (the U.S. government) and as deceptive (the government of Vietnam)—allows the U.S. government's actions to be viewed as perhaps more innocent than those of the Vietnamese (the Vietnamese know there are POWs), thus maintaining a subtle racism that is transfigured as gender.[12] The implication remains that the U.S. government was somehow tainted, as were Theweleit's soldiers, through its contact with the "dirty" female,[13] here compounded, not by class, but by race. Race is used here to couch threats of masculine violence against feminine positions. The murder of Trang echos throughout *Missing in Action* as a reminder of the capability of the masculine not only to overpower but also to eliminate the feminine, a threat that must finally be turned against the U.S. government itself. Braddock's actions against Fitzgerald underwrite the forcefulness of the scene in *Rambo: First Blood, Part II* when Rambo raises his oversized knife above Murdock's head and finally stabs it into the table by

Murdock's ear. The threat of rape and murder is combined as the threat of masculinity against femininity, though clouded by an ostensibly male/male situation.

The multiplying of the feminine that occurs in its use as signifier for both U.S. and Vietnamese governments is portrayed in opposition to the unitary and thus more powerful singularity of the masculine, a character that does not vary, waver, or negotiate. Multiplicity is the most negative feature of the feminine: it can be attached to several governments at once (Braddock has only one loyalty), be inhabited by both the male and female (as Braddock's sexuality insists, he is only male), is led by emotion to alter its decisions (unlike Fitzgerald's changing opinion of Braddock, he maintains only one purpose throughout the film), and, whether innocently or no, conspires in the repression of the masculine (both governments try to deter Braddock from finding the POWs). In this way the threat of feminine multiplicity is negated by the masculine and thus suggests, as I discuss later, that one of the strategies of the masculine in dominant U.S. culture is not to repress this multiplicity but to augment its production in order to enhance its own singularity.

Jason Rhodes, former Marine colonel, offers a speech in *Uncommon Valor* that interweaves the images of the feminine presented in the characters of the three wives. Telling his rescue team that "you men have got what it takes," he goes on:

> There's a bond between you men as strong as the bond between my son and me. 'Cause there's no bond as strong as that shared by men who've faced death in battle. You men seem to have a strong sense of loyalty because you're thought of as criminals. Because of Vietnam. You know why? Because you lost. And in this country, that's like going bankrupt.

Building on this economic motif, Rhodes suggests that the U.S. government won't return to rescue the POWs because "there's no *gain* in it." From here his theme shifts subtly to the government itself, to the "politicians that never lost a single son in Vietnam." Recapitulating *Missing in Action*, Rhodes explains, "They've been negotiating for ten years. Well, the other's side's not buying," concluding, "Gentlemen, we're the only hope these POWs have. So we're going back there. . . . And this time—this time—nobody can dispute the rightness of what we're doing!"

Rhodes here captures all of the wives' positions in the film and then links them to the government. Echoing the scenes in which he recalls his son while his wife sleeps, Rhodes insists that the bonds between these men are identical to those of father and son, effectively excluding women from their relations. But more clearly, Rhodes's insistence that "there is no bond as strong as that shared by men who've faced death in battle" targets directly the insufficiency of the mother/child bond—this mother sleeps when her child is in trouble, but the father acts. When Rhodes declares that no politician's son died in Vietnam, he is drawing attention to their alienation from these bonds as well, since they, like the mothers, have been insulated from the death in battle that draws these men together.

In the government's ten-year negotiations, Rhodes reiterates the weakness of Senator Porter and his team. But it is not accidental that the two citations of this ten-year period come here and in Mrs. Wilkes's attack on Rhodes, "It's taken me ten years to get that goddamn war out of his head." The government's negotiating posture is here aligned with efforts to repress recognition of the war and the men who fought in it, symbolized by denying the existence of men who are still prisoners of war," that is, still suffering from the government's failure to win in Vietnam.

But the clearest connection comes to the most alienating image of the feminine in the parallel between Mrs. Charts's mercenary interests in her husband and the government's economic devaluation of the Vietnam soldier. Interested only in "how much would [her husband] be paid," Mrs. Charts articulates what the government will not state directly—that these soldiers can be evaluated only in monetary terms, not, as they might have expected, in terms of patriotism, bravery, loyalty, and so on. Marshall Murdock puts an actual figure on their value in *Rambo:* "Do you think somebody's going to stand up on the floor of the United States Senate and ask for a couple of billion dollars for a couple of forgotten ghosts?" In the ledger books, these sums read "billions" versus "zero," a clear indication of the price the U.S. government is willing to pay for the POWs. As can be expected, Colonel Trautman again states the truth most baldly. When Murdock's men refuse to go down and rescue Rambo and another POW from the pursuing Vietnamese, he yells, "You goddamn mercenaries! There's men down there. *Our* men!" The helicopter pilot's reply captures the government's position succinctly, in a catechism that will echo throughout Vietnam representation of these years: "No, *your* men. Don't be a hero." In this scenario, it is the government that is mercenary, only willing to do what it can perceive monetary benefits from. Trautman's display of loyalty and value for human life is translated by Murdock's government men into a braggadocio heroism. But the most scathing indictment of Murdock and his men is in their denial of any relation except monetary to the soldiers who fought in Vietnam; they're not "our men," they tell Trautmen, but "your men."

Valerie Horowitz's speech to Major Blake in *Laotion Fragments* offers yet another turn of the feminine in its link to the government, the rendition now familiar in feminist criticism of the apparently polarized feminine positions of seductress and saint or, in this case, whore and fairy princess.[14] Daughter of the CIA chief in Vietnam, Valerie's link to the government is not as direct as Fitzgerald's but is nonetheless more insidious, since none of the soldiers fighting in Vietnam really understands the CIA's actions or decisions. Phrasing the plea that seems a combination of the Big Bad Wolf and the U. S. government's defense for entering Vietnam, Valerie asks Blake, "I'm not so bad, am I?" As a whore who uses men, Valerie evaluates them only on one basis, importantly not the one on which they value their own performances in the war: as she says, "there's a constant flow of neat young men coming every day—the best America has to offer—except they all look alike. Steely blue-eyed and dedicated. The faces never change—only their cock size." To her, as to the CIA, these men are all the same, and both she and the CIA rapidly consume "the best America has to offer" with little regard for their "faces." Their self-absorbed oblivion to the needs and characters of soldiers is underscored in the assessment that Valerie is "a lousy piece of ass—plays with herself while you're screwing her."

But immediately following her encomium of American soldiers, Valerie switches to the saint/princess character of the feminine, dreaming that "someday there'll be one who's not really married and I'll just woo the shit out of him and he'll take me away from all this and there won't be any bad memories because nobody will ever be able to talk about it." At the same time that they use these soldiers for their "cock size," both Valerie and the CIA dream of getting "away from all this," from the entanglements of Vietnam. Able to use only these soldiers as bodies, both want in fact to "marry" them (are they already married to other women or to the military and their commitments?) as knights in shining armor to take them "away from all this." And then Valerie concludes, "How's that for openers, Mister Chief Raven FAC who has a wife named Mary the same as my mother's name. Would you like to be my father too?" (p. 61). Enlisting here the imagery of virginal saints and helpless daughters, Valerie ties the sexual and the fantastic into one, standing as virgin and seductive daughter before her savior father. The roles of authority reverse, with Blake and his fellow soldiers becoming the knowledgeable, already married father figures of the war. But their forced submission to the decisions of the CIA/Valerie cause these fathers to lose the war, not through any fault of their own, but because wars cannot be run by mothers/virgins/whores/daughters. When the father's authority is challenged and he becomes only a body, a "cock size," failure is inevitable.[15]

Tracing uses of the feminine in Vietnam representation leads thus to a recognition of the feminine as a shifting and multiple signifier, applied variously to individuals, countries, governments, and sexes. As *Missing In Action* and *Uncommon Valor* both display, that multiplicity is not sequential but simultaneous, so that the feminine is portrayed in varying characters and characteristics at the same time. It finally is not, according to these narratives, the individual characteristics of the feminine that are most destructive—Mrs. Wilkes can be pushed aside, Fitzgerald can be overpowered, Trang can be killed—but their shifting multiplicity. Although Rhodes's rescue mission is successful in retrieving American POWs, he is too late to save his own son, who died earlier of disease. In the logic of the film, his son might not have died if the U.S. government had not been feminized into a negotiating posture that altered its position with every new wave of public sentiment. The ability to occupy contradictory positions simultaneously is the greatest threat to the singular masculine.

Although the feminine is used chiefly to account for failure and to provide explanations about the loss of the war, what becomes apparent is that the feminine is used finally to identify the "enemy"—that against which the soldier had to struggle in order to fight and possibly win the war in Vietnam, whether the Vietnamese, a difficult landscape, or the U.S. government itself. Not the official enemy of governments or armies, this is the enemy of the soldier. Given contemporary representations of the Vietnam veteran as emblematic of American masculinity itself and the war as a battle for the stability of masculinity in American culture, the feminine is then not merely the enemy of soldiers but the enemy of all American men.

## II

The single most destructive feature of the feminine in Vietnam representation, representing variability itself, is negotiation. Klaus Theweleit's German soldier male insists on a nonnegotiating posture:

> It is not weapons that stand at the forefront of defense. . . . it is, rather, ideological constants that offer immunity from the mire; *clarity of thought is what these men are after*. . . . Representing interests, making compromises, negotiating, reaching goals in roundabout ways, planning for the long run, or taking both sides into account: all these methods are contaminated, at once male and female, in short, mire. [italics added][16]

The negotiating posture, so common a characterization of the U.S. government in recent Vietnam representation, is tainted because it is both male and female. For this reason women are so often affiliated with the government or its positions. To be both male and female is to invite the destruction of the singular point of view from which action can occur.

Rambo, Colonel Braddock, Jason Rhodes, and others like them demonstrate the "ideological constants" that bolster their actions. Rambo makes this clearest when confronted with Marshal Murdock's techonological array of the most up-to-date computer equipment. Murdock—the feminized government official who cannot stand the Vietnamese heat, drinks refrigerated sodas, and sweats out the film in shirt and tie in contrast to Rambo's bared and tanned chest—relies for his knowledge and decisions on computer graphics, radar equipment, and special radio devices. After reviewing all of this equipment, Rambo simply replies, "I've always believed the mind is the best weapon," underscoring the singular nature of individual thought in contrast to the multiple voices of technology. Importantly, setting himself apart from the kind of masculinity conveyed by a now parodied and insufficient James Bond heroism, Rambo jettisons all of Murdock's hi-tech equipment before he parachutes into Vietnam. In fact, this equipment almost causes Rambo's death when it catches onto the airplane from which he is being dropped. And Rambo's final defeat of the

Russians comes not from any use of the hi-tech helicopter that he is flying but from outwitting the enemy, proving that "the mind is the best weapon." It is not simply that Rambo chooses not to use Murdock's methods—he will surely die if he does. "It is not weapons that stand at the forefront of defense."

As Thweleit's own language suggests, this multiple posture is not simply a contrast to the singular thought and action of the soldier male but is a direct threat to it. Sinking into this mire is "contaminating," while "ideological constants" offer "immunity" from its infection. Rambo is literally lowered into the mire of a leech pond when he is captured by the Vietnamese in *Rambo: First Blood, Part II*. Then tortured by the Russians and abandoned by Murdock, who "aborts" the rescue mission, Rambo escapes with Co's help. Purified by the rain after her death, Rambo reenters the camp alone, strengthened, and now "immune," to best all of his enemies, including Murdock and his computers.

The multiple body that has succumbed to the negotiating posture of the male/female is, in these terms, diseased, "contaminated," and capable of infecting all but the strongest soldier male resisters. The power of the multiple feminine to disrupt singularity is portrayed as extremely strong here, its effects rippling like tremors from an earthquake through society. Only males who have been in quarantine have survived without contamination—Rambo was first in a POW camp and then a U.S. prison, Braddock was in a POW camp, and Rhodes's men are gathered from various marginal areas: mental institutions, beaches, isolated art studios, and remote farmland (the only exception, and the only man not of the original team, is the black helicopter pilot, his connection to fighting contagion validated in his profession of hospital administrator).

Protected from the feminine and its disease, these veterans can become emblems of a revived masculinity that has not, like those associated with the government, been "contaminated." For this reason the most recent of Vietnam representations—films like *Gardens of Stone* and *Platoon*—return for their settings to the early years of the war (whereas *Rambo*, *Missing in Action*, and *Uncommon Valor* all occur in the present, with veterans returning to Vietnam after the war is over). In an effort to retrieve the uninfected male and return him to the present, they return to a time before contamination has occurred, before the country itself had succumbed to the influence of the multiple feminine.

Like these fictional narratives, nonfiction personal analyses of the Vietnam war repeat the pattern of the unified masculine fighting the multiple and shifting feminine. Much like Rambo and Braddock, Richard Nixon portrays himself as singly battling a feminized government, himself the hero of "ideological constants" confronting a multiple and varying enemy, Congress. "We won the war in Vietnam," Nixon declares. "Congress proceeded to snatch defeat from the jaws of victory."[17] His most pointed criticism of the actions of the Congress in relation to Vietnam is its unwillingness to maintain its commitments to support the government of South Vietnam after the U.S. troop withdrawl. It is this retreat from its promises, according to Nixon, that lost the war for South Vietnam.

Changing its position on supporting the government of South Vietnam with continued military supplies and retaliatory bombing if the North broke the treaty agreements, Congress' feminine duplicity led to weakness, inaction, and failure.

> Objective military analysts have stated that South Vietnamese soldiers were, man-for-man, better fighters than the North Vietnamese. They lacked nothing in spirit. . . . Congress turned its back on a noble cause and a brave people. South Vietnam simply wanted the chance to fight for its survival as an independent country. All that the United States had to do was give it the means to continue the battle. Our South Vietnamese friends were asking us to give them the tools so they could finish the job. Congress would not, so our allies could not. (p. 202)

This is the process of contamination. Congress, overly influenced, according to Nixon, by vocal antiwar demonstrators in the U.S., succumbed to their influence, causing it to lose its own ability to act firmly and with strength. In turn, the inaction of Congress led directly, for Nixon, to the defeat of South Vietnam. "On the eve of their battle for survival, our South Vietnamese allies were in their weakest condition in over five years" (p. 192). Nixon records the statement of General Van Tien Dung, commander of North Vietnam's forces in the South, that "we increasingly took the initiative and grew stronger, the enemy grew weaker and more passive every day" (p. 195).

A weakness that had begun with a minority voice had spread across the globe and affected not only Vietnam but other nations as well. After summarizing the atrocities that occurred after the North Vietnamese takeover of the South and the Khmer Rouge occupation of Cambodia, Nixon blames Congress and the antiwar movement for allowing these massacres to happen.

> As the plight of the Cambodian and Vietnamese peoples became publicized in the late 1970s, many antiwar figures reacted in horror to the consequences of their own policies. . . . A generous view of the antiwar movement's position would be that there was no way they could have known what would happen in the wake of our defeat. But it *was* known—and they *should have* known. (p. 208)

Nixon blames their "willful ignorance" (p. 208) for the situations in Vietnam and Cambodia, an ignorance that led to "inaction" and a "grotesquely twisted moral sense" (pp. 208–209).

But the infection did not stop even here. "After we failed to prevent Communist conquest in Vietnam, it became accepted dogma that we would fail everywhere. For six years after Vietnam, the new isolationists chanted 'No More

Vietnams' as the dominoes fell one by one: Laos, Cambodia, and Mozambique in 1975; Angola in 1976; Ethiopia in 1977; South Yemen in 1978; Nicaragua in 1979" (p. 212). These failures constitute what Nixon calls "America's first international losing streak" (p. 212), all a result of those first contaminating voices of failure who chose inaction over action, weakness over strength, and losing over winning.

In sharp contrast, Nixon's willingness to act and to enforce his commitments with power achieved what Congress could not. Before the congressional capitulation and the loss of South Vietnam, Nixon's bombing campaigns, he argues, decisively set back Communist activities. In Cambodia, for instance, "Our air strikes represented the critical bargaining chip that made a Cambodian settlement possible" (pp. 176–77). And in Laos, when Pathet Lao forces threatened to gain power, Nixon's bombing campaigns and halting of the withdrawl of mines from Hanoi harbor led to a cease-fire (p. 177). But with Congress hampering presidential powers, these advantages were lost. For Nixon the failure lay clearly with congressional inaction and variability, not with his own "ideological constant." As Nixon writes, "It was not a failure of presidential will—I was willing to act—but an erosion of congressional support. . . . In May [of 1973] I no longer could have mustered the votes necessary *to back up my strong words with strong actions*" (p. 178) [italics added]. The ability to act is, for Nixon, like for Rambo and Braddock, the key to accomplishing his single-minded goals. Congress and its feminine kin, the antiwar demonstrators, refused to acknowledge the necessity of action and instead depended on words and treaties.

> [A]ntiwar critics were naively ignorant of the fact that diplomacy cannot succeed without power to back it up. . . . Foreign leaders who oppose our course of action are seldom brought along by reason and persuasion alone. . . . [D]iplomacy is helpless unless combined with direct military pressure. Nothing would convince Congress of this simple fact of international life in 1973. (p. 179)

Reminiscent of Braddock's use of force to overpower Trang and Fitzgerald, Nixon advocates force as a tool of international policy. It is because, he writes, "we abandoned the use of power in Indochina" (p. 209) that we lost the war in Vietnam.

Closely aligned with the narrative themes of *Rambo: First Blood, Part II*, *Missing In Action*, and *Uncommon Valor*, Nixon's presidential position is directly opposed to the negotiating and weakened posture he applies to Congress during the final years of the war in Vietnam. Like these veteran-heroes, he depicts himself as acting singly against the finally overwhelming passivity of a feminized Congress that chooses "retreat" over "defeat" (p. 200). Like these heroes, he shows how decisive and straightforward action accomplishes what no amount of negotiation can—the defeat of the enemy. Nixon finally succeeds in constructing the real enemy of South Vietnam, not the North Vietnamese, but a

U.S. Congress that failed to back up "strong words with strong actions," a Congress whose contaminating influence is spreading this disease of failure and weakness throughout the globe. Nixon, firmly enmeshed within the government, his hands tied by Watergate, cannot maintain the immunity of a Rambo or a Braddock, and his cause, unlike theirs, is finally lost. The soldier male in government, no matter how willful and single-minded, cannot survive.

John Wheeler does not hesitate to link this variable, weakened, and passive attitude in the United States to what he calls the "feminization of the culture."[18]

> If the Vietnam War represented a *defilement*, then in some sense the fashionability of being a man, and of expressing oneself as a man was eclipsed. Men grew long hair. Some became "flower children." The language reflected a recoil from the verb "to tell." Instead one would prefer to "share" an idea. *We shrank from the exercise of power and strength,* which in the culture of our childhood was largely associated with masculinity. [Italics added] (p. 79)

The "defilement" that was Vietnam affected not women but men, causing them to become like women, growing long hair and wearing flowers, being immersed in Theweleit's "mire," "at once male and female." This contamination led directly to a loss of the strength and will necessary to action, so that verbs of direction, command, and hierarchy were replaced by verbs of submission, passivity, and community—of sharing rather than telling.

In the same paragraph, Wheeler moves quickly to the most drastic consequences of this feminization, not the long hair of stateside hippies but the lives of soldiers:

> When long after the war, North Vietnamese commanders told Richard Armitage that they had kept their eye fixed on political developments back stateside, they expressed a truth which most GI's sensed in the sixties. "Somehow, the irresolution back home is jeopardizing me while I'm here." . . . One thing that matters to a trooper is *his* life *in the next fifteen minutes*. One mechanism of these deaths was the rigorous controls on American troopers on engagement, pursuit, and free-fire. . . . One reason for these tight constraints was certainly the great political vigilance back home (p. 80)

—a vigilance characterized by a feminized culture. For Wheeler, as for Nixon, these feminized postures of passivity and weakness caused countless deaths both during and after the war. Whereas for Nixon the greatest threat was in the loss of country after country to Communism, for Wheeler, it is the loss of the world itself: "Because of unresolved guilt and grief over Vietnam *and of the lost idea of masculinity* [italics added], our generation has diminished its ability to defend America and is psychologically unable to implement a military draft even if plainly needed. *Nuclear deterrence is weakened* [italics in original]" (p. 203). The contamination of the feminine is therefore not to be viewed inconsequentially but significantly, not only for America, but for the world as a whole.

Because his paragraph begins with feminization (he names Jane Fonda as a particular culprit[19]) and ends with rules of engagement and free-fire, it is not difficult to trace Wheeler's connection between limitations on battle strategies and limitations on masculinity itself. As warfare is hampered, put under "tight constraints," so is the power of masculinity "to tell." What intervenes between these narrative poles of feminization and constraint is the climax of the story, death. "One thing that matters to a trooper in war is *his life in the next fifteen minutes*. One mechanism of these deaths. . . ." It is as if the feminization of culture is itself responsible for these unnamed deaths by placing masculinity under constraints so that it can no longer "exercise power and strength." Wheeler's argument is thus less about war in Vietnam than about the larger "warfare" occuring in American culture in the battle for the reclamation of masculinity from contamination and defilement. And his formula for the loss of this battle is simple: stripped of masculinity, men will die; succumbing to feminization, the country will follow.

## III

In all of these examples—*Missing In Action, Uncommon Valor, Rambo: First Blood, Part II, No More Vietnams*, and *Touched with Fire*—women or what are perceived as the feminine characteristics of weakness, passivity, nonaggression, and negotiation are shown to be responsible for America's loss of the war in Vietnam. Whether ascribed to American soldiers, the Vietnamese people, Vietnam, or the U.S. government, these features are associated with the figure that is blamed for failure. Though blame has shifted, its signifying characteristics have not. Affiliated with the feminine, this fluid and consistent shifting of positions for blame indicates that the feminine, not any of these single entities of "Vietnam" or the government, is the subject of representation here. It then becomes clear that one of the critical functions of Vietnam representation in contemporary American culture is to maintain and propagate an image of the feminine as multiple, varying, unpredictable, and, consequently, threatening and contaminating (recall Mailer's image, discussed in chapter 1, of the cancer that is infecting America) and that the *specific* depictions of war, militarism, and the "enemy" are less motivated and more liable to change.

For example, the films discussed here cannot be said to endorse either the current military or governmental structure because each of the POW rescue missions is forced to work against the U.S. government *and* military commanders. And though the films are made in locations that resemble possible future sites for U.S. combat operations more than they resemble Vietnam (Mexico, the Phillipines, St. Kitts-Nevis), their casts of characters are not representative of the proportions of potential recruits who would be fighting in such battles (the soldiers in these films are disproportionately white in comparison to current racial distributions of the American military[20]). Nor do they represent the ideal of the military soldier, as none of these heroes follows orders or works within the proper chain of command. As Lieutenant Colonel John F. Cullen, spokesperson for the U.S. Army Recruiting Command in 1985, said of Rambo, "This is not the kind of guy we want for our poster boy of the '80s."[21] Although intertwined throughout these representations, a straightforward militarism or patriotism cannot be said to be the chief goals of current or recent Vietnam narratives. Their numerous statements of loyalty to America and celebration of its fighting soldiers serve primarily as spectacles to distract from the construction and depiction of the threat of the feminine.

The chief structure of these representations is then not explicitly political, militaristic, or even simply a parade of violence. It is instead the opposition created between the multiple and contaminating feminine (contaminating because multiple) and the unitary and immune masculine, the masculine that has remained single and consistent, according to John Del Vecchio's Egan, throughout "10,000 years of human warfare perhaps 100,000 years perhaps for the entire age of man perhaps earlier."[22] All Egan or any of these characters need do is "relax" and tap into "his heritage as an American, as a man, as a human being" (p. 179). As in Del Vecchio's novel, the figures in these representations who possess this single-mindedness of "ideological constants" are consistently favored over those who alter their opinions, negotiate, or waver—over those who side with, hide behind, or are women. Charles Griswold reads this opposition even in the monuments of the Washington Mall, explaining that "Washington [as representative of the presidency] was a man of action rather than words; the Capitol is the home of endless talk, a trait traditionally, albeit tendentiously, associated with womanliness."[23] In this context, Nixon, Rambo, and Wheeler occupy the same position, presenting themselves as besieged by the feminized culture that surrounds them, unable to do their jobs effectively because of it, and unable to save the lives of those who fall prey to its influence. In the most contemporary terms, to this list must be added the projected media character of someone like Oliver North, who depicts himself as at odds with the cumbersome bureaucracy of democracy and victim of a wavering congressional opinion (at one time supporting and then withdrawing support for the Contras). His single-mindedness, pursuing his beliefs in contradiction to stated U.S. policy, marks him as the epitome of the unitary and self-contained image of the masculine produced in and through current Vietnam representation. In the eyes of the American public, his specific political positions are in most ways irrelevant; it is his image of steadfast singularity that signifies his success as a media production.

The shifting, variable, and disruptive features attributed to the feminine in Vietnam representation are the very features of the feminine celebrated by many feminists, in particular by French feminists like Luce Irigaray, Helene

Cixous, and others who call for a new style of "feminine writing" that deliberately employs these strategies of multiplicity to disrupt the unified discourse of masculinity. As Irigaray declares:

> "She" is indefinitely other in herself. That is undoubtedly the reason she is called temperamental, incomprehensible, perturbed, capricious—not to mention her language in which "she" goes off in all directions and in which "he" is unable to discern the coherence of any meaning. . . . It is therefore useless to trap women into giving an exact definition of what they mean. . . . They are already elsewhere than in this discursive machinery where you claim to take them by surprise.[24]

And in contrast to the negation of simultaneity in Vietnam representation, Irigaray says of the feminine voice in writing, "Simultaneity would be its distinctive feature."[25] Josette Feral sees this as a "simultaneity which rejects fixed and immutable meaning and the rigidity of the One. . . . Nor would this movement go in any single direction. The text would explode in all directions at once, exactly the way woman's body (and sex organs) explode into fragments" (p. 550). Much of French feminism thus foregrounds exactly the features attributed to the "enemy" in Vietnam representation.

Not only do these feminist writers speak of many of the same characteristics of multiplicity and unpredictability that plague Vietnam representation; they celebrate them. Rather than the despised and repressed, these are the features that the feminine embraces. It is, for example, Helene Cixous's tactic to foreground in the feminine the very characteristics rejected by the masculine. As Diane Griffin Crowder explains,

> Cixous' strategy for women is to adopt many of the traits stereotypically attributed to women in male discourse. Flowing, formless language, irrationality, the unconscious, maternal nurturance, rejection of power, and being closer to the body are prized in her theory of "woman's writing."[26]

These, the features characteristic of the "enemy" in Vietnam representation, are turned against masculinity itself in the theories of many French feminists to provide women a position from which to write their own narratives and characters.

The "jouissance" of the feminine in the writing of many French feminists is, for all intents and purposes, inverting the relationships between the feminine and masculine portrayed in Vietnam representation, where the feminine is consistently presented as that which is to be repressed, defeated, and overcome. The multiple that is seen as deceptive and untrustworthy by Vietnam writers is celebrated in these theories as a plurality that is generated by women's bodies themselves and not by stereotypical projections of masculinity:

> [Women's] sex organ which offers nothing to the view has no distinctive form of its own. . . . The *one* of form, the individual sex, proper name, literal meaning—supersedes, by spreading apart and dividing, this touching of *at least two* (lips) which keeps woman in contact with herself. . . . *She is neither one nor two*. She cannot, strictly speaking, be determined either as one person or as two. She renders any definition inadequate.[27]

This body *is* multiple, plural, undefinable as is the feminine that is its expression in culture. It is not then unexpected that this is the body repelled by the soldier male, the body that Rambo and the soldier male must deny in order to remain "pure." Bodily purity thus becomes inseparable from the unification of character and purpose, a unification that is threatened by the multiplicity of the feminine body and its plural manifestations.

In the eyes of these feminists, the "contamination" of masculinity by women is a necessary rather than an avoidable consequence of the feminine. As Cixous declares, "A feminine text cannot fail to be more than subversive. It is volcanic; as it is written it brings about an upheaval of the old property crust, carrier of masculine investments; there's no other way."[28] The threat perceived by the masculine in Vietnam representation is then, in these terms, quite real, for this celebration of the very feminine that masculinity attempts to reject is nothing short of, to use Cixous's frame, war.

The principal difference between the terms of portrayal of French feminist theories and Vietnam representation is a distinction between multiplicity and fragmentation, in other words, what is perceived by feminist theorists as a multiplicity to be embraced by women is portrayed by the masculine as a fragmentation of destruction. The tension between these terms is not unacknowledged by writers like Irigaray when she asks, "Must the multiple nature of female desire and language be understood as the fragmentary, scattered remains of a raped or denied sexuality?" Her answer is significant:

> The rejection, the exclusion of a female imaginary undoubtedly places woman in a position where she can experience herself only fragmentarily as waste or excess in the little structured margins of a dominant ideology, this mirror entrusted by the (masculine) "subject" with the task of reflecting and redoubling himself.[29]

Thus, the perception of fragmentation is one viewed within the frame of a masculine ideology, one that wishes to suppress female power through denying it a place of meaning. It is, as Rosi Braidotti explains, "woman's basic historical condition."[30] The multiple feminine is, however, separated from history, is women's positive experience, not of this rejection, but of their repressed selves, hidden beneath fragmentation. And, for Irigaray, the promotion of the feminine would not lead to a simple mimicking of the masculine in which the multiple would become singular as it gained power: "Woman would always remain multiple. . . . That does not mean that she would appropriate the other for herself, that she would make it her property. Property and propriety are undoubtedly rather foreign to all that is female."[31]

But, as some feminist critics have pointed out, there are dangers to this theorization of the feminine. In particular, the risk of reinstating a masculine-defined gender structure through the valorization of that which the masculine denies as feminine. Ann Rosalind Jones, in agreement with critics like Christine Delphy and Collete Guillaumin, explains: "Rather than questioning the terms of such a definition (woman is man's opposite), *feminité* as a celebration of women's difference from men maintains them. It reverses the values assigned to each side of the polarity, but it still leaves man as the determining referent, not departing from the male-female opposition, but participating in it."[32] It is this point that I would like to pursue in relation to the characterization of the feminine in Vietnam representation.

## IV

Analyses offered earlier in this chapter suggest that Vietnam representation is, in one and the same gesture, employing the multiple feminine as its signification of failure *and* promoting multiplicity as an end in itself for the feminine, responding to "contamination" not through "celebration." This is one of the strategies that Dana Polan attributes to American late capitalism and its formations in mass culture.

> while an older capitalism emphasized a psychical, financial frugality centered on the father as the principal productive force . . . the late capitalism of what we now refer to as post-industrial society . . . is a capitalism that encourages excessive expenditure, that desires a desire that is not sublimated or organized within the frame of the Oedipalized family. . . . *The moment of late capitalism may work not so much by a repression as by a positive incitation, an invitation to individuals to exceed previous boundaries, to be in excess of an analytic, literally conservative control of productivity.* [italics added][33]

Thus, the very strategies for feminine writing advocated by Cixous, Irigaray, and others—unboundedness, negation of unitary paternal authority, subversive pluralities—may, in contemporary U.S. dominant cultural formations,[34] be mimicking rather than throwing into upheaval the structures and productions of the masculine. In such a context, "feminine writing" becomes merely yet another form of "excess" rather than subversion.[35]

Polan necessarily ties the productions of capitalism to representations of sexual difference, suggesting that "the power of spectacle is inextricably linked to the functions of sexual difference in late capitalist society; that is, *the offer of a freedom from logics, from rational controls, is often held out to a male at the price of the reification of woman* [italics added]" (p. 185). This is how the operation of "feminine writing" can be used against itself: the very ends it desires are projected by capitalism onto the position of the masculine, showing the masculine as now occupying the position of diversity and a desire for a liberation from unitary authoritarian controls once ascribed to the feminine. There are two consequences of this: one, that the feminine is reinstated as the voice of authority and control against which the masculine must struggle in order to achieve "excess" and, two, that the strategy of plurality is made unavailable to the feminine as a ground for its own materialization.

Vietnam representation displays the complexity of these operations, principally by revealing that they are not separate but simultaneous, constructing the feminine as both authority and multiplicity, effectively employing each characterization to negate the power of the other. Let me work through one example.

In *Uncommon Valor,* women and the characterizations of the feminine they represent are aligned with voices of traditional authority, particularly those of the United States government, as senators, high-ranking military officials, and even IRS bureaucrats enact the positions established by the three women in the film, specifically in their combined efforts to repress continued activities relating to the war in Vietnam. What Mrs. Wilkes has been trying to get out of her husband's head for ten year is just what the U.S. government itself wants to close off references to, to the point of denying the existence of POWs when they are known to be alive. It is against this repressive authority that Rhodes and his men must pose their "excess," a "freedom from logics, from rational controls." They are defying at all stages the controls placed on them by the government, finally even buying their weapons from an underground expatriate Frenchman in Thailand when the U.S. government confiscates theirs. (Similarly, Rambo jettisons his equipment provided by the government, the only hi-tech machinery he employs being that stolen from the Russians.) Rhodes's team is composed of characters who already live on the margins of controls, enacting "excess" individually—Blaster living on beaches, Sailer in a mental institution (after being a member of a motorcycle gang), Wilksie in artist's studios—but ineffectively.

But at the same time that the women in *Uncommon Valor* are being used to inscribe voices of authority, they are presented as fragmented in their separation from each other and through the numerous ways in which the positions they represent are enacted by government officials and the Vietnamese. More important, the context of Vietnam representation in which they are framed insists on the constantly shifting nature of these positions so that they are constructed differently, from *First Blood* to *Rambo: First Blood, Part II,* for instance. These positions, unlike those of the men on Rhodes's team, cannot be rejoined into a unified force, and therefore their power, for all of their affiliation with authority, is nullified.

Thus the feminine is denied at any stage a relation to power. When speaking in voices of authority, that authority is shown to be weakened and wrong; when employing multiplicity, that diversity is depicted as a fragmentation unaware of itself. Importantly, the characterization of multiplicity is not denied the feminine but insisted on, "celebrated." Women and the positions they represent are foregrounded as plural and diverse instances of a muted and defeated authority, one that is made, in Vietnam narratives, to appear increasingly rather than decreasingly multiple.

It is here that Polan's thesis can be elaborated to address the masculine. While late American capitalism is promoting "excess" and "a freedom from logics," it does so while insisting that "excess" be subject to and available for recombination. At this historical point in time, I would suggest, the mechanism for that recombination, what Polan calls the "spectacular combining, or merging, of all sorts of residual and emergent forms" (p. 185) is the masculine point of view, a point of view that presents itself as expressing the desire for excess at the same time that it offers, through recombination, a unified centrality that channels that desire into ostensibly satisfactory forms. Thus, the individual members of Rhodes's team were powerless in their "excess" to achieve anything with their lives and were trapped within a system that betrayed them. Rejoined, their "excess" channelled by Rhodes into a reentry into the masculine, they were powerful and successful.

In contrast, the positions of the feminine are denied access to recombination except through men. Mrs. Rhodes can hope to see her son again, not through the workings of the government, but through her husband's rescue mission; to recall an earlier reference, Sam Hughes of *In Country* can only join the collectivity of Vietnam through her father and her "own" name as a man appearing on the Vietnam Memorial. In this way the feminine is denied power in Vietnam representation, its multiplicity being presented only as fragmented failure.

There is, then, an inversion taking place in the construction of multiplicity and unity in Vietnam representation. While the masculine position is vocalized as "excess," desiring liberation from rules and rational constraints (just as Rambo quickly abandons his orders and the "constraints" of the technology assigned to him), it is structured as unification through the recombination of "excess" under the centralized point of view of the masculine. In this way, late American capitalism can safely portray itself as allowing, even promoting, the expression of similar desires for "freedom" at the same time that those desires are brought under control and defined through the position of the masculine. In contrast, the position of the feminine is foregrounded as unification through its affiliation with traditional voices of authority, while it is structured through a fragmentation and diversity that lead only to failure. Consequently, the feminine allows for the expression and recuperation of authority, but only as it can finally be reintegrated into the masculine point of view, while effectively denying women and the positions of plurality they represent any access to power. By presenting traditional voices of authority as irreconcilably fragmented and by presenting the feminine as a failed plurality, American culture disallows either of these as alternate power bases for responses to the masculine, denies them except *through* the masculine.

What a reading of Vietnam representation then suggests is that a valorization of plurality as an end in itself, as a strategy for contemporary American feminism may be misdirected in the context of late American capitalism's own appropriation of plurality and "excess" as aspects of its own structures. What it also suggests is that a response directed at the operations of capitalism itself is disfunctional. To the extent that any such response ignores the overlapping constructions of gender, particularly of the masculine point of view, those operations will remain veiled to analysis. The masculine point of view's appropriation of "excess" as a stage in the recombination of centralized power formations should, at this historical moment, be a primary object of feminist concentration.

The shifting identifications of the feminine as location for loss correspond to the gradual regeneration of the masculine that has taken place in recent years in American culture. By bringing that loss "home" to rest in the government itself, Vietnam representation has succeeded not only in recuperating the veteran as the emblem for a revival of masculinity but also in denying what has been the most singly successful avenue for challenges by the American women's movement to that masculinity in recent decades—government legislation and institutionalization of civil rights. Thus by attacking the government in Vietnam representation as feminine, multiple, and weak, constructions of the masculine can negate both the authority of the government to enact civil rights and the unification of the feminine as a political force in the women's movement. Read in these terms, it becomes apparent that Vietnam representation is only topically "about" the war in Vietnam or America's military strength or political policymaking. Its true subject is the masculine response to changes in gender relations in recent decades, its real battle that of the masculine to dominate and overpower its "enemy"—the feminine.

# SIX

# THE REMASCULINIZATION OF AMERICA

Representations of the Vietnam War in American culture have become increasingly popular and increasingly foregrounded in recent years, from the "Rambo" phenomenon to television heroes' disarming willingness to reveal their previously "secret" Vietnam pasts (such as "Miami Vice"'s Sonny Crockett). As previous chapters have shown, this popularity marks more than an acceptance of the war and its veterans, though this is its presumed apologia. Instead, representations of the war have been used as a vehicle for the expansion and specification of altered gender relations in which an apparent liberation of gender roles has given way to a redefined masculinity that presents itself as separate from and independent of an opposed feminine. As I have shown in these chapters, this shift is part of a process that can best be called "the remasculinization of American culture." Let me summarize the logic of this process as I have presented it here.

The groundwork for regenerating masculinity is the mythos of masculine bonding. The masculine here represents itself as a "separate world," one that poses survival—finally the survival of masculinity itself—as depending on the exclusion of women and the feminine, a world in which men are not significantly different from each other and boundaries of race, class, education, age, geographic location, and ethnicity are overcome in favor of the ties between "men who have faced death together" *(Uncommon Valor)*. Necessary to maintaining this illusion of exclusivity is a response to the role of women in reproduction, what seems to be the surest challenge to an autonomous masculine economy. Only by appropriating reproduction to itself can the masculine succeed in sustaining that "separate world" from which women can then be fully eliminated.

Vietnam representation thus succeeds in producing an arena of masculine self-sufficiency, but as long as this project was defined solely in terms of the Vietnam War, its impact would be limited historically and demographically. The next step in the process of remasculinization was to bring that separate world "home" so that its logic could be applied to an American society in which, as John Wheeler declared, "masculinity had gone out of fashion." To this purpose, the male Vietnam veteran—primarily the white male[1]—was used as an emblem for a fallen and emasculated American male, one who had been falsely scorned by society and unjustly victimized by his own government. It is this portrayal of veterans' experiences as "class" victimization that enabled masculinity to place itself in the category of a social group in need of special consideration. No longer the oppressor, men came to be seen, primarily through the imagery of the Vietnam veteran, as themselves oppressed. It was not then difficult to insert this characterization into an already formulated cultural attitude toward the victimized that had been established in relation to civil rights and women's movements, to the point that hiring quotas and organizations like NOW were seen as depriving men of their "rights." The final step in this process was to transfer the accumulated negative features of the feminine to the government itself, the primary vehicle for legislated and enforced changes in civil rights. From this vantage point, not only could individual men cite discrimination (Jim Baake), but all men as a group could also declare their suffering at the hands of a government biased toward and operating under the aegis of the feminine.

Consequently, the Vietnam War and its veterans became the springboard for a general remasculinization of American culture that is evidenced in the popularity of figures like Ronald Reagan, Oliver North, and J. R. Ewing, men who show an open disregard for government legislation and legal decisions and favor images of strength and firmness with an independence that smacks of Rambo and confirms their faith in a separate culture based on a mythos of masculinity. At the same time, the appearance of recent television programs in which fathers play the primary parent figures—"My Two Dads," "Paradise," "Full House," "Who's Dad?," and "Year in the Life"—and, perhaps more to the point, in which men play paternal figures who help society at large—"The Equalizer," "J. J. Starbuck," "Highway to Heaven," and even "The A Team"—testifies to a renewed interest in patriarchal figures as sources of security and guidance. They are in direct line with films like *Gardens of Stone* and their portrayal of Vietnam veterans as leaders who can return an unstable America to prosperity. Monica Collins's review of the 1987 television season confirms that the "separate world" of Vietnam has come "home" to America. As she concludes, "men prevail. . . . [M]en out on the streets making them safe for the men taking care of the kids."[2]

This remasculinization has occurred, not as a result of, but certainly in consolidation with the war in Vietnam. The war and its representations have been successfully employed as vehicles for a renewed sense of American masculinity, one that has, as popular opinion would declare, altered its role and character. But as these images make clear, that alteration has not increased a flexibility of gender roles so much as it has simply redefined them in a manner that is equally excluding and, more significantly, equally damaging to women and those who are the subjects of masculine domination. A look at one of the most acclaimed of Vietnam narrations, Stanley Kubrick's *Full Metal Jacket* (1987), will display how these gender roles have become, since the years of the war, more rather than less defined and firm, and more rather than less threatening.

Nineteen hundred sixty-eight, the year of the publication of both the first essay that would later become Michael Herr's *Dispatches*[3] and the production of *The Green Berets*, marks the first appearance of popular texts about American involvement in what came to be known as the war in Vietnam. Though earlier novels had addressed, whether explicitly or cryptically, an American presence in Vietnam—Eugene Burdick and William Lederer's *The Ugly American* (1958), Graham Greene's *The Quiet American* (1955)—it was these two works, along with television reports of the war, that first brought portrayals of American combat soldiers to the attention of the American public.

Almost twenty years later, Michael Herr collaborated with Gustav Hasford and Stanley Kubrick to write the screenplay for the highly acclaimed *Full Metal Jacket*, based on Hasford's 1979 novel, *The Short-Timers*. The years between 1968 and 1987, roughly the years covered in this study, have been the temporal location for a radical shift in the ways in which the Vietnam War and its soldiers have been represented and narrated. During this time, the images and constructions of the masculine in American culture have been renegotiated and regenerated.[4] Although the terrain for this renegotiation has been called "Vietnam," as I have argued here, its real name is the feminine or, more precisely, gender itself.

*Full Metal Jacket*, a rewriting of a 1979 novel with the participation of a 1968 author, produced in 1987, captures the full circuit of change described here, principally in the alteration of its closing lines as the new ending for the cryptic LURP story Herr first told in 1968. In contrast to Herr's fear of the LURP/narrator, Joker closes the film by saying, "I'm in a world of shit but I'm alive. And I'm not afraid." The process outlined in previous chapters has come "alive" in Kubrick's film to reveal a masculinity that is "not afraid" of telling its tale.

Gustav Hasford's *The Short-Timers* is a novel about the making of Marines. From their introduction to Parris Island to their battles at Hue and Khe Sanh, Hasford follows men who change in one year from high-school reporters to platoon leaders and "killers," "indestructible men, men without fear."[5] Refusing the simple tale of "innocent turned killing machine" that is so easily told about Vietnam, Hasford insists on the complexity of his characters, men who see the war clearly and who fight it anyway. As Joker says: "I'm not the author of this farce, I'm just acting out my role. It's bad luck to wear green on stage but the war must go on. . . . I'm just a snuffy. A corporal. I don't send any body out to get blown away. I know that getting killed over here is a waste of time" (p. 161). Not the troubled boys manipulated by the "Green Machine" of a film like *The Boys in Company C*, these are men who kill and get high from it. After Rafter Man gets his first kill, he calls out, "Am I bad? Am I a menace? Am I a life *taker?* Am I a heart *breaker?*" (p. 119), and afterwards, they all "sleep like babies" (p. 122). The ambivalence of Hasford's characters is captured in Joker wearing both a peace button and a helmet decorated with "Born to Kill" written across it. These men kill if they have to, enjoy it if they can, and want the war to end, all at the same time.

There are three crucial scenes in Hasford's novel that become important points of translation for *Full Metal Jacket:* the killing of Gunnery Sergeant Gerheim by the recruit he has nicknamed "Gomer Pyle," the hunting and killing of a female sniper in Hue who has expertly picked away at the members of the Hardass Squad until they are all dead, and the confrontation with an unknown sniper at Khe Sanh who mercilessly fires rounds into members of the Lusthog Squad as they try to save those who are already down. An examination of the corresponding scenes in the novel and the film will show a shift that has occurred between 1979 to 1987—from an ambivalent gender construction to a reaffirmed and confident masculinity that defines itself in opposition to an enemy feminine.

Gomer Pyle, seemingly too dumb to understand Marine regulations and behavior, is berated by Sergeant Gerheim until he breaks, becoming a crack recruit, finally selected as the "outstanding recruit from Platoon 30-92" (p. 24). After graduation, he is heard talking to his rifle, Charlene: "I LOVE YOU! DON'T YOU UNDERSTAND? I CAN DO IT. I'LL DO ANYTHING!" (p. 27). When Sergeant Gerheim comes in, Pyle, who has loaded a full magazine into his rifle, fires point blank and kills Gerheim, accusing him of trying to take Charlene: "NO! YOU CAN'T HAVE HER! SHE'S MINE!" (p. 29). Shortly afterward, he places the rifle barrel in his own mouth and fires.

When Joker arrives in Hue and joins Cowboy's Lusthog Squad, he is told about a sniper who has killed another squad in their platoon. After "shooting off fingers, toes, ears—everything" (p. 109), the sniper finally kills all nine members of the squad who came out to try and rescue each other. Cowboy's squad chases this sniper into a row of mansions until she finally emerges in full view: "She is a child, no more than fifteen years old, a slender Eurasian angel with dark, beautiful eyes, which, at the same time, are the hard eyes of a grunt" (p. 116). Although Rafter Man fires several rounds into her, she does not die. As they gather around her maimed body, the squad members debate what to do with her. Animal Mother wants to "leave the gook for the mother-loving rats" (p. 119), but Joker says, "We can't just leave her here" (p. 119). Finally, Joker tries to place himself in her position: "I look at the sniper. She whimpers. I try to decide what I would want if I were down, half dead, hurting bad, surrounded by my enemies. I look into her eyes, trying to find the answer. She sees me. She recognizes me—I am the one who will end her life" (p. 120). Joker raises his gun and fires directly into her head.

Later, on a patrol at Khe Sanh, the squad encounters another sniper, one who operates by much the same strategy of partially wounding one man and then picking off the rest who come to his rescue. With three men down, yet still alive, Cowboy orders the rest of the squad to retreat, knowing they will all be killed if they try to save each other, while he runs out to the dying men. Seeing Cowboy run out to his men, the sniper begins to laugh, a laughter that "seems to radiate from the jungle floor, from the jade trees, from the monster plants, from within our own bodies" (p. 175). Soon, Joker starts laughing too, and he knows that "sooner or later, the squad will be laughing" (p. 175). When the laughter ceases, Cowboy, hit by the sniper in both legs, fires his forty-five pistol into the head of each wounded soldier. He then raises the pistol to his own, only to have it shot from his hand by the sniper. Ordering the rest of the squad to move out, Joker raises his rifle and fires, not at the sniper, but at Cowboy:

> *Bang*. I sight down the short metal tube and I watch my bullet enter Cowboy's left eye. My bullet passes through his eye socket, punches through fluid-filled sinus cavities, through membranes, nerves, arteries, muscle tissue, through the tiny blood vessels that feed three pounds of gray butter-soft high protein meat where brain cells arranged like jewels in a clock hold every thought and memory and dream of one adult male *Homo sapiens*. (p. 178)

Joker now becomes sergeant of the squad, they start on their return to base, and the novel ends, the sniper never found.

Hasford shows us a war in which we see no American soldier killed by a Vietnamese (the deaths at Hue are told to Joker and not narrated in the novel): Gerheim is shot by Pyle, Rafter Man is run over by an American tank, Alice, Doc Jay, and the New Guy are killed by Cowboy, and Cowboy by Joker. The only face-to-face meeting with a Vietnamese concludes in Joker killing point blank a woman who is no longer armed. It is finally this that the sniper is laughing at, this that Joker sees out in the jungle—that this is a war in which Americans were fighting what is inside themselves more than the Vietnamese.

> The ugly that civilians choose to see in war focuses on spilled guts. To see human beings clearly, that is ugly. To carry death in your smile, that is ugly. War is ugly because the truth can be ugly and war is very sincere. . . . The squad is silent, waiting for orders. Soon they will understand. Soon they won't be afraid. The dark side will surface and they'll be like me; they'll be Marines.
>
> Once a Marine, always a Marine. (pp. 175–76)

As Joker says, "God has a hard-on for Marines because we kill everything we see" (p. 150), especially, Hasford reveals, each other.

*The Short-Timers* is thus an open-ended novel, one in which the laughter of the sniper in the jungle has not been silenced and the Marines returning home are far from heroes. It is a novel in which the "enemy" is never really seen and seems finally to have become the soldiers themselves. The threat posed by the sniper is not deterred and the squad goes on, now led by Joker, but basically unchanged. More important, the novel does not conclude with these soldiers reaching any insight or understanding about war and society; they deliver no messages such as are found in *Platoon*. Instead, they march into the jungle, trying "very hard not to think about anything important" (p. 180).

Reading *The Short-Timers* through the frame of gender that has defined this study, it becomes apparent that the open-endedness of Hasford's novel parallels the undelineated boundaries between masculine and feminine in his narrative.

This is not a novel in which the masculine "wins," but instead one in which the masculine struggles against itself and loses. The early scenes between Pyle and Gerheim are the most polarized gendered confrontations of the novel, as Pyle, seemingly unfit for the Marine Corps, finally kills the hyper-masculine diatribe of Sergeant Gerheim. But by killing himself as well, Pyle explodes the simple dichotomy between masculine and feminine posed at the start of the novel in the apparently "failed" manhood of Pyle harrassed and exposed by Gerheim's "successful" masculinity. What Hasford shows here is that neither the masculine nor the feminine "survives" as soldiers in this Vietnam.

With the appearance of the female sniper, it seems as if the novel might be reestablishing a boundary of gender, with the feminine slowly slaughtering (symbolically castrating) the masculine soldier. But Joker's first description of her delays such a simple conclusion. Although she is "a child," "a slender Eurasian angel," he says that her eyes "are the hard eyes of a grunt" (p. 116), marking her final characterization as that of a Marine and not a woman. And though she is killed, and, it would seem, the feminine along with her, the second sniper, unseen and unidentified by gender, survives. Hasford even denies Joker any privileged view of gender determination, as he shows Joker participating in rather than disclosing gender images. Although Joker says the sniper reveals "his" position, seeming to identify the gender of this second sniper and reinstate a gender polarization, he also referred to the first sniper as "he" before seeing her. Joker, who was wrong the first time, cannot be used as a reliable witness to gender, as Hasford successfully undercuts Joker's attempts to "know" the enemy by "his" gender. Consequently, it cannot be said that either the feminine or the masculine is precisely defined at the end of this novel. The dual deaths of Pyle and Gerheim early in the novel show the consequences of enforced gender opposition—death for both sides. The remainder of Hasford's novel refuses to reestablish gender as the matrix for integration of the war or its soldiers.

*Full Metal Jacket* appears eight years after Hasford's novel and at the culmination of a masculine regeneration that began with *First Blood* and continued with *Rambo: First Blood, Part II*, *Missing In Action*, *Missing in Action 2*, *Platoon*, and *Gardens of Stone*. Its depiction of the same three scenes—Gerheim's death and the encounters with the two snipers—marks a sharp change in the open-ended and gender-ambivalent narrative written by Hasford. *Full Metal Jacket* alters the features of Hasford's novel, all in ways that operate to pinpoint and foreground the feminine in confrontation with the masculine. The film shuts down the novel's ambiguity and reinstates a clarified rejection of the feminine and restitution of the masculine.

The hillbilly slowness that is Pyle's character in the novel is translated into a soft, overweight, undisciplined, babyish innocence in the film. Lawrence Pratt becomes Leonard Lawrence, with references to Lawrence of Arabia and the undoubted homosexual connotations of that name immediately establishing Pyle's sexual difference. It is only by invoking male homosexuality that difference could be maintained in an environment where Hartmann (Gerheim's character in the novel) addresses all of his recruits as "ladies." When Pyle makes mistakes, Hartmann places him in yet another marginal role as a baby, having him suck his thumb and walk with his pants pulled down. Far more than in the novel, Pyle's character is explicitly made the feminine contrast to the masculinization of the recruits. Hartmann even recognizes Pyle's threat as "contamination," linking him yet again to the feminine fears of Theweleit's soldier males.[6] When Pyle fails to climb an obstacle, Hartmann shouts, "I'm going to wring your balls off so you can't contaminate the rest of the world."

Where the novel's dual murder of Pyle and Gerheim opens the way to gender ambivalence, the same scene in the film takes place in the enclosed space of a latrine rather than in the open barracks, suggesting that the tightened masculine community Kubrick is trying to establish in the film is more directly threatened by these gendered murders than is the questioning stance of Hasford's perspective. The gender relations that Hasford interrogates in the novel must be deferred by Kubrick's masculine community. This shift is the first step in delineating gender lines that become firmly established by the film's close in the sniper scenes. Kubrick, Herr, and Hasford's screenplay collapses the two sniper scenes of the novel into one, with the gruesome dismemberment of Cowboy's squad occurring at Hue, not Khe Sanh. The laughing sniper of the jungle is written out of the screenplay and replaced by the woman found in the broken mansions of Hue killed by Joker.

The differences between the two scenes with the sniper are significant. The black soldier named "Alice" in the novel (another instance of Hasford's gender ambivalence) becomes "Eightball" in the film, eliminating any possible gender interpretation of the encounter except as it is directed against the sniper. And instead of Cowboy going out to shoot the dying squad members, he is himself shot and killed, not by Joker, but by the sniper. Though Rafter Man does still fire at her, Joker finds her first; his rifle jams and she turns and fires at him. Rafter Man then comes in from behind and shoots her. Finally, though Joker again kills her, she has asked him explicitly to do it. After saying her prayers in Vietnamese, she turns to Joker and says, "G.I. Shoot Me" again and again. Each of these changes, though seemingly minor, moves the screenplay into a more definitive depiction of the feminine as enemy and rewrites the novel as a story of a gendered opposition between masculine and feminine, a battle that the masculine must win in order to survive the war.

No longer responsible for their own deaths, the American soldiers who die in *Full Metal Jacket* are killed by the Vietnamese. And the most deaths portrayed in the film are at the hand of the single female sniper. Where Joker sees her first accidentally in the novel, their meeting in the film is deliberate and dramatic. When his gun jams, she fires multiple rounds at him, hitting only the post he is hiding behind. Not sniping at or stumbling over him, she is purposefully trying to kill him, creating a sense of confrontation between masculine and feminine that is not in the novel. The strongest threat to the survival of American soldiers in this film is thus nothing other than a single female sniper, the feminine itself.

Joker's only "confirmed kill" in the film is this sniper. But even this is altered in such a way that he is absolved of her death. She has told him to shoot her; it is not his desire or responsibility. He is fulfilling her wish, not his own. The masculine is thus cleansed in this film of any involvement with death. The soldiers have not killed each other nor have they killed irresponsibly or even wilfully. The impetus for death lies wholly with the enemy, and that enemy is shown only as female.

The unidentified laughing sniper who closes Hasford's novel is thus fully identified by the camera as feminine, no longer anonymously laughing but showing identifiable terror in the face of her enemies. Any ambiguity is closed down in this embodiment of danger as female. While the most urgent threat posed to American soldiers in the novel was a polarized gender scheme in which men killed each other and themselves trying to fulfill masculine guarantees, the film translates this into a far more simplistic and bifurcated scenario in which the survival of masculinity is threatened directly and only by a castrating female characterization.

The clearest indication of the alteration in narrations is the ending. The men in *The Short-Timers* go back to Khe Sanh on the same trail they went in, having lost half of their squad in defeat to an unknown sniper who continues to haunt the jungle around them. But Kubrick's soldiers, having killed the sniper, move on, no longer alone but gathered with others who are entering Hue to clean out the enemy. Heading for the Perfume River, they group forces and begin singing the theme song from "Mickey Mouse" as they walk through the burning city. Not retreating through a dense jungle in loss, these soldiers are marching through a city of rubble, their song ringing off the charred ruins of Hue. Having located and defeated the feminine that was mercilessly "sniping" at them, they now join with other men to sing an oddly celebratory tune of American childhood, only this time the "club" is all male and they are moving out to kill more of the enemy, now identified and vulnerable to their collective power.

Three additional points reinforce a reading of *Full Metal Jacket* as a firm delineation of gender boundaries and reinstatement of the masculine in opposition to a feminine enemy. One is a scene repressed by Kubrick's screenwriting team and the other two are apparently gratuitous scenes added to the film and not present in the novel.

In the film, when Joker first finds Cowboy's squad in Hue, he gets into a verbal showdown with Animal Mother that seems unmotivated in the film. Each tops the other's last taunt to the eager cheers of the rest of the squad until Cowboy puts a stop to what is escalating into a full-scale fight. Similarly, throughout the novel, Joker and Animal Mother have a running battle over who gives orders to the squad, who has more experience, and who is more "hard-core." But their first disagreement comes, not simply as a result of their different personalities, as it seems in the film, but because Joker objects to Animal Mother having chased a thirteen-year-old Vietnamese girl "with his dick hanging out" (p. 90). Although T.H.E. Rock says "she was just a baby," Animal Mother declares, "If she's old enough to bleed, she's old enough to butcher" (p. 91). At this point, Joker and Animal Mother quickly get into a fight that ends only when Cowboy stops the two of them from shooting at each other (again, Americans killing Americans). What comes out in the film as simply a battle of male egos is in fact a repression of rape, a denial of masculine violence against the feminine, necessitated by the film rewriting gender as a confrontation between a purified masculine and a threatening and castrating feminine. In its regenerated form, the masculine must be seen as only a victim of the ruthless strategies of the feminine, not as responsible for its own oppressions and violence, allowing the masculine to relieve itself of the role of oppressor. The film is thus repressing out of its audience's awareness the very factor that confirms gender boundaries between men and women, the threat of rape.

Equally important, repressing this scene allows Joker's subsequent killing of the Vietnamese sniper to seem less gruesome and almost charitable. When he could not catch this thirteen-year-old girl, Animal Mother recalls another girl they encountered in the jungle leading an NVA rifle squad: "She was a lot younger than the one I saw today. . . . I didn't get to fuck that one either. But that's okay. That's okay. I shot her motherfucking face off" (p. 92). Although it seems at this point in the novel that Animal Mother's actions are diametrically opposite to Joker's, we must recall Joker's own killing of the sniper, when "[o]ne round enters the sniper's left eye and as the bullet exits it tears off the back of her head" (p. 120). In effect, Joker "shot her motherfucking face off," making him more like Animal Mother than we would like to believe, a realization the film does not allow us to have. In the film, Joker remains "pure" in his unambiguously masculine murders, shooting only a sniper who tried to kill him, not other Americans and not blowing the "motherfucking face off" fifteen-year-old girls. But Animal Mother's formulation makes clear that shooting "her motherfucking face off" and raping the girl are equivalent, the shooting adequate compensation for not raping. The corrolation between these two episodes in the novel forces a recognition of masculine violence as rape, of shooting the enemy as raping the enemy. By not including Animal Mother's action and not showing the death of the sniper, *Full Metal Jacket* allows for the repression of the violence that underlies the gender system.

In contrast to this repressed scene of rape, *Full Metal Jacket* adds two scenes not in the novel, both of Vietnamese prostitutes approaching American soldiers. Both precede the attack of the sniper and thus establish a frame of reference for Vietnamese women that will color the later appearance of the sniper. In the first instance, a Vietnamese prostitute approaches Joker and Rafter Man in Da Nang, saying "Me so horny." Joker bargains with her over her price when suddenly two small boys steal Rafter Man's camera and the episode ends, marking the prostitute as commodity. Later, after they enter Hue, a Vietnamese soldier approaches the squad as pimp for a prostitute. Again they bargain, but she refuses to "boom-boom with soul brother" because she thinks Eightball is "too beaucoup." When he shows her his penis, she changes her mind, suggesting that it is not "too big."

There are several things going on here. First, that both of these episodes occur before we see the sniper establishes a context for viewing Vietnamese women in the film that does not exist in the novel and gives the encounter with the sniper stronger sexual overtones than it otherwise would have. A Hispanic soldier, for example, added to the squad for the film, stands over the dying sniper and says, "No more boom-boom for this baby-san," a phrase not included in the novel. By using the vocabulary of the prostitute only a few minutes earlier—"boom-boom"—a connection is made between sniper and prostitute, sheerly on the basis of their being women. Where Joker calls her "a grunt" in the novel, no such gender-crossing epithet is allowed here; she is only woman and only prostitute.

Second, although the sniper in the film is young, she is clearly not fifteen years old, and both of the prostitutes are older, whereas all of the female Vietnamese mentioned in the novel are under fifteen. *Full Metal Jacket* is substituting not only adults for children but prostitutes for female children. Whereas the girls of *The Short-Timers* are innocent of sexual connotations—Animal Mother chasing a girl who is trying to get away from him and the sniper as devoted to her fight as the grunts are—the women of *Full Metal Jacket* are overtly sexual, propositioning men who are at all times seated, not initiating sexual encounters on their own. Masculinity thus remains passive and subject to the explicit sexual overtures of women who represent only sex. And while the first episode is cut off, even the second shows only Animal Mother leading the prostitute off to a collapsed building. Joker and the other soldiers still remain pure, though they too have ostensibly contracted with the prostitute. Kubrick, Herr, and Hasford thus succeed in translating an ambivalent gender characterization of a female sniper into a deliberate and clearcut sexual stereotyping of women as whores (in which all female children inevitably become adult prostitutes), further underscoring the barriers between masculine and feminine in this film.

Thus, in the close to two decades between the publication of Herr's first essay and the appearance of Kubrick's *Full Metal Jacket*, the depiction of gender has become more rather than less clearly defined. More to the point, it appears that the enemy has been both defined *and* eliminated, enabling a triumphant masculine to emerge from the rubble of Vietnam in childlike celebration, ready to conquer its symbolically weakened foe.

The prostitutes and sniper are not only women but Asian, and it could be just as important to understand their construction as "enemy" in terms of their race. What suggests then that these passages should be read primarily through a framework of gender rather than race? Relevant is certainly the long tradition in Hollywood film of racial stereotyping, especially of Asians in war films.[7] More to the point, what indicates that these scenes can be read more forcefully as evidence of a regeneration of masculinity than of white dominance? or that a reading that sees only the racial polarities here would be missing the very mechanism through which those polarities are enacted? Although I can do so only briefly, I want to answer these questions by referring to some of the complex relations between gender and race in contemporary U.S. cultural representation. Specifically, as a look at Kubrick's *Full Metal Jacket* shows, gender is used as a vehicle for racial oppression and therefore must be acknowledged as the primary category for the construction of relations of power and dominance in current U.S. dominant cultural representations. In these terms, any reinforcement of systems of dominance that favor whites in America should be read in relation to the patterns of remasculinization set out here.

In the second encounter with the prostitute in *Full Metal Jacket*, she refuses to have sex with Eightball, the black soldier in the squad ("Alice" in the book), saying "No boom-boom with soul brother." What at first might appear to be a sign of racial identification—she and the black soldier against the whites[8]—is soon explained as nothing more than racial stereotyping itself, as she says Eightball is "Too beaucoup" and her pimp explains, "Too big." When Eightball unzips his pants and shows her his penis, she changes her mind and agrees.

Earlier, before they entered combat, Joker and Rafter Man hear a joke told in their barracks: "How do you stop five black dudes from raping a white chick?—Throw 'em a basketball." Before any response can be made, incoming rounds announce the arrival of the Tet Offensive, 1968, and the men leave their tents to defend the base. This joke left hanging in midair—a joke that the ensuing explosions expose as threatening to the comaraderie of battle—is finally dealt with in the prostitute's reaction. Her denial of sexual difference between black and white—he is obviously not "too beaucoup"—is a defeat of one of the strongest stereotypes of American racism, that black men's penises are larger than white's,[9] thus eliding differences betwen men through the reassertion of their difference from women. More to the point, the negation of racial barriers that underlies so much of Vietnam representation is maintained only at the expense of women, as the insistence on their difference from men prevents any recognition of what women share with men of color—oppression by white men. The unacknowledged sexual tension defused here is a reply to the overt racial hostility raised in the joke, a hostility that taps into traditions of racial and sexual animosity in its reference to relations between black men and white women. But because the encounter with the prostitute is also based on racial difference, it seems to respond directly to the joke and suggest that these racial differences are only jokes and stereotypes, not realities. The sexual difference between men and women is used to defer racial differences which are, through this "joke" and through the prostitute who must carry their burden, elided and apparently eliminated.

More than this, the prostitute's evaluative acquiescence not only defuses any racial tensions remaining about black men and white women by denying the need for concern, her look effectively castrates the black man and leaves him powerless. He has exposed himself to the entire squad and shown to them as well that he is not "too beaucoup." The prostitute's gaze here—one that the camera does not follow because it cannot afford to verify (or contradict)—is surrogate for that of the other men. Her judgment reveals theirs, as Animal Mother steps in between Eightball and the prostitute and leads her off, saying "Niggers wait at the end of the line." She has been made the vehicle for their emasculation of him. Likewise, though he is collecting her money, her Asian soldier pimp is equally castrated, as this squad of primarily white men takes her from him for overtly sexual usage. Although the Asian solider seems to be on a level with the Americans through the exchange of "goods," they finally possess and control her body in a way he does not.

Similarly, after shooting the sniper, the Hispanic soldier raises sexuality as a reference in his declaration, "No more boom-boom for this baby-san." After Joker shoots her, it is again this soldier who concludes, "Hard core man. Fuckin' hard core." (A similar line is spoken in the novel by Alice, the black soldier, but without the sexual connotations; importantly, racial difference is maintained.) Like Eightball's penis, the Hispanic soldier has exposed himself to the squad in his introduction of sexuality, and, like Eightball, he has been effectively emasculated in his own admission that Joker is more "hard-core" than he. Although the same could be said for all the other squad members, no others have raised the sexual and therefore have not made themselves available for castration.

In a genre whose most consistent refrain is the eradication of racial difference, these scenes of one of Vietnam's most recent war narratives reveal the interrelationship between gender and race. While race is vocally negated as a category through discussions of "brotherhood" and bonding—"An AK round don't care what color your paint job is"—scenes like these in *Full Metal Jacket* display the links between gender, sexuality, and the defusion of racial tension. As in the scene from *The 13th Valley* in which a Native American and black soldier investigate the "mystery of the Orient" and in Lieutenant Brooks's fantasy of himself sucking white Egan's penis, sexuality and gender difference are foregrounded as a spectacle to divert attention and tension away from racial difference. In each case, women are the operatives for this defusion, primarily as vehicles for the castrating gaze of the white male.

These scenes and the many like them that punctuate Vietnam representation begin to reveal the complex operations of patriarchal structures in contemporary U.S. culture. The interrelations between, for example, gender and race that have been described here are typical of current modes of operation for patriarchy, in which gendered representation is used as a vehicle for the defusion of racial tension and difference. It is clear, if only from these few references, that gender and race intimately intersect in dominant narratives but that gender is the primary mechanism through which race is addressed, not vice versa, and that racial difference is economically dealt with at the expense primarily of women.

What a further, more detailed examination of American cultural representation would reveal is a constant shifting of relations between issues of gender, race, class, and sexual preference, so that at no two historical periods would their intersections be identical.[10] As components or modes of operation for patriarchal structures, these categories are historically contextualized so that different channels for the negotiation and maintenance of patriarchal power are exercised at different moments. While one category is foregrounded, others are being addressed in subtle and less apparent ways. For example, in recent years, much feminist work that challenges patriarchal structures of gender relations has focused on the positions and relations of women to men, often paying less attention to racial, class, or sexual differences between women and between men. As in *Full Metal Jacket*, men of color are effectively castrated as a mechanism for reproducing the illusion of racial equality. Consequently, patriarchal oppression of, for instance, homosexuals and blacks in America has been able to increase in its efficiency and complexity, while "feminism" seems to have gained ground.[11]

Consequently, it is necessary to pay close attention to the specific historical manifestations of patriarchal structures.[12] Only in such terms can the accurate interrelations between gender, race, class, sexual preference, and other forms of patriarchal expression be understood. Primarily, as Gerda Lerner suggests,[13] it is through gender that other forms of oppression and structures for dominance are enacted, but the foregrounding of those forms depends on contextual historical situations dictated by economic, social, or political needs. Thus, where structures of gender may at one time be employed to respond to class tensions, they may be used at another to respond to anxieties about racial or sexual difference. And where at one point class issues may be foregrounded to repress awareness of gender systems (as in Victorian England), at another, race may be used to accomplish the same thing (as in the Plantation South). In each case, the complex intersections between all of the manifestations of dominance in patriachal structures will vary according to historical moment and location and must be specified in each situation in order to be adequately understood and challenged.

At this time in U.S. dominant culture, gender is being foregrounded as a category through which issues of race, class, sexual preference, and other forms of difference are being denied. Vietnam representation reveals the ways in which contemporary popular narratives are repressing class or race differences as relevant concerns. Instead, through the remasculinization of American culture that is now taking place, gender differences have been reaffirmed as a primary interpretive frame for U.S. social relations. And, to the extent that feminist criticism foregrounds as well only issues of gender, it is in many ways complicit with the programs set out in Vietnam representations.

Because constructions of masculinity and femininity are being used in American mass culture to repress awareness of other forms of patriarchal dominance, it is methodologically important to maintain a distinction between patriarchy and masculinity. Masculinity is the primary mechanism for the articulation, institutionalization, and maintenance of the gendered system on which patriarchy is based. The structural expression of patriarchal interests takes place through what I have earlier called the masculine point of view, distinct from masculinity in that it marks specific males as expendable in order to maintain the larger frame of masculine narration. But because patriarchal structures address and set into operation relations of dominance between classes, races, and other groups of people defined in relation to patriarchal interests, it is important to stress the ways in which masculinity is itself only one of those mechanisms, along with images of blacks, lesbians, Hispanics, the poor, gays, workers, mothers, Asians, and so on. Although masculinity is by far the category of privilege within patriarchy, in such terms it is itself constructed and manipulated by interests other than those defined by gender.

For this reason an examination of masculinity, not as a direct oppressor of women, but as a category of definition itself is important to any feminist understanding of the operations of patriarchy. By assuming a monolithic and stable identity between masculinity and patriarchy, patriarchy manages to shield itself from real challenges to its structures of dominance. Lerner suggests that it is through the control of symbolic relations that men's dominance over women has become institutionalized, so that an assumed "natural" disposition of women's position becomes "a metaphor defining power relations in such a way as to mystify them and render them invisible" (p. 211). Similarly, by repressing masculinity as a mechanism for the operation of patriarchy and invoking it instead as synonymous with patriarchy, gender relations, for all of the study and investigation of women's relations to power, remain mystified and invisible.

War is the most severe consequence of the mystification of gender and the concomitant mystification of power relations that occurs within patriarchy. In particular, wars are the most historically visible specifications of patriarchal power relations, foregrounding race, class, nation, "culture," property, and so on in their different manifestations. A historical study of warfare as a point of contact for patriarchal relations would be very useful to feminist study and would provide an alternative means of interpreting warfare than has generally been offered by historians or political theorists. It is not accidental that many feminist critics and writers have turned to addres issues of warfare in recent years—among them Judith Hicks Stiehm, Nancy Hartsock, Marge Piercy, Christa Wolf, Betty A. Reardon, Jean Bethke Elshtain, Marguerite Duras, Sandra Gilbert, Joan Didion, Nancy Huston, and Susan Gubar.[14] Although some feminists still discuss war as antithetical to women's identity,[15] the writers mentioned here have recognized the extent to which warfare is a subject that should not be excluded as having nothing to do with women's concerns but is one that may instead provide insight into the very operations that feminism is working to disclose.

War is a crucible for the distillation of social and cultural relations, so that within its frame modes of discourse become more prominent, to the point of appearing almost simplistic. This apparent simplicity has itself functioned as part of the mystification of warfare and its related power structures. But, as I have tried to show here, war and its representations offer markers for more widespread cultural analyses. Issues of masculine bonding, narrative form, reproduction, political relations, epistemology, racial difference, and subjectivity have all been intertwined throughout the Vietnam War and its representations. In addition, all have intersected with structures of gender in such a way that there can finally be no adequate understanding of that war and its place in American culture without an understanding of its gendered relations.

Similar statements could be made about all wars, principally because war is the distilled expression of relations of social and cultural dominance. Jean Bethke Elshtain suggests that war has a significant place in societies because it crystallizes social identities: "wars destroy and bring into being men *and* women as particular *identities* by canalizing energy and giving permission to narrate. Societies are, in some sense, the sum total of their 'war stories'."[16] In particular, war accomplishes this effect by formalizing a notion of collective identity for those who engage in it: "War creates *the* people. War produces power, individual and collective. War is the cultural property of peoples, a system of signs that we read without much effort because they have become so familiar to us" (p. 167).

But when considering warfare as a mark of patriarchal operations, Elshtain's description seems just reversed. It is not so much that war "creates" identities as it provides a forum for the articulation of identities already implicit within the systems of dominance and power within patriarchy. To see war as "producing" power is still to perceive it as something in some ways separate from other kinds of social and power relations. But war is not separate from society and cannot therefore "produce" something that is not already inherent within it. To suggest that it can is to accept the ability of the masculine point of view to "produce" and "create" of itself.

Instead, war should be seen more as an eruption of systems already at work in patriarchal structures, a focalization of tensions already in operation. What Betty A. Reardon says about the military—that it is "the distilled embodiment of patriarchy"[17]—can be expanded to apply to all of the aspects of warfare, as it becomes the vehicle for the specification of social relations. Warfare thus does not "create" identities within patriarchy so much as it allows for their negotiation and articulation.

Andrea Dworkin identifies part of this operation when she describes the tensions that exist for men between "the law that protects male power—basic fundamentalism, religious or secular—and men's wanting to break that law: exercise the privileges of power for the sake of pleasure." As she goes on to explain, "men disagree about how much license men should have to break the laws that men make to protect male power."[18] Replacing Dworkin's citation of "men" here with "the masculine," it is possible to read her analysis of the tension between law and license as an impetus for warfare, with war as the ground on which these tensions as they exist in society are tested. In particular, within the military regimen—what constitutes the "law" of warfare—individual license is explored in the decisions each soldier makes about the means to defeat the enemy, whether that be killing, imprisoning, torturing, "relocating," raping, burning, bombing, or propagandizing. Narratives like *Apocalypse Now* epitomize this tension, as Kurtz has clearly taken "license" too far and now must get back "on the boat" or be killed himself by the representative of the law.

Dworkin asks a number of questions about that law that can surely be applied to an analysis of warfare:

> How much license can men take without destroying the effectiveness of the laws that formally restrain them in order to protect their power as men? . . . Which laws are fundamental, essential, to maintaining the authority of men over women? Which laws are fundamental, essential, to keeping male dominance the basis of how society is organized, how rights are apportioned, how power is distributed? (p. 160)

These questions are answered for society in general as they are worked out in war, in the particular instances of domination and the specifications of power. Thus, at those moments when social order in American society seems most in flux and unstable—the post-Depression era, the industrial versus agricultural conflicts of pre-Civil War times, the advent of the Atomic Age, or the civil rights movements of the sixties—war appears as the arena in which an alternate social order is tested as a means for reestablishing social balance. And because, as Lerner suggests, relations of dominance at work in the gender system are patterns for other power relations, the renegotiated balance between law and license is worked out in terms of masculine and feminine.

War provides the optimum forum within which to answer these questions of law and license because it is perceived as a circumstance in which "the World" seems removed and irrelevant, or its limitations on behavior seem not to apply. As Daniel Egan claimed, "We got a separate culture out here. And in some respects it's better."[19] In that "separate culture," one that seems to strip away other forms of social relations such as class, race, ethnicity, sexuality, geographical background, age, and education, the laws that define relations of dominance can be foregrounded and tested, in balder and more simplistic terms than would apply within the larger society—"If they're not all VC now, they could fuckin' well become VC."[20]

But what has happened in recent decades is that the arena of warfare that had once been more clearly separated from other social formations[21] has become the umbrella signifier for American culture as we exist under the label of the "Cold War," the "battle between the sexes," the "war on poverty," and so on.

While clearly many of these labels serve only as metaphors, the expansion of the terminology of warfare to general social relations enables a more fluid application of the specifications of war to society as a whole. The widespread usage of the vocabulary of warfare in public life—in politics, Wall Street, business, journalism, even literary theory—accompanies a consistent appearance of war narratives in American popular culture—from World War II films to television's "Combat," "M*A*S*H," and "Tour of Duty." All combine in recent decades to produce a cultural ego more sensitive to the reformulations of law and license that take place in war.

What this discourse of warfare also means is that American culture is equally to be defined in recent decades by a foregrounding of the structures of dominance expressed in the system of gender. Within the vocabulary of war that has been in force since the 1950s—since, in effect, Soviet acquisition of nuclear technology—relations of dominance have been renegotiated in American society, relations that, while expanding some areas of "license" in civil rights, have reinstated the "law" of the masculine point of view as a general cultural formation. It is for this reason that I have referred to these decades as a period of the "remasculinization of America," where the limits of the masculine have been tested, both in war itself and in the discourse of war, and reestablished as law.

Jean Bethke Elshtain concludes that the modern world follows Hegel's belief that

> War-constituted solidarity is immanent within the state form. But the state, hence the nation, comes fully to life only with war. Peace poses the specific danger of sanctioning the view that the atomized world of civil society is absolute. In war, however, the state as a collective being is tested, *and the citizen comes to recognize the state as the source of all rights*. [italics added][22]

What the discourse of warfare at operation in recent decades in U.S. society thus suggests is that, along with the renegotiation of masculinity has come a renegotiation and reempowerment of the state in such a way that war as a general social condition is used to heighten the ability of the state to proclaim itself "the source of all rights." It is this simultaneous movement of the regeneration of the state that makes the advances of feminism, civil and minority rights, and so on suspect within the discourse of warfare, as they have achieved their goals primarily via state legislation and power. Consequently, rather than a direct challenge, these movements have been used to confirm to an extent, under the vocabulary of war, the general remasculinization of American culture.

A novel like Joan Didion's *Democracy* stands as cultural witness to what I have been describing here. Opening with the detonation of a nuclear bomb at a Pacific test site in 1952, the novel moves through the intervening years of the Vietnam War and ends in 1975, while its date of publication, 1984, brings it to cover the decades discussed here. Didion's novel stands as testimony to the pervasiveness of a discourse of warfare, especially because it at no point addresses war directly. There are no scenes of combat, although the main character, Inez Victor, is related to people who traverse Vietnam without entering the war. Her lover, Jack Lovett, became involved in Vietnam during the early days of American advisors and continued working for the U.S. government in an undercover capacity. Her daughter, Jessie, decides to go to Vietnam to work, taking a job as a waitress in a Saigon bar. Her son, Adlai, does a college internship and stages a "vigil for the liberation of Saigon."[23] And her husband, Harry Victor, is a member of the U.S. Senate and campaigns for the presidency on an antiwar ticket. But Inez, who has no direct involvement in the war, ends the novel in Kuala Lumpur working in a refugee center for Southeast Asians, vowing to remain there "until the last refugee was dispatched" (p. 234), while her daughter, rescued from Vietnam by Jack Lovett, ends the novel in Mexico City, writing a novel about Maximilian and Carlota.

The discourse of warfare is, in *Democracy*, not merely a backdrop for one woman's story, but is the structuring frame that designates a time different from that which existed before 1952. As the narrator/author records, "In 1955 . . . I had first noticed the quickening of time. In 1975 time was no longer just quickening but collapsing, falling in on itself, the way a disintegrating star contracts into a black hole" (p. 72). As each character in some way touches Vietnam, they mark their connection to this new time that is best known by its relation to the war. But because those connections, epitomized by Jack Lovett's mysterious profession, are never fully clear, the war spills over into life and seems not to be separated from it.

To escape that discourse, both Inez and her daughter must leave the United States, living as exiles in Third World cities, refugees from their own country's warfare. Both Harry Victor and Adlai remain, Harry becoming special envoy to the Common Market and Adlai a clerk for a federal judge in San Francisco. That the men stay and thrive in this discourse while the women must seek refuge from it marks its gendered character and declares the simultaneous reaffirmations of the masculine and the state, both regenerated through the discourse of war as social structure. For Didion, the war is not a specific but a general feature of these decades so that those who are not "in" the war must live by its rules or become exiles to its system.

It is thus that the discourse of warfare is linked to the process of remasculinization current in American culture. Far more than simply saying that war is a "man's world," such a formulation traces the specific operations whereby gender relations in American culture have been redefined in recent years through the complex representation and dissemination of a discourse of warfare linked primarily to the Vietnam War. It has been principally through this discourse that an ambivalent and apparently increasing breakdown of gender articulations has become specified to redefine the constructions of masculine and feminine in even firmer and more exclusionary terms, so that women are effectively eliminated from the masculine narration of war and the society of which it is an emblem, either by the masculine point of view from which the stories are told or by themselves as exiled "refugees" from U.S. social relations. In either case, masculine and feminine have become more rather than less polarized, more rather than less distinct, more rather than less threatening. And because of the seminal position of gender dominance in relation to other forms of dominance in U.S. culture, power relations defined through race, sexual preference, ethnicity, class, and so on are becoming equally polarized.

Consequently, in order to respond effectively to current gender constructions in American culture, feminism needs to focus attention on the primary vehicle for the remasculinization of American society now taking place—the discourse of warfare. To perceive and respond to war as the antithesis to peace is to continue to allow this system its mastery of many areas of cultural existence. What I have tried to outline here as the specific usages of the Vietnam War and those who fought in it can be expanded to provide a reading of dominant American cultural formations that now base much of their expressive efficiency on a discourse developed around that war. Far from arguing for a causal relation between the Vietnam War and the remasculinization that occurs coincident with it, I hope to have suggested instead that the war has been an eruption of gender relations and anxieties surrounding the maintenance and continuation of dominance structures in recent decades. To either dismiss or focus on that war as a point of origin for contemporary U.S. crises is thus a misguided effort, one that finally expends its energy reinforcing rather than altering the larger structures of patriarchal interests that prompted the war.

As long as the representational images reflecting that war continue their operation, the discourse of warfare that affects other aspects of U.S. culture will maintain its currency. As the advertisements for *Missing in Action* declared, "It ain't over until the last man comes home." This is the voice that echoes throughout contemporary American culture, reminding us of its project of remasculinization through the discourse of warfare—reminding us of the intimacy of gender and war.

"I'll tell you how intimate: they were my guns and I let them do it."

# Notes

## PREFACE

1. Gerda Lerner, *The Creation of Patriarchy* (New York: Oxford University Press, 1986), p. 239.

2. Eve Kosofsky Sedgwick, *Between Men: English Literature and Male Homosocial Desire* (New York: Columbia University Press, 1985).

3. For a discussion of World War II film narratives, see Jeanine Basinger's *The World War II Combat Film: Anatomy of a Genre* (New York: Columbia University Press, 1986).

4. In addition to elaborating these issues in chapter 3, I discuss them further in "Masculinity as Excess in Vietnam Films: The Father/Son Dynamic of American Culture," *Genre* (forthcoming).

5. Kristen Thompson, "The Concept of Cinematic Excess," in *Narrative, Apparatus, Ideology: A Film Theory Reader*, ed. Philip Rosen (New York: Columbia University Press, 1986): pp. 130–43.

6. Anthony Easthope, *What a Man's Gotta Do: The Masculine Myth in Popular Culture* (London: Paladin, 1986), p. 7.

7. Michael Herr, *Dispatches* (New York: Avon, 1978), p. 70.

## 1. FACT, FICTION, AND THE SPECTACLE OF WAR

1. Edwin McDowell, "Publishing: Everyone Seems to Be Doing Books on Vietnam," *New York Times*, December 2, 1983.

2. Although *Rambo III* has not had the box office success of its predecessors, it is still expected to make $160 million in theater sales in the United States and to have, as did *First Blood* and *Rambo: First Blood, Part II*, a considerable market outside the U.S. For example, *Rambo III* broke box office records in Puerto Rico and the Philippines and made $8 million in its first ten days on the Japanese market. These figures do not include the substantial video sales anticipated for the film.

3. *First Blood* (1982) earned approximately $57 million dollars at the box office, and its partner, *Rambo: First Blood, Part Two* (1985) earned the third highest opening gross in movie history until that time. A film that cost $30 million to make, *Rambo* collected $100 million in its first month of release, and its novelization sold so well that it held a place on the best-seller list of the *New York Times*. Both films are still at the top of sales and rentals in videocassettes (most video stores keep four or five copies of *Rambo* on hand). *Missing in Action 2—The Beginning*, released in late November 1984, had grossed $22 million by year's end, holding the number one spot during its first week of release and remaining in the top fifty grossing films through early February.

4. Owing both to the recent appearance of these programs and the structural differences of the televisual apparatus from film, I will not address these television programs in this study. For a discussion of both television series, see John Carlos Rowe's essay in *Genre*'s special issue on Vietnam Studies (forthcoming).

5. An indication of public opinion in 1988 about service in Vietnam is that Dan Quayle was criticized for *not* having gone to the war.

6. Richard Nixon, *No More Vietnams* (New York: Arbor House, 1985), p. 164. All subsequent references in the text will be to this edition.

7. Norman Mailer, *The Armies of the Night: History as a Novel, the Novel as History* (New York: Signet, 1968), p. 209. All subsequent references will be to this edition.

8. Loren Baritz, *Backfire: A History of How American Culture Led Us into Vietnam and Made Us Fight the Way We Did* (New York: Ballantine, 1985), p. 226.

9. Barbara Tuchman, *The March of Folly: From Troy to Vietnam* (New York: Knopf, 1984), pp. 376–77.

10. Quoted in Richard Halloran, *To Arm a Nation: Rebuilding America's Endangered Defenses* (New York: MacMillan, 1986), p. 65.

11. Edward N. Luttwak, *The Pentagon and the Art of War: The Question of Military Reform* (New York: Simon and Schuster, 1985), p. 268.

12. Quoted in Alan Tonelson, Review of *To Arm a Nation*, *New York Times Book Review*, November 30, 1986, p. 7.

13. Philip Beidler, *American Literature and the Experience of Vietnam* (Athens: University of Georgia Press, 1982), p. 32.

14. Examples include the following accounts, whether singly or in collection: those of individual soldiers—Al Santoli's *Everything We Had*, Peter Goldman and Tony Fuller's *Charlie Company: What Vietnam Did To Us*, and Mark Baker's *Nam;* POW accounts—Zalin Grant's *Survivors* and J. C. Pollock's *Mission M.I.A.*; soldier's families—C. D. B. Bryan's *Friendly Fire* and Myra MacPherson's *Long Time Passing;* journalists—Oriana Fallaci's *Nothing, and So Be It*, Michael Herr's *Dispatches*, Kate Webb's *On the Other Side: 23 Days with the Viet Cong;* medical personnel—Lynda Van Devanter's *Home before Morning*, Ronald J. Glasser's *365 Days*, Keith Walker's *A Piece of My Heart*, and Kathryn Marshall's *In a Combat Zone;* even radio announcers, such as Chris Noel's *Matter of Survival* and *Good Morning, Vietnam*. Significantly, this list is a mixture of fiction and nonfiction, personal narrative and collected narration, which indicates the difficulty of categorizing Vietnam representation.

15. Richard Ohmann details this dichotomy in his reading of *Catcher in the Rye* ("The Shaping of the Canon in U.S. Fiction, 1960–1975," *Critical Inquiry* 10 [September 1983]: 199–223), suggesting that the opposition of individual to society is not only a repeated motif in American literature but a function of that society's efforts to have the individual seek the source of any dissatisfaction within him/herself, as does Holden Caulfield, rather than in the society at large.

16. Jean-François Lyotard, *The Postmodern Condition: A Report on Knowledge*, trans. Geoff Bennington and Brian Massumi (Minneapolis: University of Minnesota Press, 1984), p. 37.

17. Although Barthes's definitions are useful here, his descriptions of the readerly text and its exploration and disruption of the conditions of the classic narrative cannot be applied to Vietnam narrative directly, though its nonnarrative format shares many of the features of the readerly text (Roland Barthes, *S/Z*, trans. Richard Miller [New York: Hill and Wang, 1974]). Some of the complexities of such parallels are indicated in both Dana Polan and Tania Modleski's suggestion that Barthes's categories align themselves with a subtext of high and popular culture (Dana Polan, "Brief Encounters: Mass Culture and the Evacuation of Sense," in *Studies in Entertainment: Critical Approaches to Mass Culture*, ed. Tania Modleski [Bloomington: Indiana University Press, 1986], pp. 167–88; Tania Modleski, "The Terror of Pleasure: The Contemporary Horror Film and Postmodern Theory," in *Studies in Entertainment*, ed. Modleski, pp. 155–67).

18. Janice Radway's study of the modern Gothic romance ("The Utopian Impulse in Popular Literature: Gothic Romance and 'Feminist' Protest," *American Quarterly* 33, no. 2 [1981]: 140–62) astutely pinpoints the critical difference of focusing on endings rather than middles, in particular, of valorizing the more repressive closure of Gothic romances, in which marriage to the previously shunned man is expected, over the more expressive plot developments in which women characters exercise independence and vocalize dissatisfactions with social structures.

19. Quoted in John Clark Pratt, *Vietnam Voices: Perspectives on the War Years, 1941–1982* (New York: Penguin, 1984), pp. 650–51.
20. Beidler, *American Literature*, p. 3.
21. Ibid., p. 8.
22. Quoted in Stanley Karnow, *Vietnam: A History* (New York: Viking, 1983), p. 247, 248.
23. Quoted in Al Santoli, *To Bear Any Burden* (New York: Ballantine, 1985), p. 227.
24. Quoted in Peter Goldman and Tony Fuller, *Charlie Company: What Vietnam Did to Us* (New York: Ballantine, 1983), p. 71.
25. Quoted in Pratt, *Vietnam Voices*, p. 653.
26. Baritz, *Backfire*, p. 30.
27. Michael Herr, *Dispatches* (New York: Avon, 1978), p. 65. All subsequent references will be to this edition.
28. David A. Maurer, *The Dying Place* (New York: Dell, 1986), p. 42.
29. William E. Holland, *Let a Soldier Die* (New York: Dell, 1984), p. 186.
30. Herr, *Dispatches*, p. 170.
31. William Broyles, Jr., "Why Men Love War," *Esquire*, November 1984, p. 62.
32. Georges Bataille, *Death and Sensuality: A Study of Eroticism and the Taboo* (New York: Walker, 1977), pp. 141–42.
33. Broyles, "Why Men Love War," p. 62.
34. William Eastlake, *The Bamboo Bed* (New York: Avon, 1969), p. 49. All subsequent references are to this edition.
35. Quoted in Keith Walker, *A Piece of My Heart: The Stories of 26 American Women Who Served in Vietnam* (Novato, Calif.: Presidio, 1985), p. 206.
36. David H. Van Biema, "With a $100 Million Gross(out), Sly Stallone Fends Off *Rambo's* Army of Adversaries," *People*, July 8, 1985, p. 37.
37. Timothy S. Lowry, *And Brave Men, Too* (New York: Berkley Books, 1985), p. 23.
38. Steve Neale, "Masculinity as Spectacle: Reflections on Men and Mainstream Cinema," *Screen* 24, no. 6 (1983): 8.
39. The female body is not "technologized" in the sense I mean here in Vietnam representation. Instead, as I discuss in chapter 3, the female body is mechanized as an unmotivated reproductive machine. Mechanization of the female body is designed to detract from women's power over their own bodies and over reproduction, whereas technologization of the male body is employed to enhance the power, invincibility and stability of the male body.
40. Broyles, "Why Men Love War," p. 61.
41. Herr, *Dispatches*, p. 65.
42. Broyles, "Why Men Love War," p. 62.
43. John Ellis, *Visible Fictions: Cinema, Television, Video* (London: Routledge, Kegan, Paul, 1982), p. 41.
44. William Pelfry, *The Big V* (New York: Avon, 1972), p. 67.
45. Quoted in Mark Baker, *Nam* (New York: Berkley Books, 1981), p. 23.
46. Philip Caputo, *A Rumor of War* (New York: Ballantine, 1977), p. 255.
47. Quoted in Walker, *Piece of My Heart*, p. 207.
48. Quoted in Pratt, *Vietnam Voices*, p. 652.
49. Mikkel Borsch-Jakobsen, "The Freudian Subject: From Ethics to Politics," lecture, University of Washington, February 5, 1987.
50. John M. Del Vecchio, *The 13th Valley* (New York: Bantam, 1982), p. 1.
51. Ellis, *Visible Fictions*, p. 44.
52. Vladimir Propp, *The Morphology of the Russian Folktale*, trans. Lawrence Scott (Austin: University of Texas Press, 1968).
53. Caputo, *Rumor of War*, p. 289.
54. Jacques Derrida, "Implications: Interview with Henri Ronse," in *Positions*, trans. Alan Bass (Chicago: University of Chicago Press, 1981), p. 12.

55. Judith Hicks Stiehm, *Bring Me Men and Women: Mandated Change at the U.S. Air Force Academy* (Berkeley: University of California Press, 1981), p. 284.

56. Cecilia Tichi, "Video Novels," *Boston Review* 13, no. 3 (June 1987): 13.

57. Dana Polan insightfully discusses these and other shared features of avant-garde and mass culture in his critique of theories of mass culture ("Brief Encounters").

58. Teresa de Lauretis, *Alice Doesn't: Feminism, Semiotics, Cinema* (Bloomington: Indiana University Press, 1984), chap. 5.

59. Andy Warhol became the spokesperson for performativity when he called for a future society in which everyone would be a "star" for one second.

60. John Wheeler, *Touched with Fire: The Future of the Vietnam Generation* (New York: Avon, 1984), p. 52.

61. Herr, *Dispatches*, p. 145.

62. Norman Mailer, *The Armies of the Night*, p. 241.

63. Lyotard, *Postmodern Condition*, p. 77.

64. Broyles, *Brothers in Arms*, p. ix.

65. Kathryn Marshall, *In the Combat Zone: An Oral History of American Women in Vietnam, 1966–1975* (Boston: Little, Brown, 1987), p. 3.

66. Broyles, *Brothers in Arms: A Journey from War to Peace* (New York: Knopf, 1986), p. ix.

67. Herr, *Dispatches*, p. 1.

68. Goldman and Fuller, *Charlie Company*, p. xv.

69. Similarly, Roman Jakobson describes the movement between metaphor—the "structural"—and metonymy—the "spectacular"—in the formation of poetic language ("The Metaphoric and Metonymic Poles," in *Critical Theory since Plato*, ed. Hazard Adams [New York: Harcourt, Brace, Jovanovich, 1971], pp. 1113–17). Here, I am suggesting the interaction between these two strategies—the structural and the spectacular—as the basis for the formation of contemporary cultural language.

70. Broyles, "Why Men Love War," p. 62.

71. Nixon, *No More Vietnams*, p. 159.

72. Wallace Terry, *Bloods: An Oral History of the Vietnam War by Black Veterans* (New York: Ballantine, 1984), p. xiv. Blacks were more likely to be drafted (28 percent as opposed to 24 percent for whites); more likely, once in the military, to go to Vietnam (55 percent as opposed to 47 percent for whites); and more likely to serve in heavy combat (34 percent as opposed to 29 percent for whites, though the figure was even higher for Hispanics, 41 percent of whom served in heavy combat). But the source for these figures, *Myths and Realities: A Study of Attitudes toward Vietnam Era Vets*, concludes that "exposure to heavy combat was not so much a product of racial discrimination as of class discrimination." Using education levels as a relative indication of class, the authors note that 54 percent of Vietnam era veterans who did not complete high school served in Vietnam and 24 percent served in heavy combat, as opposed to 35 percent and 5 percent respectively for college graduates (United States, Senate, Committee on Veterans' Affairs, 92nd Congress, 2nd sess., *Myths and Realities: A Study of Attitudes toward Vietnam Era Vets* [Washington: Government Printing Office, 1980]).

73. Quoted in Pratt, *Vietnam Voices*, p. 669.

74. Del Vecchio, *13th Valley*, p. 444.

75. Quoted in Al Santoli, *Everything We Had* (New York: Ballantine, 1981), p. 69.

76. Caputo, *Rumor of War*, p. 312.

77. Quoted in Baker, *Nam*, p. 172.

78. Quoted in Santoli, *Everything We Had*, p. 5.

79. Joan Didion's *Democracy* (New York: Simon and Schuster, 1984) is one of the few Vietnam novels to present this position explicitly and thereby begin to deconstruct it. Didion includes herself as character, narrator, and novelist in her narrative and openly questions issues of authority, facticity, history, and justice. In doing so, she avoids the creation of a "godlike" authority, which is present in Nixon, Mailer, and Herr.

80. Eastlake, p. 1.

81. Beidler, *American Literature,* p. 26.

82. Nixon, *No More Vietnams,* p. 9. Adolf Hitler, in *Mein Kampf,* articulated the identification of the unthinking masses as feminine: "The people, in an overwhelming majority, are so feminine in their nature and attitude that their activities and thoughts are motivated less by sober consideration than by feeling and sentiment" (New York: Reinal and Hitchcock, 1940, p. 237).

83. Jessica Benjamin makes this point clearly in her reading of *The Story of O* ("The Bonds of Love: Rational Violence and Erotic Domination," *Feminist Studies* 1 [Spring, 1980]: 158–69), as she notes that for effective domination, the dominator must maintain some level of individuality in the subject for the relationship of domination to be maintained. If the full tendencies of domination are exercised, the dominator must disappear with the erasure of the dominated as subject.

84. René Girard, *Deceit, Desire, and the Novel,* trans. Yvonne Freccero (Baltimore: Johns Hopkins University Press, 1965).

85. Eve Kosofsky Sedgwick, *Between Men: English Literature and Male Homosocial Desire* (New York: Columbia University Press, 1985), pp. 14–15.

86. Nancy Hartsock, *Money, Sex, and Power: Toward a Feminist Historical Materialism* (Boston: Northeastern University Press, 1983).

87. Kaja Silverman, "Fragments of a Fashionable Discourse," in *Studies in Entertainment,* ed. Modleski, p. 142.

88. This is Herr's spelling of LRRP (long-range reconnaissance patrol).

89. I specify "feminine" and "masculine" here because terms like "tits" and "balls," though referencing male and female body parts, are clearly gender constructed and interpreted. As Herr's comments show, these terms have less to do with body features than with gendered characteristics.

90. Klaus Theweleit's reading of the "soldier male" in German culture speaks resonantly here, as he describes their stance on negotiation in clear gender terms: "Representing interests, making compromises, negotiating, reaching goals in roundabout ways, planning for the long run, or taking both sides into account: all these methods are contaminated, at once male and female, in short, mire" (*Male Fantasies,* vol. 1, trans. Stephen Conway [Minneapolis: University of Minnesota Press, 1987], p. 388).

91. Marilyn French, *Beyond Power: On Women, Men, and Morals* (New York: Ballantine, 1985), p. 72.

92. Frederic Jameson, "Metacommentary," *PMLA* 86, no. 1 (January 1971): 9.

93. Quoted in Pratt, *Vietnam Voices,* 650–51.

94. The numerous and often contradictory critical interpretations of *Platoon* testify to this apparent undecidability. See, for example, the discussion in *Cineaste,* vol. 15, no. 4: 4–9. See also Richard Corliss's summary of diverse interpretations of the film in "*Platoon:* Viet Nam, the Way It Really Was, On Film," *Time,* January 26, 1987, pp. 54–62.

95. Corliss, "*Platoon,*" p. 55.

96. Quoted in Polan, "Brief Encounters," p. 177.

97. As Nancy Hartsock insightfully queries, why does the recent proliferation of theoretical positions attacking the stability of the subject and the interpretability of language occur simultaneously with women's achievement of subjectivity and access to language? ("Epistemology and Minority Discourse: Towards a Feminist Reconstitution of Knowledge," lecture, Conference on New Gender Scholarship, February 14, 1987, University of Southern California). Like the abandonment of logic, this strategy denies its own proposed bases for power at the moment when those bases become available to those excluded from power.

98. Guy Debord, *Society of the Spectacle* (Detroit: Black and Red, 1983), p. 29. While utilizing Debord's model here of the spectacle, I want first to emphasize that a

shortcoming of Debord's thesis is that he does not read capitalism in relation to gender and, second, express my disagreement with his use of terms like "center," which I think are inappropriate for discussing the construction of gender.

99. For a summary and explanation of the arguments of deconstruction, see Christopher Norris, *Deconstruction: Theory and Practice* (London: Methuen, 1982).

100. Ohmann, "Shaping of the Canon."

101. Wheeler, *Touched with Fire*, p. 141.

## 2. "THAT MEN WITHOUT WOMEN TRIP"

1. John M. Del Vecchio, *The 13th Valley* (New York: Bantam, 1982), p. 145. All subsequent references in the text are to this edition.

2. Charles R. Anderson, *The Grunts* (New York: Berkley Books, 1976), p. 187.

3. William Turner Huggett, *Body Count* (New York: Deli, 1973), p. 424. All subsequent references in the text will be to this edition.

4. Anderson, *Grunts*, p. 4.

5. See Robin Wood, *Hollywood from Vietnam to Reagan* (New York: Columbia University Press, 1986), p. 167. A similar point is made by Jeanine Basinger in *The World War II Combat Film: Anatomy of a Genre* (New York: Columbia University Press, 1986), pp. 61–62.

6. Quoted in Wallace Terry, *Bloods: An Oral History of the Vietnam War by Black Veterans* (New York: Ballantine, 1984), p. 242.

7. Quoted in Ibid., p. 38.

8. Quoted in Ibid., p. 151.

9. Richard Halloran, *To Arm a Nation: Rebuilding America's Endangered Defenses* (New York: MacMillan, 1986), p. 87.

10. William Broyles, Jr. "Why Men Love War," *Esquire*, November 1984, p. 58.

11. William Eastlake, *The Bamboo Bed* (New York: Avon, 1969), p. 61.

12. Robert Roth, *Sand in the Wind* (Boston: Little, Brown, 1973), p. 329.

13. James Webb, *Fields of Fire* (Englewood Cliffs, N.J.: Prentice Hall, 1978) p. 136.

14. William Broyles, Jr., *Brothers in Arms: A Journey from War to Peace* (New York: Knopf, 1986), p. 199.

15. Edward Said's *Orientalism* (New York: Harcourt, Brace, 1979) identifies most clearly the major features of racial prejudice directed at the "Orient" in Western society. John W. Dower's study of racism toward Asians during World War II, *War without Mercy: Race and Power in the Pacific War* (New York: Pantheon, 1986) is especially enlightening.

16. J. C. Pollock, *Mission, M.I.A.* (New York: Dell, 1982), p. 116.

17. Anderson, *Grunts*, pp. 136–37.

18. Quoted in Broyles, *Brothers in Arms*, p. 199.

19. Although Lionel Tiger, along with other sociologists and cultural theorists, labels the bonds formed between men as the "male bond" (*Men in Groups* [New York: Random House, 1969]), I find the term "masculine bond" preferable because it emphasizes the extent to which this bond is itself a cultural and not a biological contract.

20. Marilyn French, *Beyond Power: On Women, Men, and Morals* (New York: Ballantine, 1985), p. 87.

21. Judith Hicks Stiehm, *Bring Me Men and Women: Mandated Change at the U.S. Air Force Academy* (Berkeley: University of California Press, 1981), p. 3.

22. Eve Kosofsky Sedgwick, *Between Men: English Literature and Male Homosocial Desire* (New York: Columbia University Press, 1985), p. 160.

23. Ibid., p. 39. For accounts of women in combat under conditions of "necessity," see Shelley Saywell's *Women in War* (New York: Viking, 1985).

24. Nancy C. M. Hartsock, *Money, Sex, and Power: Toward a Feminist Historical Materialism* (Boston: Northeastern University Press, 1983), p. 190.

25. See Nancy Chodorow's *The Reproduction of Mothering: Psychoanalysis and the Sociology of Gender* (Berkeley: University of California Press, 1978) for a detailed analysis of these consequences for male and female children.

26. Stiehm, *Bring Me Men and Women*, p. 295.

27. As I argue in more detail in later chapters, this retrieval of the soldier should not be read as a closing of the circle of masculinity and a sign of its disintegration, but instead as a pattern of negotiations, a response to alterations in the historical construction of gender that will enable the masculine to accommodate itself to varied gender structures and thereby reassert its sufficiency.

28. Bobbie Ann Mason, *In Country* (New York: Harper and Row, 1985), p. 244. All subsequent references in the text are to this edition.

29. For a fuller discussion of how women and the feminine are portrayed in Vietnam films, see my "Friendly Civilians: Images of Women and the Feminization of the Audience in Vietnam Films" (*Wide Angle* 7, no. 4 [October, 1985]: 13–23).

30. Pollock, *Mission*, p. 118.

31. Sedgwick, *Between Men*, p. 160.

32. John Clark Pratt, *The Laotian Fragments* (New York: Viking, 1974), p. 149.

33. Andrea Dworkin, *Pornography* (New York: Perigee, 1981), p. 50.

34. Del Vecchio, *13th Valley*, p. 1.

35. Quoted in Susan Brownmiller, *Against Our Will: Men, Women and Rape* (New York: Simon and Schuster, 1975), p. 107.

36. For a more detailed reading of this complex and fascinating novel, see my "Tattoos, Scars, Diaries, and Writing Masculinity," in *American Representations of the Vietnam War*, edited by John Carlos Rowe and Rick Berg (New York: Columbia University Press, forthcoming).

37. Larry Heinemann, *Paco's Story* (New York: Penguin, 1986), p. 178.

38. Del Vecchio, *13th Valley*, p. 481–82.

39. Dworkin, *Pornography*, p. 23.

40. Luce Irigaray, "When the Goods Get Together," in *New French Feminisms*, ed. Elaine Marks and Isabelle de Courtivron (New York: Schocken Books, 1980), p. 107.

41. Terry Eagleton, *Literary Theory: An Introduction* (Oxford: Oxford University Press, 1983), pp. 132–33.

42. Sedgwick, *Between Men*, p. 89.

43. Richard Klein, "Review: *Homosexualities in French Literature*," *Modern Language Notes* 95, no. 4 (May 1980): 1077.

44. Edward F. Murphy, *Vietnam Medal of Honor Heroes* (New York: Ballantine, 1987). Murphy records numerous cases of Medal of Honor winners throwing themselves on grenades or explosives to protect the men around them (pp. 38, 50, 60, 68). *The Boys in Company C* depicts such an act, done in this case to protect Vietnamese children.

45. Broyles, "Why Men Love War," p. 65.

46. John Wheeler, *Touched with Fire: The Future of the Vietnam Generation* (New York: Avon, 1984), p. 16.

47. John Hellman, *American Myth and the Legacy of Vietnam* (New York: Columbia University Press, 1986), p. 207.

48. Charles Reich, *The Greening of America: How the Youth Revolution is Trying to Make America Livable* (New York: Random House, 1970), pp. 215–16.

49. Even a critic who does read male bonding in American literature through gender does so from the masculine point of view. Joseph A. Boone's essay, "Male Independence and the American Quest Genre: Hidden Sexual Politics in the All-Male Worlds of Melville, Twain and London," (in *Gender Studies: New Directions in Feminist Criticism*, ed. Judith Spector [Bowling Green, Ohio: Bowling Green State University Popular

Press, 1986], pp. 187–218) suggests that nineteenth-century narratives of male bonding challenged the heterosexual status quo of the romance genre by positing a "feminine" side of their heroes' characters. But, as Boone shows, the introduction of women into these narratives, as in Jack London's *The Sea Wolf*, disrupts the possibilities for such male expansion. Boone also fails to explore the possibility of female bonding or a "masculine" side to the female character. It is as if such bonding and its accompanying breakdown in "conventional sexual categorization" in American literature, whether of Vietnam or the "Pequod," cannot be accomplished except through the masculine collective.

50. Nina Baym, "Melodramas of Beset Manhood: How Theories of American Fiction Exclude Women Authors," in *The New Feminist Criticism*, ed. Elaine Showalter (New York: Pantheon, 1985), p. 78.

51. Peter Marin, "What the Vietnam Vets Can Teach Us," *Nation*, November 27, 1982, p. 562.

52. Pollock, *Mission*, p. 95.

53. Hellman's use of this term recalls Annette Kolodny's description of the dominating metaphor of American myth: "regression from the cares of adult life and a return to a primal warmth of womb or breast in a feminine landscape" (*The Lay of the Land: Metaphor as Experience and History in American Life and Letters* [Chapel Hill: North Carolina University Press, 1975], p. 6). By not questioning the gendered quality of this myth or the terminology that supports it, Hellmann is re-creating it in a critical vocabulary.

54. Philip D. Beidler, *American Literature and the Experience of Vietnam* (Athens: University of Georgia Press, 1982), p. xiii.

55. The Russian Formalists supply the best vocabulary for understanding these formulations, as they identify the dialectical relations between dominant and alternate discourses operating at a particular cultural moment. Herr's writing, part of the dominant, is not noticed, whereas Emerson's, an alternate form, is. What I am suggesting here is that such formulations work equally well for gender considerations as they do for literary ones. See Roman Jakobson, "The Dominant," in *Readings in Russian Poetics: Formalist and Structuralist Views*, ed. Ladislaw Matejka and Krystyna Pomorska (Cambridge, Mass.: MIT Press, 1971), pp. 82–88.

56. Oliver Stone, *Platoon*, screenplay (New York: Vintage, 1987), p. 128.

57. Michael Clark's fine essay, "The Silent Mirror of Vietnam" (*LSA* 6, no. 3 [Fall, 1983]: 10–15) is one of the best of such studies. For a review essay of essays on the memorial, see Peter Ehrenhaus's contribution to *Critical Studies in Mass Communication* 6.1 (1989): 92–94.

58. Charles L. Griswold, "The Vietnam Veterans Memorial and the Washington Mall: Philosophical Thoughts on Political Iconography," *Critical Inquiry* 12, no. 4 (1986): 713.

59. Susan Brownmiller, *Femininity* (New York: Fawcett Columbine, 1984), p. 15.

60. I want to distinguish my usage of this term from Kristen Thompson's ("The Concept of Cinematic Excess," in *Narrative, Apparatus, Ideology: A Film Theory Reader*, ed. Philip Rosen [New York: Columbia University Press, 1986]: 130–43), where she defines "excess" as material aspects of filmic narratives that "are not contained by its unifying forces" (p. 130). In identifying aspects of cultural narrative and not elements of individual films, I am suggesting that masculinity as excess disrupts the "unifying forces" of cultural narrative in its insistent repetition and assertion of the force of gender. As this study argues, it is at these points that we can best "read" those cultural narratives. I discuss the question of excess in more detail in "Masculinity as Excess in Vietnam Films: The Father/Son Dynamic of American Culture" (*Genre*, forthcoming).

61. Joe Klein, *Payback* (New York: Ballantine, 1984), p. 365.

62. J. L. Austin, *How to Do Things with Words* (Cambridge, Mass.: Harvard University Press, 1962), pp. 99–100.

63. Loren Baritz, *Backfire: A History of How American Culture Led Us into Vietnam, and Made Us Fight the Way We Did* (New York: Ballantine, 1985), p. 328.

64. Dave Barry, "Beer-Ad-Inspired Patriotism Is Better Than None at All," *Miami Herald* June 29, 1986.

65. I follow here Nancy Chodorow's distinction between "difference" and "differentiation" in a psychoanalytic context: "Difference and differentiation are, of course, related to and feed into one another. . . . However, it is possible to be separate, or be differentiated, without caring about or emphasizing difference, without turning the cognitive fact into an emotional, moral, or political one. In fact, assimilating difference to differentiation is defensive and reactive, *a reaction to not feeling separate enough*" [italics added] ("Gender, Relation, and Difference in Psychoanalytic Perspective," in *The Future of Difference*, ed. Hester Eisenstein and Alice Jardine [Boston: G. K. Hall, 1980], p. 8).

66. Judith Williamson, "Woman Is an Island: Femininity and Colonization," in *Studies in Entertainment*, ed. Tania Modleski (Bloomington: Indiana University Press, 1986), p. 101.

67. Rosalind Coward, *Female Desires: How They Are Sought, Bought and Packaged* (New York: Grove, 1985), p. 150.

68. Hartsock, *Money, Sex, and Power*, p. 198.

69. Jean Franco, "The Incorporation of Women: A Comparison of North American and Mexican Popular Narrative," in *Studies in Entertainment*, ed. Modleski, p. 123.

70. As Richard Dyer states in his discussion of images of Paul Robeson's body, "Representations of blacks then function as the site of *remembering and denying* the inescapability of the body in the economy" (*Heavenly Bodies: Film Stars and Society* [New York: St. Martin's Press, 1986], p. 139). Dyer's insightful arguments suggest the ways in which race and gender intersect through representations of the body, in particular, through the denial of the body in cultural productions.

## 3. FALSE LABORS

1. Tom Mayer, "A Birth in the Delta," in *The Weary Falcon* (Boston: Houghton Mifflin, 1971), p. 168. All subsequent references in the text are to this edition.

2. In this way, the narrative refers to the period during the 1950s and early 1960s when it was standard American medical practice for women to be drugged unconscious during delivery.

3. John Wheeler, *Touched with Fire: The Future of the Vietnam Generation* (New York: Avon, 1984), pp. 140–41.

4. William Broyles, Jr., *Brothers in Arms: A Journey from War to Peace* (New York: Knopf, 1986), p. 201.

5. William Eastlake, *The Bamboo Bed* (New York: Avon, 1969), p. 249.

6. William Broyles, Jr., "Why Men Love War," *Esquire*, November 1984, p. 61.

7. There are numerous cases of men who did not fight in combat in the Vietnam War—whether through draft deferrel, draft avoidance, having a noncombat position in Vietnam—who state they regret this condition. Christopher Buckley writes in an August 1983 article for *Esquire*, "I didn't suffer with them [veterans]. I didn't watch my buddies getting wiped out next to me. And though I'm relieved, at the same time I feel as though part of my reflex action is not complete. . . . I haven't served my country. I've never faced life or death. I'm an incomplete person" (quoted in Wheeler, *Touched with Fire*, p. 124). James Fallows's now famous essay, "What Did You Do in the Class War, Daddy?" was one of the earliest public "confessions" of having "missed" something important in life by not having served in the war. As he says elsewhere, "I don't know anyone who has changed his views about the rightness or the wrongness of the war—but for some there

is this feeling that a normal way station on the route to masculinity has been missed" (in Myra MacPherson, *Long Time Passing: Vietnam and the Haunted Generation* [New York: Signet, 1984], p. 180). On the other side, there are some feminist writers whose assertions about childbirth and its significance echo the claims Broyles wishes to make for warfare and men. Sheila Kitzinger, for example, says that "The experience of bearing a child is central to a woman's life. . . . It is unlikely that any experience in a man's life is comparably vivid" (*The Experience of Childbirth* [Harmondsworth, England: Penguin, 1974], p. 17).

8. Wheeler, *Touched with Fire*, p. 156.

9. Tiger distinguishes aggression, which is "related to mastery" (*Men In Groups* [New York: Random House, 1969], p. 170), from violence, which is the product of human interaction with the environment and is not oriented toward producing or maintaining a hierarchical set of relations.

10. Elaine Morgan's study of apes and human evolution responds directly to Tiger's emphasis on male bonding by showing it more a product of Tiger's own perspective than of relations among apes. In particular, she criticizes Tiger's selection of two groups of apes—the baboon and the macaque—as sources for his study. As she points out, these are the two most aggressive and hierarchical of ape species, in disproportionate number to all other species, which are far friendlier, form less violent hierarchies, and depend less on aggression for maintenance of group coherence. In addition, she argues that Tiger's qualification for bonding, a selectivity on the part of males that he finds absent in the "aggregation" of females, excludes not only females but "99 percent of all males as well" (*The Descent of Woman* [New York: Bantam, 1973], p. 206), focusing disproportionately on an elite group of "bachelor males" who are fighting for group dominance. By examining the frequency of grooming habits and nurturing behaviors, Morgan argues instead that females show more group cohesion than males, showing a kind of bonding, the significance of which Tiger's analysis deliberately ignores, (pp. 206–7).

11. Rosalind Coward, *Female Desires: How They Are Sought, Bought and Packaged* (New York: Grove, 1985), p. 91.

12. Judith Hicks Stiehm, *Bring Me Men and Women: Mandated Change at the U.S. Air Force Academy* (Berkeley: University of California Press, 1981), p. 296.

13. Nicole-Claude Mathieu, "Biological Paternity, Social Maternity," *Feminist Issues* 4, no. 1 (Spring, 1984): 64.

14. This parallel between women and the land shows the continued relevance of Annette Kolodny's arguments (*The Lay of the Land: Metaphor as Experience and History in American Life and Letters* [Chapel Hill: University of North Carolina Press, 1975]).

15. Mathieu, "Biological Paternity," p. 64.

16. Robyn Rowland, "Technology and Motherhood: Reproductive Choice Reconsidered," *Signs* 12, no. 3 (Spring 1987): 525.

17. Stiehm, *Bring Me Men and Women*, p.296.

18. Nancy C. M. Hartsock, *Money, Sex, and Power: Toward a Feminist Historical Materialism* (Boston: Northeastern University Press), 1983.

19. While Hartsock interprets this appropriation in terms of the masculine control of creativity and rhetoric (*Money, Sex, and Power*, p. 197), I am emphasizing here the much more literal appropriation of reproduction itself, rather than its metaphors. Although it would seem that an appropriation of biological reproduction would be impossible, recent cultural narratives have been hinting at such possibilities. *Enemy Mine*, a film about an "androgynous" lizardlike alien creature, is significant here because the actor who plays the alien, Lou Gosset, Jr., has such a deeply "male" voice that his subsequent admission that "he" is pregnant seems less a sign of androgyny than of a pregnant male. That the baby is delivered by Caesarean is also in keeping with any possible male reproduction. In the premier episode of *St. Elsewhere* in 1987, a Vietnam veteran not only believed he

was pregnant and experienced "morning sickness," but convinced several of the young male doctors of this as well. In an acted out birthing, he "delivers" a memory of killing a child in Vietnam during the war. Neatly, his wife becomes pregnant during this time, as if she exists only to carry out "his" pregnancy.

20. Klaus Theweleit's account of the narratives of members of the German Freikorps shows the same technique, in which numerous dates, names, and figures are recorded, but never the name of their wives (*Male Fantasies*, vol. 1, trans. Stephen Conway [Minneapolis: University of Minesota Press, 1987], pp. 3–18).

21. Andrea Dworkin, *Pornography* (New York: Bantam, 1982), p. 222.

22. Hartsock, *Money, Sex, Power*, p. 253.

23. There are other Vietnam narratives in which a birth takes place: an episode of "China Beach"; an episode of "Tour of Duty"; and, though it is not about Vietnam, Samuel Fuller's *The Big Red One*, made in 1980, has a scene of childbirth in a tank. There are also World War II films in which a birth takes place—*Stand By for Action* (1943), *So Proudly We Hail* (1943)—but the scenarios of birth and the attitude toward mother and child are different. The pattern of reproduction and war narratives as it changes over time deserves separate attention as a focus for historical changes in gender constructions.

24. Peter Travers, "Picks and Pans," *People*, June 24, 1985, p. 10.

25. Jacques Derrida, "Choreographies," *Diacritics* 12, no. 2 (Summer 1982): 76.

26. Robin Wood, *Hollywood from Vietnam to Reagan* (New York: Columbia University Press, 1986), p. 294.

27. The insistence on "ease" and a lack of inhibition on the part of men suggests the weight of social constraint and limitation falls on men and not women. Chapter 4 discusses this characterization of victimization in more detail.

28. Toril Moi, *Sexual/Textual Politics: Feminist Literary Theory* (New York: Methuen, 1985), p. 65.

29. Joseph A. Boone's essay on the nineteenth-century American quest narratives of Melville, Twain, and London, "Male Independence and the American Quest Genre: Hidden Sexual Politics in the All-Male Worlds of Melville, Twain and London" (in *Gender Studies: New Directions in Feminist Criticism*, ed. Judith Spector [Bowling Green, Ohio: Bowling Green University Popular Press, 1986]: pp. 187–218) interestingly recapitulates Wood's pattern in indicating that Wood's thesis is not singular but typical of a larger critical pattern now appearing in scholarship about male bonding, masculinity, and male homoeroticism. Focusing entirely on the masculine point of view in the narratives he chooses—Ishmael, Billy Budd, Huck—Boone suggests, like Wood, that Huck, for example, can "cross boundaries of class, race and sex with startling ease" (p. 200), while Ishmael himself assumes an "androgynous" position of incorporating the feminine into his already established masculine character. In each case, the feminine is incorporated, or, more precisely, appropriated to the character of the hero in such a way that Boone's claim for its challenge to traditional heterosexual norms is *only* a masculine statement.

30. Donald Pfarrer, *Neverlight* (New York: Laurel, 1982), p. 72. All subsequent references in the text will be to this edition.

31. Jessica Benjamin, "The Bonds of Love: Rational Violence and Erotic Domination," *Feminist Studies* 1 (Spring 1980): 42.

32. Zoe Sofia, "Exterminating Fetuses: Abortion, Disarmament, and the Sexo-Semiotics of Extraterrestrialism," *Diacritics* 14, no. 2 (Summer 1984): 51.

33. James Webb, "When My Son Was Born," *Parade*, June 16, 1985, p. 8. This is the opening line of the essay.

34. Mary O'Brien, *The Politics of Reproduction* (Boston: Routledge and Kegan Paul, 1981), p. 53.

35. As these quotations show, O'Brien leaps from "male" to "men" with startling

alacrity. Her elision of the biological and the social suggests a direct cause-effect relation between reproduction and patriarchy. For all of Mary Daly's own tendencies to fall into this trap, she offers a cogent critique of positions like O'Brien's: "to conclude that 'womb envy' is the key to phallocratic deception and to fixate on female biological fertility would be just another way of falling into the trap of demonic deception" (*Gyn/Ecology: The Metaethics of Radical Feminism* [Boston: Beacon Press, 1978], pp. 46–7), that is that women are limited to their biological functions. I find O'Brien's thesis suggestive but not exhaustive.

36. Wheeler, *Touched with Fire*, p. 85.

37. Mary Daly discusses an unpublished essay by Anne Dellenbaugh, "Parthenogenesis: Why We've Never Heard about It," to argue that this is a feature of Western culture as a whole, in which "a deliberate effort is being made to remove creativity from women and re-establish it in the realm of male domination and control. Thus, the christian 'Virgin Birth' is a link between primordial mythic parthenogenesis and technological attempts to establish the 'father' as the one 'true parent' through cloning" (*Gyn/Ecology*, pp. 83–84).

38. Gena Corea, *The Mother Machine: Reproductive Technologies from Artificial Insemination to Artificial Wombs* (New York: Harper and Row, 1985), p. 289.

39. Rowland, "Technology and Motherhood," p. 526.

40. Robyn Rowland, "Reproductive Technologies: The Final Solution to the Woman Question?" In *Test-Tube Woman: What Future for Motherhood?*, ed. Rita Arditti, Renate Duelli Klein, and Shelley Minden (Boston: Pandora, 1984), p. 363.

41. Loren Baritz, *Backfire: A History of How American Culture Led Us into Vietnam, and Made Us Fight the Way We Did* (New York: Ballantine, 1985), p. 34. Rambo personally kills eight Russian and a score of Vietnamese soldiers and bombs or shoots several hundred more; *People* magazine counts forty-four dead by Rambo's hands alone, estimating an average of one murder every 2.1 minutes of the film.

42. Jean-François Lyotard, *The Postmodern Condition: A Report on Knowledge*, trans. Geoff Bennington and Brian Massumi (Minneapolis: University of Minnesota Press, 1984), p. 37.

43. Peter Marin, "What the Vietnam Vets Can Teach Us," *Nation*, November 27, 1982, p. 562.

44. Susan Rubin Suleiman, "Pornography, Transgression, and the Avant-Garde: Bataille's *Story of the Eye*," in *The Poetics of Gender*, ed. Nancy K. Miller (New York: Columbia University Press, 1986), p. 120. Georges Bataille, "The Notion of Expenditure," in *Visions of Excess: Selected Writings, 1927–1939*, ed. Allan Stoekl (Minneapolis: University of Minnesota Press, 1985), p. 117.

45. Wheeler, *Touched with Fire*, p. 131.

46. J. C. Pollock, *Mission, M.I.A.* (New York: Dell, 1982), p. 94.

47. Suleiman, "Pornography, Transgression, and the Avant-Garde," p. 130.

48. Corea, *The Mother Machine*, p. 262.

49. Luce Irigaray, *Ce sexe qui n'est pas un* (Paris, 1977).

50. Domna Stanton, "Difference on Trial: A Critique of the Maternal Metaphor in Cixous, Irigaray, and Kristeva," in *The Poetics of Gender*, ed. Nancy K. Miller, p. 171.

51. Klaus Theweleit, *Male Fantasies* vol. 1, trans. Stephen Conway (Minneapolis: University of Minnesota Press, 1987), p. 270.

52. Hartsock, *Money, Sex, and Power*, p. 242.

53. Broyles, "Why Men Love War," p. 58.

54. In "Masculinity as Excess in Vietnam Films: The Father/Son Dynamic of American Culture" (*Genre*, forthcoming), I argue that it is the exchange of power and positionality between father and son that constrains and controls the excess of gender in American culture. It would be, in Theweleit's terms, the father/son paradigm that enables "reterritorialization." Additionally, because such paradigms foreground the child

as son, discussion of the father/daughter and mother/daughter relationship offer, as I argue in chapter 3 of *Reproducing Fathers* (manuscript in progress), greater possibilities for the disruption of patriachal powers.

## 4. "DO WE GET TO WIN THIS TIME?"

1. John Chrysostom, "Homilies on St. John, xxv.2," in *A Select Library of the Nicene and Post-Nicene Fathers of the Christian Church*, vol. xiv, ed. Philip Schaff (New York: Christian Literature, 1980), p. 80.

2. Some of these effects are discussed in the numerous collections of essays that are or will be appearing that address the Vietnam War. Essays in these collections range from discussing film and fiction to pop music, comic books and cartoons, Vietnam memorials, and other aspects of American culture: *Wide Angle* 7, no. 4 (October 1985); *Cultural Critique* 3 (Spring 1986), ed. Richard Berg and John Carlos Rowe; *Search and Clear: Responses to Selected Literature and Films of the Vietnam War*, ed. William J. Searle (Bowling Green, Ohio: Bowling Green University Popular Press, 1988); *The Cultural Legacy of Vietnam: Uses of the Past in the Present*, ed. Peter Ehrenhaus and Richard Morris (Ablex Press, forthcoming); *Tell Me Lies about Vietnam: Cultural Battles for the Meaning of the War*, ed. Alf Louvre and Jeffrey Walsh (England: Open University Press, forthcoming); *Vietnam Images: War and Representation*, ed. James Aulich and Jeffrey Walsh (London: Lumiere Macmillan, 1988); *Critical Studies in Mass Communication* 6.1 (1989), ed. Harry Haines; *Genre*, ed. Gordon O. Taylor (forthcoming).

3. Lucian Truscott in *The Wounded Generation: America after Vietnam*, ed. A. D. Horne (Englewood Cliffs, N.J.: Prentice-Hall, 1981), p. 107.

4. A similar pattern is noticed by Nancy K. Miller in her critique of Denis Donoghue's reading of anger expressed in some feminist criticism. Miller interprets Donoghue's reading to ask: "Are the women really angry (as in really guilty) or are they just getting carried away by the sound of their own voice: is this a 'real fury in the words' (a fake rage like a fake orgasm?)" ("Men on Feminism," in *Men in Feminism*, ed. Alice Jardine and Paul Smith [New York: Methuen, 1987], p. 138).

5. John Wheeler, *Touched with Fire: The Future of the Vietnam Generation* (New York: Avon, 1984), p. 141.

6. Numerous women have written on their experiences in the antiwar movement in the sixties and its relation to their increasing awareness of the women's movement. Some of these statements are included in: Marge Piercy's *Vida* (New York: Summit, 1979), Myra MacPherson's *Long Time Passing* (New York: Signet, 1984), Susan Jacoby's essays (see Jacoby's essay in *The Wounded Generation*, ed. A. D. Horne), Gloria Emerson's *Winners and Losers: Battles, Retreats, Gains, Losses, and Ruins from the Vietnam War* (New York: Penguin, 1972).

7. Truscott in *Wounded Generation*, ed. Horne, p. 108.

8. Lance Morrow, "A Bloody Rite of Passage," *Time*, April 15, 1985, p. 22.

9. Wheeler, *Touched with Fire*, p. 148.

10. Judith Hicks Stiehm, *Bring Me Men and Women: Mandated Change at the U.S. Air Force Academy* (Berkeley: University of California Press, 1981), p. 227.

11. Samuel Osherson, *Finding Our Fathers: The Unfinished Business of Manhood* (New York: The Free Press, 1986), p. 11.

12. Wheeler, *Touched with Fire*, pp. 16–17.

13. *American Heritage Dictionary*, ed. William Morris (Boston: Houghton Mifflin, 1978), p. 887.

14. Wheeler, *Touched with Fire*, p. 17.

15. George Swiers uses a similar analogy in identifying what he calls the "demented-vet portrayals" of 1970s: "No grade-B melodrama was complete without its standard

vet—a psychotic, ax-wielding rapist every bit as insulting as another one-time creature of Hollywood's imagination, the shiftless, lazy, and wide-eyed black" ("'Demented Vets' and Other Myths: The Moral Obligation of Veterans," in *Vietnam Reconsidered: Lessons from a War,* ed. Harrison E. Salisbury [New York: Harper and Row, 1984], p. 198).

16. The most complete narratives of POWs are contained in Zalin Grant's *Survivors: American POWs in Vietnam* (New York: Berkley Books, 1975). The 1987 film *Hanoi Hilton* depicts some of the scenes narrated in *Survivors*. In addition to providing evidence of victimization, the narratives of POWs support racism as well by reinforcing an American identity in contradistinction to a third-world people.

17. Tom Morganthau, "We're Still Prisoners of War," *Newsweek*, April 15, 1985, p. 34.

18. Ron Kovic, *Born on the Fourth of July* (New York: Pocket Books, 1976), p. 134.

19. Quoted in *Charlie Company: What Vietnam Did to Us*, ed. Peter Goldman and Tony Fuller (New York: Ballantine, 1983), p. 88.

20. Ruben Treviso, "Hispanics and the Vietnam War," in *Vietnam Reconsidered,* ed. Salisbury, p. 185.

21. These figures were compiled from *Myths and Realities: A Study of Attitudes toward Vietnam Era Vets*, U.S. Senate Committee on Veterans' Affairs, *Hearings*, 92nd Congress, 2d sess. (Washington: Government Printing Office, 1980) and Treviso, "Hispanics and the Vietnam War."

22. Figures quoted in Horne, ed., *Wounded Generation,* p. 10.

23. Quoted in Morrow, "Bloody Rite of Passage," p. 59.

24. Michael Herr, *Dispatches* (New York: Avon, 1978), pp. 13–14.

25. Loren Baritz, *Backfire: Vietnam—A History of How American Culture Led Us into Vietnam, and Made Us Fight the Way We Did* (New York: Ballantine, 1985), pp. 285–86.

26. Stanley Karnow, *Vietnam: A History* (New York: Viking, 1983), p. 323.

27. Quoted in Al Santoli, *To Bear Any Burden: The Vietnam War and Its Aftermath in the Words of Americans and Southeast Asians* (New York: Ballantine, 1985), pp. 118–24). For a summary discussion of the extent to which American interests were invested in Vietnamese government corruption, see Barbara W. Tuchman's "America Betrays Herself in Vietnam," in her *The March of Folly: From Troy to Vietnam* (New York: Knopf, 1984, chap. 5). We must keep in mind that these constructions of connection, service, and duty were interpreted in quite other ways by the Vietnamese themselves and that the term "corruption" applies principally to the identification of American interests.

28. Joe Klein, *Payback* (New York: Ballantine, 1984), p. 272.

29. U.S. Congress, Senate, Committee on Veterans' Affairs, *Hearings*, 96th Congress, 2d sess. (Washington: Government Printing Office, 1980).

30. Morrow, "Bloody Rite of Passage," pp. 23–24.

31. *New York Times,* May 26, 1984.

32. *Myths and Realities*, p. 85.

33. Jean Bethke Elshtain, *Women and War* (New York: Basic Books, 1987), p. 218.

34. The most prominent exception to this is Vietnamese director Ho Quang Minh's film, *Karma* (1986), which records the impact of the war on a South Vietnamese family. Ho Quang Minh plans two other films to complete his trilogy, one a view of the war for a North Vietnamese family and the other for an American family.

35. These figures are compiled from various government documents (*Myths and Realities*, and U.S. Veterans' Administration, *Annual Report* [Washington: Government Printing Office, 1983]). There is some disagreement about the number of women serving in the Vietnam-era military. Early figures of 2 percent *(Myths and Realities)* were rejected in favor of the more recent 3.2 percent *(Annual Report)*.

36. Rambo's representativeness as a white male would seem to be contradicted by

his early and brief assertion in *Rambo: First Blood, Part II* that he is part Indian. But Sylvester Stallone's widely proclaimed Italian heritage outweighs "Rambo"'s statement as a cultural signifier and draws him back into the circle of a white American male who can effectivley capitalize on his absorbed "heritage," appropriating it within his image rather than being challenged by it. Secondarily, Rambo's image from *First Blood*, in which no such statement was made, was already fully established as a cultural artifact. His subsequent acknowledgment of Native American ancestry thus stands, not as a detractor from his image as a white male, but as reinforcement, both of his "natural" abilities as a soldier and, more importantly, of his genuine "Americanness." As Harry Haines explains, "[Rambo's] Indian origins enable him to move deftly through the jungle, using the natural environment as a weapon; his German origins explain his superior command of technology and strategy" ("The Pride Is Back: *Rambo, Magnum, P.I.*, and the Return Trip to Vietnam," in *The Cultural Legacy of Vietnam: Uses of the Past in the Present*, ed. Peter Ehrenhaus and Richard Morris [Ablex Press, forthcoming]).

37. The television program "Tour of Duty" includes black and Hispanic soldiers, though the officers are white.

38. Morrow, "Bloody Rite of Passage," p. 24.

39. Haines, *The Pride Is Back*, (forthcoming).

40. Morrow, "Bloody Rite of Passage," p. 24.

41. David H. Van Biema, "With a $100 Million Gross(out), Sly Stallone Fends Off *Rambo*'s Army of Adversaries," *People*, July 8, 1985, p. 37.

42. Mircea Eliade, *The Sacred and the Profane* (New York: Harcourt, 1959), p. 131.

43. The power of Norris's role here to regenerate masculinity within and without *Missing in Action* becomes doubled when it is known that his own brother died in a POW camp (Peter Travers, "Picks and Pans," *People*, June 24, 1985, pp. 9–10).

44. Klaus Theweleit, *Male Fantasies* vol. 1, trans. Stephen Conway (Minneapolis: University of Minnesota Press, 1987), p. 420.

45. These themes are in sharp contrast to an earlier film like Hal Ashby's *Coming Home*, in which the veteran-as-victim is celebrated, with Luke rejecting the war and its masculine values in favor of the feminism and femininity of Sally Hyde (a feminism that, problematically, he is instrumental in bringing about). He accepts not only a more passive and negotiating posture, but is firmly established in a domesticity as well. Finally, his disability marks his rejection of the masculine body, and his love scenes with Sally Hyde reinforce his association with her sexuality. *Coming Home*, like *First Blood*, is the representation of veterans to which *Rambo: First Blood, Part II* and *Missing in Action* are responding.

46. Jeanine Basinger sees some Vietnam films, *Uncommon Valor* in particular, as merely variations of World War II combat narratives (*The World War II Combat Film: Anatomy of a Genre* [New York: Columbia University Press, 1986], p. 122).

47. Jean Franco makes a similar argument for the popularity of Harlequin romances, in which their "use of the archaic evokes more than a manorial setting; it also slips in, as if they were a fact of nature, gender relationships in which men have both power and knowledge, and in which women have to be tutored" ("The Incorporation of Women: A Comparison of North American and Mexican Popular Narrative," in *Studies in Entertainment*, ed. Tania Modleski [Bloomington: Indiana University Press, 1986], p. 126).

48. Richard Nixon's study, *No More Vietnams* (New York: Arbor House, 1985), discusses each of these topics in detail as constructive outcomes of the Vietnam war. See Elaine Scarry's "Injury and the Structure of War" for an acute analysis of these explanatory structures (*Representations* 10 [1985]: 1–52).

49. Wheeler, *Touched with Fire*, p. 4.

50. Elshtain, *Women and War*, p. 247.

51. Truscott in *Wounded Generation*, ed. Horne, p. 133.

52. Swiers, "Demented Vets," p. 200.

53. John Wheeler, in *Wounded Generation*, ed. Horne, p. 130.

54. Elshtain, *Women and War*, p. 220.

55. Wheeler, *Touched with Fire*, p. 202.

56. Richard Corliss, "*Platoon:* Viet Nam, the Way It Really Was, on Film," *Time*, January 26, 1987, p. 59.

57. Carolyn Heilbrun in her book *Toward a Recognition of Androgyny* (New York: Harper and Row, 1973) is chief among those who argue that androgynous characters who can incorporate both the masculine and the feminine represent positive movements for feminism.

58. The issue of reintegration sets these current Vietnam films apart from earlier Hollywood war films, which generally tell the tale of a marginalized, ostracized protagonist (male) being reintegrated into the larger structure of the military, the nation, or the male community, a reintegration often signified by a woman's acceptance (*Operation Pacific* [1951]). Those who are not reintegrated are eliminated (*From Here to Eternity* [1953] or *In Harm's Way* [1965] or *Green Berets* [1968]). In contrast, Rambo and Braddock are even more marginalized at the close of their films than at their beginnings, emphasizing the individual over the community.

## 5. "ACT BEFORE THE FIGHTING BREAKS OUT"

1. For a further explanation of and use of this term, see my "Debriding Vietnam: The Resurrection of the White American Male," *Feminist Studies* 14, no. 3 (Fall 1988): 525–45.

2. This situation is drawn in David A. Willson's novel, *REMF Diary: A Novel of the Vietnam War Zone* (Seattle: Black Heron Press, 1988), a parody of Vietnam personal narratives that discuss the difficulties of the war. In *REMF Diary*, the main character laments the loss of air conditioning, flavors of ice cream, and shirts in the laundry.

3. Lucian Truscott in *The Wounded Generation: America after Vietnam*, ed. A. D. Horne (Englewood Cliffs, N.J.: Prentice-Hall, 1981), p. 110.

4. Studies like Richard Halloran's *To Arm a Nation: Rebuilding America's Endangered Defenses* (New York: MacMillan, 1986) and Edward N. Luttwak's *The Pentagon and the Art of War: The Question of Military Reform* (New York: Simon and Schuster, 1984) have offered statistical and analytical arguments that the American soldier was and remains superior to his counterparts.

5. Quoted in Al Santoli, *Everything We Had* (New York: Ballantine, 1981), p. 7.

6. Peter Travers, "Picks and Pans," *People*, June 24, 1985, p. 10.

7. For a development of the ways in which the character of the veteran was "feminized" in Vietnam film, see my "Friendly Civilians: Images of Women and the Feminization of the Audience in Vietnam Film" (*Wide Angle* 7, no. 4 [October 1985]: 13–23).

8. Michael Herr, *Dispatches* (New York: Avon, 1978), p. 1.

9. John M. Del Vecchio, *The 13th Valley* (New York: Bantam, 1982), p. 103.

10. John Clark Pratt, *The Laotian Fragments* (New York: Viking, 1974), p. 37. All subsequent references in the text will be to this edition.

11. This is in keeping with Steve Neale's suggestion that "in a heterosexual and patriarchal society, the male body cannot be marked explicitly as the erotic object of another male look" and that that look "must be motivated in some other way, its erotic component repressed," in this case through violence ("Masculinity as Spectacle: Reflections on Men and Mainstream Cinema," *Screen* 24, no. 6 [1983]: 8).

12. As Edward Said has shown, Western depictions of Asians are in general trans-

lated through gender terms as "feminine" and sexualized (*Orientalism* [New York: Harcourt Brace, 1979]).

13. Klaus Theweleit, *Male Fantasies* vol. 1, trans. Stephen Conway (Minneapolis: University of Minnesota Press, 1987).

14. This opposition is discussed in Shiela Ruth, *Issues in Feminism: A First Course in Women's Studies* (Boston: Houghton Mifflin, 1980).

15. In this way, the father's/male body is mythified and castration averted.

16. Theweleit, *Male Fantasies*, pp. 387–88.

17. Richard Nixon, *No More Vietnams* (New York: Arbor House, 1985), p. 165.

18. John Wheeler, *Touched with Fire: The Future of the Vietnam Generation* (New York: Avon, 1984), p. 79.

19. Fonda's recent apology for her activities during the Vietnam War continues the feminine characteristics discussed here. As she said in her 20/20 interview (June 17, 1988), "My intentions were never to hurt [U.S. soldiers] or make their situation worse. . . . I was trying to help end the killing and the war *but there were times when I was thoughtless and careless about it* and I'm . . . very sorry I hurt them" [italics added].

20. As of 1984, blacks comprised 32.5 percent and Hispanics 4.3 percent of the U.S. Army (figures quoted by Ruben Treviso in "Hispanics and the Vietnam War," in *Vietnam Reconsidered: Lessons From A War,* ed. Harrison E. Salisbury [New York: Harper and Row, 1984], p. 185, though Treviso suggests that because percentages are calculated on the basis of self-declaration, Hispanics are considerably undercounted).

21. Quoted in David H. Van Biema, "With a $100 Million Gross(out), Sly Stallone Fends Off *Rambo*'s Army of Adversaries," *People*, July 8, 1985, p. 36.

22. Del Vecchio, *13th Valley*, p. 179.

23. Charles L. Griswold, "The Vietnam Veterans Memorial and the Washington Mall: Philosophical Thoughts on Political Iconography," *Critical Inquiry* 12, no. 4 (1986): 695.

24. Luce Irigaray, "This Sex Which Is Not One," trans. Claudia Reeder, in *New French Feminisms*, ed. Elaine Marks and Isabelle de Courtivron (New York: Schocken Books, 1980), p. 103.

25. Quoted in Josette Feral, "Writing and Displacement: Women in Theatre," trans. Barbara Kerslake, *Modern Drama* 27, no. 4 (1984): 550.

26. Diane Griffin Crowder, "Amazons and Mothers? Monique Wittig, Helene Cixous and Theories of Women's Writing," *Contemporary Literature* 24, no. 2 (1983): 143.

27. Irigaray, "This Sex Which Is Not One," p. 101.

28. Helene Cixous, "The Laugh of the Medusa," in *New French Feminisms*, p. 258.

29. Irigaray, "This Sex Which Is Not One," p. 104.

30. Rosi Braidotti, "Envy: or With Your Brains and My Looks," in *Men in Feminism*, ed. Alice Jardine and Paul Smith (New York: Methuen, 1987), p. 237.

31. Irigaray, "This Sex Which Is Not One," p. 104.

32. Ann Rosalind Jones, "Writing the Body: Toward an Understanding of l'Ecriture Feminine," in *The New Feminist Criticism*, ed. Elaine Showalter (New York: Pantheon, 1985), p. 369.

33. Dana Polan, "Brief Encounters: Mass Culture and the Evacuation of Sense," in *Studies in Entertainment: Critical Approaches to Mass Culture*, ed. Tania Modleski (Bloomington: Indiana University Press, 1986), p. 178.

34. The emphasis here is to suggest that the theorizations of French feminism are not inaccurate but may be figured differently in cultural formations that are institutionalized and structured in different ways than those in France.

35. The use of "excess" here is to be distinguished from that offered in chapter 2, where it has a specifically gendered usage. To distinguish between this earlier usage and Polan's I will continue to designate Polan's term with quotation marks.

## 6. THE REMASCULINIZATION OF AMERICA

1. Although remasculinization works primarily to the benefit of white males, because of the structured oppression of women within patriarchal relations, all men would, to some extent, benefit from this process. But in spite of the ideology of collectivity, remasculinization is not a project of equivalence. Other forms of difference—race, class, sexual preference, age, and so on—are employed to maintain a hierarchy of privilege within masculinity. In specific circumstances, women are enabled to have a kind of privilege over men, but this privilege is by and large a product of associations with men or institutions constructed on a basis of masculine relations.

2. Monica Collins, "Next Season It'll Be a Man's Game," *USA Today*, May 19, 1987, p. 3D.

3. As a correspondent for *Esquire* from 1967 to 1970, Michael Herr wrote four essays that would later comprise the bulk of *Dispatches:* "Hell Sucks" (*Esquire*, August 1968, pp. 66–69); "Khesanh" (*Esquire*, September 1969, pp. 118–23); "Conclusion at Khesanh" (*Esquire*, October 1969, pp. 118–23); and "The War Correspondent: A Reappraisal" (*Esquire*, April 1970, pp. 95–101).

4. I have borrowed this term from Robyn Wiegman's study of male bonding in American culture, *Negotiating the Masculine: Configurations of Race and Gender in American Culture* (Ph.D. diss., University of Washington, 1988).

5. Gustav Hasford, *The Short-Timers* (New York: Bantam, 1979), p. 19. All subsequent references in the text will be to this edition.

6. Klaus Theweleit, *Male Fantasies* vol. 1, trans. Stephen Conway (Minneapolis: University of Minnesota Press, 1987).

7. For detailed discussions of such stereotyping, see John W. Dower's *War without Mercy: Race and Power in the Pacific War* (New York: Pantheon, 1986) and Jeanine Basinger's *The World War II Combat Film: Anatomy of a Genre* (New York: Columbia University Press, 1986), chap. 1.

8. There are a few narratives that acknowledge racial identification, but they are written primarily by women. Both Louise Erdrich's *Love Medicine* (New York: Holt, Rinehart and Winston, 1984) and Leslie Marmon Silko's post–World War II novel *Ceremony* (New York: Signet, 1977) provide explicit scenes in which Native American soldiers see themselves in relation to Asians and opposed to whites. In sharp contrast to *Full Metal Jacket,* Erdrich has a Vietnamese woman who is being interrogated and has been raped by white soldiers look directly at Henry Lamartine, a Chippewa soldier, who imagines her look to say, "You me. Same same" (p. 138).

9. For a full discussion of the significance of this stereotype in American culture, see Trudier Harris's *Exorcizing Blackness: Historical and Literary Lynching and Burning Rituals* (Bloomington: Indiana University Press, 1984).

10. For a discussion of race and gender in American culture, see Wiegman, *Negotiating the Masculine*.

11. There have been numerous recent critiques of feminist criticism's own neglects. Among them are Jane Gaines, "White Privilege and Looking Relations: Race and Gender in Feminist Film Theory," *Cultural Critique* 4 (1986): 66; Lucie Arcuthnot and Gail Seneca's "Pre-Text and Text in *Gentlemen Prefer Blonds*" (*Film Reader* 5 [1981]: 13–23); Chris Strayer's "*Personal Best:* Lesbian/Feminist Audience" (*Jump Cut* 29 [1984]: 40–44); and Craig Owens, "Outlaws: Gay Men in Feminism," in *Men in Feminism,* ed. Alice Jardine and Paul Smith (New York: Methuen, 1987), p. 221.

12. See, for example, Hortense Spillers's excellent "Mama's Baby, Papa's Maybe: An American Grammar Book," *Diacritics* (Summer 1987): 65–82.

13. Gerda Lerner, *The Creation of Patriarchy* (New York: Oxford University Press, 1986), p. 239.

14. See, for example, the collection, *Behind the Lines: Gender and the Two World Wars*, ed. Margaret Randolph Higgonet et al. (New Haven: Yale University Press, 1987).

15. Betty A. Reardon suggests, for example, that "Because of their more intimate physical connection to the life cycle, women understand that the future is not an abstract condition in a remote time" (*Sexism and the War System* [New York: Teachers College Press, 1985], p. 86) and then uses this as a basis for arguing that women are more likely than men to work toward a "preferred future" (p. 86) that does not include war.

16. Jean Bethke Elsthain, *Women and War* (New York: Basic Books, 1987), p. 166.

17. Reardon, *Sexism*, p. 15.

18. Andrea Dworkin, *Intercourse* (New York: Free Press, 1987), p. 160.

19. Del Vecchio, *13th Valley*, p. 444.

20. John Clark Pratt, *Vietnam Voices: Perspectives on the War Years, 1941–82* (New York: Penguin, 1984), p. 651. A more recent example would be Ronald Reagan's insistent reference to the Soviet Union as an "evil empire."

21. Examples include ancient Greek societies in which warriors formed a class within society and were not a function of social membership, as well as the limitations in the Middle Ages on what kinds of lands—agricultural, church-owned—could not be trespassed for warfare. Jean Bethke Elshtain discusses these circumstances briefly in her study *Women and War.*

22. Elshtain, *Women and War,* pp. 74–75.

23. Joan Didion, *Democracy* (New York: Simon and Schuster, 1984), p. 206.

# Bibliography


Anderson, Charles R. *The Grunts*. New York: Berkley, 1976.

Arbuthnot, Lucie, and Gail Seneca. "Pre-Text and Text in *Gentlemen Prefer Blonds*." *Film Reader* 5 (1981):13–23.

Austin, J. L. *How To Do Things with Words*. Cambridge, Mass.: Harvard University Press, 1962.

Baker, Mark. *Nam*. New York: Berkley, 1981.

Baritz, Loren. *Backfire: A History of How American Culture Led Us into Vietnam and Made Us Fight the Way We Did*. New York: Ballantine, 1985.

Barry, Dave. "Beer-Ad-Inspired Patriotism Is Better Than None at All." *Miami Herald*, June 29, 1986.

Barthes, Roland. *S/Z*. Translated by Richard Miller. New York: Hill and Wang, 1974.

Basinger, Jeanine. *The World War II Combat Film: Anatomy of a Genre*. New York: Columbia University Press, 1986.

Bataille, Georges. *Death and Sensuality: A Study of Eroticism and the Taboo*. New York: Walker, 1977.

———. "The Notion of Expenditure," in *Visions of Excess: Selected Writings, 1927–1939*, ed. Allen Stoekl. Minneapolis: University of Minnesota Press, 1985, pp. 116–30.

Baym, Nina. "Melodramas of Beset Manhood: How Theories of American Fiction Exclude Women Authors." In *The New Feminist Criticism*, edited by Elaine Showalter, pp. 63–81. New York: Pantheon, 1985.

Beidler, Philip D. *American Literature and the Experience of Vietnam*. Athens: University of Georgia Press, 1982.

Benjamin, Jessica. "The Bonds of Love: Rational Violence and Erotic Domination." *Feminist Studies* 1 (Spring 1980): 158–69.

Berg, Richard, and John Carlos Rowe, eds. "American Representations of Vietnam." *Cultural Critique* 3 (Spring 1986).

Boone, Joseph. "Male Independence and the American Quest Genre: Hidden Sexual Politics in the All-Male Worlds of Melville, Twain and London." In *Gender Studies: New Directions in Feminist Criticism*. Edited by Judith Spector, pp. 187–218. Bowling Green, Ohio: Bowling Green State University Popular Press, 1986.

Borch-Jacobsen, Mikkel. "The Freudian Subject: From Ethics to Politics." Lecture delivered February 5, 1987, at the University of Washington.

Braidotti, Rosi. "Envy: or With Your Brains and My Looks." In *Men in Feminism*. Edited by Alice Jardine and Paul Smith, pp. 233–242. New York: Methuen, 1987.

Brownmiller, Susan. *Against Our Will: Men, Women and Rape*. New York: Simon and Schuster, 1975.

———. *Femininity*. New York: Fawcett Columbine, 1984.

Broyles, William Jr. "Why Men Love War." *Esquire*, November 1984, p. 55.

———. *Brothers in Arms: A Journey from War to Peace*. New York: Knopf, 1986.

Bryan, C. D. B. *Friendly Fire*. New York: Bantam, 1976.

Burdick, Eugene, and William Lederer. *The Ugly American*. New York: Norton, 1958.

Caputo, Philip. *A Rumor of War*. New York: Ballantine, 1977.

Chodorow, Nancy. *The Reproduction of Mothering: Psychoanalysis and the Sociology of Gender*. Berkeley: University of California Press, 1978.

———. "Gender, Relation, and Difference in Psychoanalytic Perspective." In *The*

*Future of Difference*. Edited by Hester Eisenstein and Alice Jardine, pp. 3–20. Boston: G. K. Hall, 1980.

Chrysostom, John. "Homilies on St. John, xxv.2." *A Select Library of the Nicene and Post-Nicene Fathers of the Christian Church,* vol. 14. Edited by Philip Schaff. New York: Christian Literature, 1980.

*Cineaste* 15.4. "*Platoon* on Inspection." Edited by Robert Sklar: 4–9.

Cixous, Helene. "The Laugh of the Medusa." In *New French Feminisms*. Edited by Elaine Marks and Isabelle de Courtivron: 245–65.

Clark, Michael. "The Silent Mirror of Vietnam." *LSA* 6, no. 3 (Fall 1983):10–15.

Collins, Monica. "Next Season, It'll Be a Man's Game." *USA Today,* May 19, 1987, p. 3D.

Corea, Gena. *The Mother Machine: Reproductive Technologies from Artificial Insemination to Artificial Wombs*. New York: Harper and Row, 1985.

Corliss, Richard. "*Platoon:* Viet Nam, the Way It Really Was, on Film." *Time,* January 26, 1987, pp. 54–62.

Coward, Rosalind. *Female Desires: How They Are Sought, Bought and Packaged*. New York: Grove, 1985.

*Critical Studies in Mass Communication*. Edited by Harry W. Haines. Forthcoming.

Crowder, Diane Griffin. "Amazons and Mothers? Monique Wittig, Helene Cixous and Theories of Women's Writing." *Contemporary Literature* 24, no. 2 (1983): 117–45.

Daly, Mary. *Gyn/ecology: The Metaethics of Radical Feminism*. Boston: Beacon, 1978.

Debord, Guy. *Society of the Spectacle*. Detroit: Black and Red, 1983.

de Lauretis, Teresa. *Alice Doesn't: Feminism, Semiotics, Cinema*. Bloomington: Indiana University Press, 1984.

———. *Technologies of Gender.* Bloomington: Indiana University Press, 1987.

Del Vecchio, John M. *The 13th Valley*. New York: Bantam, 1982.

Derrida, Jacques. "Implications: Interview with Henri Ronse." In *Positions*. Translated by Alan Bass, pp. 1–15. Chicago: University of Chicago Press, 1981.

———. "Choreographies." *Diacritics* 12, no. 2 (Summer 1982): 66–77.

Didion, Joan. *Democracy*. New York: Simon and Schuster, 1984.

Dower, John W. *War without Mercy: Race and Power in the Pacific War.* New York: Pantheon, 1986.

Duras, Marguerite. *The War: A Memoir.* Translated by Barbara Bray. New York: Pantheon, 1986.

Dworkin, Andrea. *Pornography*. New York: Bantam, 1982.

———. *Intercourse*. New York: The Free Press, 1987.

Dyer, Richard. *Heavenly Bodies: Film Stars and Society.* New York: St. Martin's Press, 1986.

Eagleton, Terry. *Literary Theory: An Introduction*. Oxford: Oxford University Press, 1983.

Easthope, Antony. *What a Man's Gotta Do: The Masculine Myth in Popular Culture*. London: Paladin, 1986.

Eastlake, William. *The Bamboo Bed*. New York: Avon, 1969.

Ehrenhaus, Peter. "The Vietnam Memorial," *Critical Studies in Mass Communication,* 6.1 (1984): 92–94.

Ehrenhaus, Peter, and Richard Morris, *The Cultural Legacy of Vietnam: Uses of the Past in the Present*. Norwood, N.J.: Ablex, forthcoming.

Eliade, Mircea. *The Sacred and the Profane*. New York: Harcourt, 1959.

Ellis, John. *Visible Fictions: Cinema, Television, Video*. London: RKP, 1982.

Elshtain, Jean Bethke. *Women and War.* New York: Basic, 1987.

Emerson, Gloria. *Winners and Losers: Battles, Retreats, Gains, Losses, and Ruins from the Vietnam War.* New York: Penguin, 1972.

Erdrich, Louise. *Love Medicine*. New York: Holt, Rinehart, and Winston, 1984.

Fallaci, Oriana. *Nothing, and So Be It*. Translated by Isabel Quigly. Garden City, N.Y.: Doubleday, 1972.

Feral, Josette. "Writing and Displacement: Women in Theatre." Translated by Barbara Kerslake. *Modern Drama* 27, no. 4 (1984):549–64.

Franco, Jean. "The Incorporation of Women: A Comparison of North American and Mexican Popular Narrative." In *Studies in Entertainment: Critical Approaches to Mass Culture*. Edited by Tania Modleski, pp. 119–39. Bloomington: Indiana University Press, 1986.

French, Marilyn. *Beyond Power: On Women, Men, and Morals*. New York: Ballantine, 1985.

Gaines, Jane. "White Privilege and Looking Relations: Race and Gender in Feminist Film Theory." *Cultural Critique* 4 (1986): 56–79.

*Genre* (special issue). Edited by Gordon O. Taylor. Forthcoming.

Girard, Rene. *Deceit, Desire, and the Novel*. Translated by Yvonne Freccero. Baltimore: Johns Hopkins University Press, 1965.

Glasser, Ronald. *365 Days*. New York: George Braziller, 1971.

Goldman, Peter, and Tony Fuller. *Charlie Company: What Vietnam Did to Us*. New York: Ballantine, 1983.

Grant, Zalin. *Survivors: American POWs in Vietnam*. New York: Berkley, 1975.

Greene, Graham. *The Quiet American*. New York: Penguin, 1955.

Griswold, Charles L. "The Vietnam Veterans Memorial and the Washington Mall: Philosophical Thoughts on Political Iconography." *Critical Inquiry* 12, no. 4 (1986): 688–720.

Haines, Harry. "The Pride is Back: *Rambo, Magnum, P.I.*, and the Return Trip to Vietnam." In *The Cultural Legacy of Vietnam: Uses of the Past in the Present*. Edited by Peter Ehrenhaus and Richard Morris. Norwood, N.J.: Ablex Press, forthcoming.

Halloran, Richard. *To Arm a Nation: Rebuilding America's Endangered Defenses*. New York: MacMillan, 1986.

Harris, Trudier. *Exorcising Blackness: Historical and Literary Lynching and Burning Rituals*. Bloomington: Indiana University Press, 1984.

Hartsock, Nancy C. M. *Money, Sex, and Power: Toward a Feminist Historical Materialism*. Boston: Northeastern University Press, 1983.

———. "Epistemology and Minority Discourse: Towards a Feminist Reconstitution of Knowledge." Lecture delivered at Conference on New Gender Scholarship, February 14, 1987, University of Southern California.

Hasford, Gustav. *The Short-Timers*. New York: Bantam, 1979.

Heilbrun, Carolyn. *Toward a Recognition of Androgyny*. New York: Harper and Row, 1973.

Heinemann, Larry. *Paco's Story*. New York: Penguin, 1986.

Hellman, John. *American Myth and the Legacy of Vietnam*. New York: Columbia University Press, 1986.

Herr, Michael. *Dispatches*. New York: Avon, 1978.

Higgonet, Margaret Randolph et al., eds. *Behind the Lines: Gender and the Two World Wars*. New Haven: Yale University Press, 1987.

Hitler, Adolf. *Mein Kampf*. New York: Reynal and Hitchcock, 1940.

Holland, William E. *Let A Soldier Die*. New York: Dell, 1984.

Horne, A. D., ed. *The Wounded Generation: America after Vietnam*. Englewood Cliffs, N.J.: Prentice-Hall, 1981.

Huggett, William Turner. *Body Count*. New York: Dell, 1973.

Irigaray, Luce. "This Sex Which Is Not One." In *New French Feminisms*. Edited by

Elaine Marks and Isabelle de Courtivron, pp. 99–107. New York: Schocken Books, 1980.

———. "When the Goods Get Together." In *New French Feminisms*. Edited by Elaine Marks and Isabelle de Courtivron, p. 107–111. New York: Schocken Books, 1980.

Jakobson, Roman. "The Dominant." In *Readings in Russian Poetics: Formalist and Structuralist Views*. Edited by Ladislaw Matejka and Krystyna Pomorska, pp. 82–88. Cambridge, Mass.: MIT Press, 1971.

———. "The Metaphoric and Metonymic Poles." In *Critical Theory since Plato*. Edited by Hazard Adams, pp. 1113–17. New York: Harcourt Brace Jovanovich, 1971.

Jameson, Frederic. "Metacommentary." *PMLA* 86, no. 1 (January 1971): 9–18.

Jeffords, Susan. "Friendly Civilians: Images of Women and the Feminization of the Audience in Vietnam Films." *Wide Angle* 7, no. 4 (October 1985): 13–23.

———. "Debriding Vietnam: The Resurrection of the White American Male." *Feminist Studies* 14, no. 3 (Fall 1988): 525–45.

———. "Masculinity as Excess in Vietnam Films: The Father/Son Dynamic in American Culture." *Genre*, forthcoming.

———. "Tattoos, Scars, Diaries and Writing Masculinity." In *American Representations of the Vietnam War,* ed. John Carlos Rowe and Rick Berg. New York: Columbia University Press, forthcoming.

Jones, Ann Rosalind. "Writing the Body: Toward an Understanding of l'Ecriture Feminine." In *The New Feminist Criticism*. Edited by Elaine Showalter, pp. 361–79. New York: Pantheon, 1985.

Karnow, Stanley. *Vietnam: A History*. New York: Viking, 1983.

Kitzinger, Sheila. *The Experience of Childbirth*. Harmondsworth, England: Penguin, 1974.

Klein, Joe. *Payback*. New York: Ballantine, 1984.

Klein, Richard. Review. *Homosexualities in French Literature*. *Modern Langauge Notes* 95, no. 4 (May 1980): 1077.

Kolodny, Annette. *The Lay of the Land: Metaphor as Experience and History in American Life and Letters*. Chapel Hill: University of North Carolina Press, 1975.

Kovic, Ron. *Born on the Fourth of July*. New York: Pocket, 1976.

Lerner, Gerda. *The Creation of Patriarchy*. New York: Oxford University Press, 1986.

Louvre, Alf, and Jeffrey Walsh. *"Tell Me Lies About Vietnam": Cultural Battles for the Meaning of the War.* Milton Keynes, England: Open University Press, forthcoming.

Lowry, Timothy S. *And Brave Men, Too*. New York: Berkley Books, 1985.

Luttwak, Edward N. *The Pentagon and the Art of War: The Question of Military Reform*. New York: Simon and Schuster, 1985.

Lyotard, Jean-François. *The Postmodern Condition: A Report on Knowledge*. Translated by Geoff Bennington and Brian Massumi. Minneapolis: University of Minnesota Press, 1984.

McDowell, Edwin. "Publishing: Everyone Seems to Be Doing Books on Vietnam." *New York Times*, December 2, 1983.

MacPherson, Myra. *Long Time Passing: Vietnam and the Haunted Generation*. New York: Signet, 1984.

Mailer, Norman. *The Armies of the Night: History as a Novel, the Novel as History*. New York: Signet, 1968.

Marin, Peter. "What the Vietnam Vets Can Teach Us." *Nation*, November 27, 1982, p. 1.

Marshall, Kathryn. *In the Combat Zone: An Oral History of American Women in Vietnam, 1966–1975*. Boston: Little, Brown, 1987.

Mason, Bobbie Ann. *In Country*. New York: Harper and Row, 1985.

Mathieu, Nicole-Claude. "Biological Paternity, Social Maternity." *Feminist Issues* 4, no. 1 (Spring 1984):63–72.

Maurer, David A. *The Dying Place*. New York: Dell, 1986.

Mayer, Tom. "A Birth in the Delta." In *The Weary Falcon*, pp. 149–75. Boston: Houghton Mifflin, 1971.

Miller, Nancy K. "Man on Feminism: A Criticism of His Own." In *Men in Feminism*. Edited by Alice Jardine and Paul Smith, pp. 137–46. New York: Methuen, 1987.

Modleski, Tania. "The Terror of Pleasure: The Contemporary Horror Film and Postmodern Theory." In *Studies in Entertainment: Critical Approaches to Mass Culture*. Edited by Tania Modleski. Bloomington: Indiana University Press, 1986: 155–67.

Moi, Toril. *Sexual/Textual Politics: Feminist Literary Theory*. New York: Methuen, 1985.

Morgan, Elaine. *The Descent of Woman*. New York: Bantam, 1973.

Morganthau, Tom. "We're Still Prisoners of War." *Newsweek*, April 15, 1985, p. 34.

Morrow, Lance. "A Bloody Rite of Passage." *Time*. April 15, 1985, p. 20.

Murphy, Edward F. *Vietnam Medal of Honor Heroes*. New York: Ballantine, 1987.

Neale, Steve. "Masculinity as Spectacle: Reflections on Men and Mainstream Cinema." *Screen* 24.6 (1983):2–17.

Nixon, Richard. *No More Vietnams*. New York: Arbor House, 1985.

Noel, Chris. *A Matter of Survival*. Boston: Branden, 1987.

Norris, Christopher. *Deconstruction: Theory and Practice*. London: Methuen, 1982.

O'Brien, Mary. *The Politics of Reproduction*. Boston: Routledge and Kegal Paul, 1981.

Ohmann, Richard. "The Shaping of the Canon in U.S. Fiction, 1960–1975," *Critical Inquiry* 10 (September 1983):199–223.

Osherson, Samuel. *Finding Our Fathers: The Unfinished Business of Manhood*. New York: The Free Press, 1986.

Owen, Craig. "Outlaws: Gay Men in Feminism." In *Men in Feminism*. Edited by Alice Jardine and Paul Smith. New York: Methuen, 1987: 219–233.

Pelfry, William. *The Big V*. New York: Avon, 1972.

Pfarrer, Donald. *Neverlight*. New York: Laurel, 1982.

Phillips, Jayne Ann. *Machine Dreams*. New York: E. P. Dutton, 1984.

Piercy, Marge. *Woman on the Edge of Time*. New York: Fawcett Crest, 1976.

———. *Vida*. New York: Summit, 1979.

———. *Gone to Soldiers*. New York: Summit, 1987.

Polan, Dana. "Brief Encounters: Mass Culture and the Evacuation of Sense." In *Studies in Entertainment: Critical Approaches to Mass Culture*, pp. 167–88. Edited by Tania Modleski. Bloomington: Indiana University Press, 1986.

Pollock, J. C. *Mission M.I.A*. New York: Dell, 1982.

Pratt, John Clark. *The Laotian Fragments*. New York: Viking, 1974.

———. *Vietnam Voices: Perspectives on the War Years, 1941–1982*. New York: Penguin, 1984.

Propp, Vladimir. *The Morphology of the Folktale*. Translated by Lawrence Scott. Austin: University of Texas Press, 1968.

Radway, Janice. "The Utopian Impulse in Popular Literature: Gothic Romance and 'Feminist' Protest." *American Quarterly* 33, no. 3 (1981):140–62.

Reardon, Betty A. *Sexism and the War System*. New York: Teachers College Press, 1985.

Reich, Charles. *The Greening of America: How the Youth Revolution Is Trying to Make America Livable*. New York: Random House, 1970.

Roth, Robert. *Sand in the Wind*. Boston: Little, Brown, 1973.

Rowe, John Carlos. *Genre*, forthcoming.

Rowe, John Carlos, and Rick Berg. *American Representations of the Vietnam War*. New York: Columbia University Press, forthcoming.

Rowland, Robyn. "Reproductive Technologies: The Final Solution to the Woman Question?" In *Test-Tube Woman: What Future for Motherhood?* Edited by Rita Arditti, Renate Duelli Klein, and Shelley Minden, pp. 356–71. Boston: Pandora, 1984.

———. "Technology and Motherhood: Reproductive Choice Reconsidered." *Signs* 12, no. 3 (Spring 1987): 512–29.

Ruth, Shiela. *Issues in Feminism: A First Course in Women's Studies*. Boston: Houghton Mifflin, 1980.

Said, Edward. *Orientalism*. New York: Harcourt, Brace, 1979.

Santoli, Al. *Everything We Had*. New York: Ballantine, 1981.

———. *To Bear Any Burden: The Vietnam War and Its Aftermath in the Words of Americans and Southeast Asians*. New York: Ballantine. 1985.

Saywell, Shelley. *Women in War.* New York: Viking, 1985.

Scarry, Elaine. "Injury and the Structure of War." *Representations* 10 (1985):1–52.

Searle, William J. *Search and Clear: Critical Responses to Selected Literature and Films of the Vietnam War.* Bowling Green, Ohio: Bowling Green University Popular Press, 1988.

Sedgwick, Eve Kosofsky. *Between Men: English Literature and Male Homosocial Desire*. New York: Columbia University Press, 1985.

Silko, Leslie Marmon. *Ceremony.* New York: Signet, 1977.

Silverman, Kaja. "Fragments of a Fashionable Discourse." In *Studies in Entertainment*. Edited by Tania Modleski, pp. 139–155. Bloomington: Indiana University Press, 1986.

Sofia, Zoe. "Exterminating Fetuses: Abortion, Disarmament, and the Sexo-Semiotics of Extraterrestrialism." *Diacritics* 14, no. 2 (Summer 1984):47–60.

Stanton, Domna C. "Difference on Trial: A Critique of the Maternal Metaphor in Cixous, Irigaray, and Kristeva." In *The Poetics of Gender.* Edited by Nancy K. Miller. pp. 157–83. New York: Columbia University Press, 1986.

Stiehm, Judith Hicks. *Bring Me Men and Women: Mandated Change at the U.S. Air Force Academy.* Berkeley: University of California Press, 1981.

Stone, Oliver. *Platoon*. Screenplay. New York: Vintage, 1987.

Strayer, Chris. "*Personal Best:* Lesbian/Feminist Audience." *Jump Cut* 29 (1984):40–44.

Suleiman, Susan Rubin. "Pornography, Transgression, and the Avant-Garde: Bataille's *Story of the Eye*." In *The Poetics of Gender.* Edited by Nancy K. Miller: 117–37.

Swiers, George. "'Demented Vets' and Other Myths: The Moral Obligation of Veterans." In *Vietnam Reconsidered: Lessons From a War.* Edited by Harrison E. Salisbury, pp. 196–202. New York: Harper and Row, 1984.

Terry, Wallace. *Bloods: An Oral History of the Vietnam War by Black Veterans*. New York: Ballantine, 1984.

Theweleit, Klaus. *Male Fantasies*. Vol. 1. Translated by Stephen Conway. Minneapolis: University of Minnesota Press, 1987.

Thompson, Kristin. "The Concept of Cinematic Excess." In *Narrative, Apparatus, Ideology: A Film Theory Reader.* Edited by Philip Rosen, pp. 130–43. New York: Columbia University Press, 1986.

Tichi, Cecelia. "Video Novels." *Boston Review* 13, no. 3 (June 1987):12–15.

Tiger, Lionel. *Men in Groups*. New York: Random House, 1969.

Tonelson, Alan. Review of *To Arm A Nation* by Richard Halloran. *New York Times Book Review,* November 30, 1986, p. 7.

Travers, Peter. "Picks and Pans." *People,* June 24, 1985, pp. 9–10.

Treviso, Ruben. "Hispanics and the Vietnam War." In *Vietnam Reconsidered: Lessons from a War.* Edited by Harrison E. Salisbury. New York: Harper and Row, 1984: 184–87.

Tuchman, Barbara. *The March of Folly: From Troy to Vietnam*. New York: Knopf, 1984.

U.S. Senate. Committee on Veterans' Affairs. *Myths and Realities: A Study of Attitudes toward Vietnam Era Vets*. 92nd Congress, 2d sess. Washington: Government Printing Office, 1980.

U.S. Senate. Committee on Veterans' Affairs. *Hearings*. 96th Congress, 2d sess. Washington: Government Printing Office, 1980.

U.S. Veterans' Administration. *Annual Report*. Washington: Government Printing Office, 1983.

Van Biema, David H. "With a $100 Million Gross(out), Sly Stallone Fends Off *Rambo*'s Army of Adversaries." *People*, July 8, 1985, pp. 34–38.

Van Devanter, Lynda. *Home before Morning*. New York: Warner, 1983.

Walker, Keith. *A Piece of My Heart: The Stories of 26 American Women Who Served in Vietnam*. Novato, Calif.: Presidio, 1985.

Walsh, Jeffrey, and James Aulich, *Vietnam Images: War and Representation*. London: Lumier Macmillan, 1988.

Webb, Kate. *On the Other Side: 23 Days with the Viet Cong*. New York: Quadrangle, 1972.

Webb, James. "When My Son Was Born." *Parade*, June 16, 1985, pp. 8–10.

———. *Fields of Fire*. Englewood Cliffs, N.J.: Prentice-Hall, 1978.

Wheeler, John. *Touched with Fire: The Future of the Vietnam Generation*. New York: Avon, 1984.

Wiegman, Robyn. *Negotiating the Masculine: Configurations of Race and Gender in American Culture*. Ph.D. dissertation, University of Washington, 1988.

*Wide Angle* 7, no. 4 (October, 1985).

Willson, David A. *REMF Diary*. Seattle: Black Heron Press, 1988.

Williamson, Judith. "Woman Is an Island: Femininity and Colonization." In *Studies in Entertainment*, pp. 99–119. Edited by Modleski.

Wolf, Christa. *Cassandra*. Translated by Jan Van Heurck. New York: Farrar, Straus, Giroux, 1984.

Wood, Robin. *Hollywood from Vietnam to Reagan*. New York: Columbia University Press, 1986.

# INDEX